China Companion

D0701209

CHINA
COMPANION

*A Guide to 100 Cities,
Resorts and Places of Interest in the
People's Republic of China*

Evelyne Garside

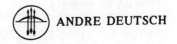 ANDRE DEUTSCH

First published 1981 by
André Deutsch Ltd
105 Great Russell Street London WC1
Second edition 1983

Copyright © 1981 by Evelyne Garside
All rights reserved

Maps and plans by Colin Edwards, Dave Indge, Bob Bonner,
Chris Sheppard, Al Spry

ISBN 0 233 97270 6

Printed in Great Britain by
St Edmundsbury Press, Bury St Edmunds, Suffolk

Contents

MAPS AND PLANS
in the text

in the appendix

Preface and Acknowledgements

When I went to China for the first time, in 1968, I landed at Shanghai and was immediately confronted with the outward signs of the ongoing Cultural Revolution: giant portraits of Mao Zedong (Mao Tse-tung), revolutionary music echoing in the terminal building, soldiers checking my passport and luggage. I felt I was putting my head in the lion's mouth, but I was so curious about China that I would not have changed places with anyone.

Tourist travel was restricted to a dozen cities then, but in some ways was less formally organized than it is now. The first time I arrived in Guangzhou (Canton) I was not met by anyone from China Travel Service. During the two years of my first stay in China, I always travelled by train in the 'hard class', and never met another foreigner, except in the dining car. Chinese passengers would line up in the corridor to talk or listen to me, giving me the newspaper to read aloud and demanding my comments, asking me about my country and the world, and then refusing to believe what I told them. No Chinese oral exam I took while I was a student was ever that tough!

Eight years later, in 1976, I came back, this time with my husband and two small daughters. I was not anxious any more, but on the contrary had a strange feeling of coming home. Everything was so familiar, the ritual at the Hong Kong border had not changed, and I even recognized some of the China Travel Service staff. Arriving in Beijing (Peking), the wind, the dust, the people, the buildings were the same. Sadly, though, the walls had gone, pollution had become so bad that the sky was more often yellow than blue, and the Western Hills on the horizon sometimes remained hidden for months.

Travel had become easier. I made my first journey — to Shandong — within two months of my arrival, and a few weeks later to Xi'an, Yan'an and Dazhai. Before the summer had settled in, I had also been to Guilin and a couple of times to Tianjin. The Tangshan earthquake interrupted my programme, but by the end of the first year, I had travelled some 15,000 km.

I had hoped to study Chinese at the Foreign Languages school in Beijing, but as a diplomat's wife, I was not eligible for a place. My husband suggested that instead I use the Chinese I already knew to research and write a guidebook to Beijing. Heartened by the crisp and sunny autumn weather, I bicycled about, exploring the city in the company of a photographer friend, Julie Munro. After a while I decided that what was really needed was a guide, not just to Beijing, but to the whole of China, to supply some of the information badly needed by increasing numbers of visitors. I had been in the country eighteen months, had visited all the cities then open to tourists, and felt I could write the book easily.

Within the next few months, however, the Chinese suddenly opened all but four provinces to foreigners; some of these places had been closed since the early 1950s. So for the next year, I made another dozen journeys, long and short, out from Beijing. My third daughter, Rebecca, was born between a trip to Sichuan and the Yangzi Gorges, and another one to Henan. By the time she arrived she was already a well-travelled person.

Though we remained in China for more than three years, it was not physically possible for me to visit every place myself or to keep up with all the changes. Certain friends helped greatly by taking with them on their travels a questionnaire which they kindly completed for me. Thus I am indebted to Charles Aylmer for information on Taishan, to Flora Botton for Kunming, to Nigel Wade for Leshan, to Helen Alexander for Hefei, to Jinlin Pai for Tianjin, to Anne-Marie Ma for Emeishan, to my husband Roger Garside for Xinjiang province, to Krystyna Horko for Shenyang, and to Elisabeth MaCullum and John Fraser for Tibet. I was lucky enough to have good companions on every journey, and I would like to thank Bobbi Clift, Elisabeth MaCullum, Helen Mitchel, Wendy Phillips and Richenda George for their cheerful presence.

Some China Travel Service guides were outstanding, and I remember particularly Miss Ma in Jinan, Mr Liu in Chengdu and Mrs Shi in Luoyang. They were knowledgeable, friendly and efficient. I am also very grateful to Mr Zhu, chief interpreter at the British Embassy in Beijing, who helped me organize my itineraries, handled my travel applications and booked my tickets. He was always courteous and efficient.

Robert N. Tharp, who spent the first thirty years of his life in China and taught for fifteen years at Yale University, patiently went over the typescript for mistakes in transcription, spelling and translation. I felt strengthened and encouraged by his interest in my book and owe him a great debt of gratitude. Of the many published sources in Chinese, English and French on which I depended, a selection of those presently available in English is listed at p. 270.

I owe the greatest thanks to Roger, my husband, for having encouraged and sometimes even pushed me into starting this guidebook. I would also like to thank the warm-hearted substitute mothers who took care of my daughters when I was travelling and writing: Pan ayi, our Chinese housekeeper, and Diana Jackson, our children's nanny; and Joele Swift and Becky Smith who looked after them after we moved to California, when I was finishing the book. My thanks also go to Marianne Schippereit who typed the final version, wrestling successfully with a tide of Chinese words with which she was not familiar, and who also corrected some mistakes in English — my mother tongue being French. Lastly, for Catharine Carver, who edited this book with a vigilant eye for details and accuracy, and improved my prose without distorting its meaning, no thanks are enough.

E.G.
Carmel, California
October 1979

Addenda to the Second edition

Areas marked ▨ on the maps on pages 4–5, 137 and 211 are now open to tourists.

Visitors are no longer required to declare the amount of foreign currency they bring in, but can exchange it for Foreign Currency Certificates (waihuijuan) as needed, to purchase goods in China. (page 7)

Inoculations against smallpox and cholera are no longer required, but it is advisable to be vaccinated against polio, tetanus, diphtheria and typhoid. (page 8)

January 1982

Abbreviations

CCP Chinese Communist Party
CTS China Travel Service, the Chinese tourist agency
KMT Kuomintang (in Pinyin, Guomindang), the nationalist party,
     at present the ruling party in Taiwan; KMT government
     =Nationalist government.
PLA People's Liberation Army, also known as the Red Army.

NOTE

Chinese place-names and other proper names throughout this book
are given in the Pinyin form of phonetic transcription officially
adopted by the government of the People's Republic in 1979. For
the background on this system of transcription see p. 25; notes on
the pronunciation of names rendered in this form are given at p. 257

E.G.

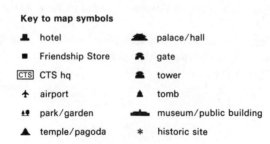

Key to map symbols

▲	hotel	▲	palace/hall
■	Friendship Store	▲	gate
CTS	CTS hq	▲	tower
✦	airport	▲	tomb
▲♥	park/garden	▲	museum/public building
▲	temple/pagoda	*	historic site

I
INTRODUCTION

China has had an almost magic appeal for Westerners since Marco Polo's journeys in the thirteenth century to the empire of the Great Khan. Adventurous travellers were lured to China by the fantastic account Marco Polo gave of the empire's wealth in gold, pearls, silk and spices; others went hoping to win over to Christianity its large population of heathens.

Times have changed. Now a potential market of 900 million people attracts large numbers of businessmen to China, while politicians come to establish contact with an increasingly significant international power, and tourists are eager to see with their own eyes a fabulous and as yet little-known country.

Until 1978, the Chinese had done almost nothing to encourage tourism or to supply visitors who did come with information about the country. There is still very little tourist information available locally. At the time of writing, for example, there is no detailed street map of Beijing (Peking) in English or French; the scant literature on Beijing's historical monuments includes a booklet on the Forbidden City which gives a very patchy historical account and does not even mention its museum, the richest in China. China Travel Service has just begun publication of a series of city guides in English, but they lack much of the information tourists expect to find in a guide book. This book is designed to supply some of this information.

PRACTICAL INFORMATION

Who visits China?   Many tour operators in western countries now organize group visits of foreigners to China. All aspects of the visit are arranged by the tour operator: visas, itinerary, accommodation, transport, etc. A list of such operators can be obtained through Chinese embassies abroad, or by writing direct to the Head Office of China International Travel Service, 6 East Changan Avenue, Beijing, People's Republic of China.

Businessmen contact initially the relevant National Foreign Trade Corporation. They are issued with an invitation which is then submitted with the application for a visa, to the embassy of the People's Republic of China in the country concerned. Information on the different Foreign Trade Corporations can be obtained from any Chinese embassy abroad.

All kinds of official delegations — athletes, performing artists, politicians, scientists, etc. — visit China every year. Their visits are arranged either by their own government or by their organization. Foreign students and teachers also come, most of them under the terms of agreements between their government and the Chinese government.

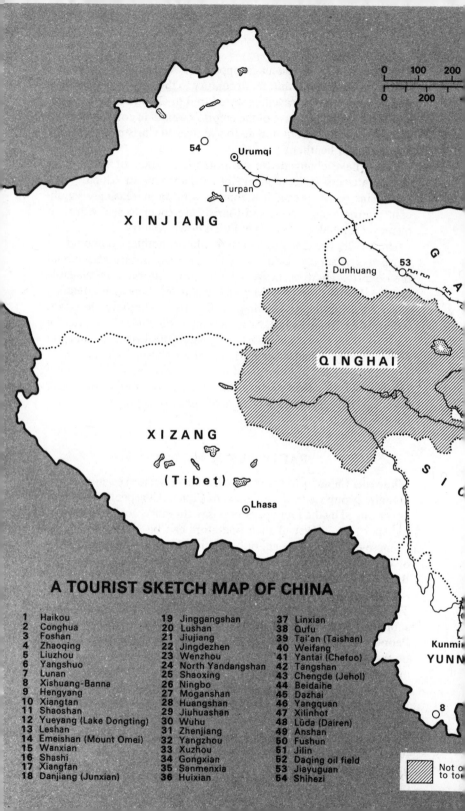

	0	100	200
	0		200

54

⊙ Urumqi

Turpan

X I N J I A N G

○ Dunhuang

53 ⊙

G

A

Q I N G H A I

X I Z A N G

(Tibet)

⊙ Lhasa

S I C

A TOURIST SKETCH MAP OF CHINA

1 Haikou
2 Conghua
3 Foshan
4 Zhaoqing
5 Liuzhou
6 Yangshuo
7 Lunan
8 Xishuang-Banna
9 Hengyang
10 Xiangtan
11 Shaoshan
12 Yueyang (Lake Dongting)
13 Leshan
14 Emeishan (Mount Omei)
15 Wanxian
16 Shashi
17 Xiangfan
18 Danjiang (Junxian)

19 Jinggangshan
20 Lushan
21 Jiujiang
22 Jingdezhen
23 Wenzhou
24 North Yandangshan
25 Shaoxing
26 Ningbo
27 Moganshan
28 Huangshan
29 Jiuhuashan
30 Wuhu
31 Zhenjiang
32 Yangzhou
33 Xuzhou
34 Gongxian
35 Sanmenxia
36 Huixian

37 Linxian
38 Qufu
39 Tai'an (Taishan)
40 Weifang
41 Yantai (Chefoo)
42 Tangshan
43 Chengde (Jehol)
44 Beidaihe
45 Dazhai
46 Yangquan
47 Xilinhot
48 Lüda (Dairen)
49 Anshan
50 Fushun
51 Jilin
52 Daqing oil field
53 Jiayuguan
54 Shihezi

Kunmi

YUNN

8 ○

Not o
to to

Experts usually come to live and work in China for periods of two to three years, although some of them have been in the country for twenty years or more. They sign individual employment contracts with the Chinese organization concerned. Increasingly, they are recruited by foreign organizations engaged in educational and other exchanges.

Chinese nationals living abroad can obtain an entry visa by joining one of the tourist groups in their country of residence, or a special tour for overseas Chinese. Others may come for a private visit at the invitation of a relative living in China. Friends and relatives of foreign residents in China (diplomats, journalists, etc.) can apply for a visa upon presentation of a personal invitation from their friend or relative.

How to get there. Airlines which operate regular flights to and from China include China's national airline CAAC, Air France, Japan Airlines, Swissair, Pakistan Airlines, Aeroflot, Tarom (Romania) and Ethiopian Airlines. A few more major airlines are likely to join the list once the modernization of Beijing, Shanghai and Guangzhou (Canton) airports has been completed. CAAC operates charter flights between Hong Kong and Guangzhou during the busy trade and tourist seasons.

A rather slow but interesting way of getting to China is by train, via the Trans-Siberian Railway; the journey from Moscow to Beijing takes five days or more. The other much-used railway route into China is via Hong Kong and the Kowloon-Guangzhou railway. There is an express non-stop service, but on the slow trains passengers cross the Lowu bridge on foot and have a long wait (with lunch) on the Chinese side of the border before boarding the Chinese train. It is worth travelling this way once at least, for the experience.

The only regular passenger service by sea is a Hydrofoil link between Hong Kong and Guangzhou. Your travel agent can provide a list of shipping companies that organize cruises to China.

Customs and currency. All non-diplomatic visitors arriving in China are required to fill in a Baggage Declaration for Inwards Passengers and to present their baggage for inspection by the customs. Only one of each of the following items can be imported per visitor for personal use: watch, portable radio, tape recorder, camera, cine camera (below 8mm), typewriter, sewing machine, fountain pen and calculator. Few tourists would think of bringing more than one sewing machine for use during a visit to China, but you will save yourself a long argument at the customs by having only one of each of the items mentioned, and a minimum amount of jewellery. Taking the items declared out again poses no problem, but you will again be expected to present them for inspection when leaving the country.

The importation of firearms, explosives, narcotics and propaganda material anti the People's Republic of China is strictly prohibited. This last does not include books about China published abroad which present a critical view of the country, but it does include propaganda material published in Taiwan. You can import duty-free 600 cigarettes and 2 bottles of spirits per person (size not stated).

Each visitor is allowed to purchase a reasonable amount of goods (handicrafts, antiques, jewellery) up to a total value of ¥10,000 (in practice there seems to be no limit), and to take them out of China upon presentation of the invoices and receipts to the customs. Antiques can only be exported if they bear a red wax seal indicating that they were made after 1840.

All non-diplomatic visitors are required to declare the amount of foreign currency in their possession when entering the country, though there is no restriction on the amount they can take in. All exchange memos must be kept together with the visitor's copy of the Declaration of Foreign Currencies and Bills for presentation to the customs upon leaving the country.

Most Travellers' Cheques are accepted by the People's Bank of China; any Chinese embassy abroad or the Office of China Travel Service (H.K.) Ltd. can give you a list of those accepted. The People's Bank of China issues Travellers' Cheques in Chinese currency which can be changed back into foreign currency if unused (Chinese currency cannot be exported). Credit cards are rarely accepted.

It is advisable to change a small amount of money immediately on arrival (at the border or at the airport), since, even as a guest in a hotel, one is often expected to pay for drinks on the spot. Moreover, internal flights are often subject to delay or cancellation and you may have to wait for hours in an airport or spend a night *en route*.

The Chinese currency is called *Renminbi* (pronounced as spelt). The unit is the *yuan*, which is divided into ten *jiao*, in turn divided into ten *fen* or cents. *Yuan* notes are issued in denominations of 1,2,5 and 10, *jiao* notes in denominations of 1,2 and 5, and *fen* as coins in denominations of 1,2 and 5.

To complicate matters, in spoken Chinese *yuan* becomes *kuai* and *jiao* becomes *mao,* though *fen* remains *fen*. For example, the price ¥21.75 will be given verbally as 'Twenty-one *kuai,* seven *mao,* five' (the *fen* is often omitted), which your interpreter will translate as 'Twenty-one *yuan* seventy-five'. But if you go to Sichuan province you will find that there they use the written form *jiao* for the spoken *mao*. Don't despair; the sales people are honest and you can always have them write down the price.

Quarantine. A valid smallpox certificate and cholera certificate are required when entering China from Hong Kong.

What to bring to make life easier. Generally speaking, you should bring practical, conservative clothes and comfortable, sturdy, non-slippery shoes; avoid man-made fibres which will be maltreated in the laundry and uncomfortable to wear in the extremely dry or humid weather.

From November to March, for the North you will need very warm clothes, shoes and underwear; for the South, where it may be warm, some denim and cotton shirts. From May to September, it will be hot and humid almost everywhere, particularly in July and August. Cotton clothes are the most comfortable. If you come during the monsoon (July), a really waterproof raincoat is essential. October and April are usually temperate. It may freeze in the Northeast and be very warm in the South, so you will need both medium-weight winter clothing and summer clothes.

Until 1979, you could not buy any foreign brands of consumer goods in China, apart from Swiss watches at a very high price. You may have heard that Coca-Cola has now come to the Middle Kingdom, but don't take this to mean that you can buy what you want anywhere in China. Imported alcohol, soft drinks, cigarettes are only available in the larger hotels in the cities or in some Friendship Stores, and can be purchased only with foreign currency. It is wise to arrive with a supply of your favourite whisky or gin, cigarettes, some tonic concentrate (to mix with the local soda), instant coffee, powdered milk, sugar, tea bags (coffee or black tea is usually only available at mealtimes in the dining room of your hotel or in the restaurant car). Bring a supply of books, magazines, a radio-cassette recorder and tapes. Bring plenty of film and do not have it processed in China.

If you want to avoid wasting time in a hospital, bring all your medical requirements with you (aspirin, cold and cough medicine, settlers, mosquito repellant, ointment for insect bites, antiseptic, adhesive plasters, etc.). You may, however, reach a point at which you would prefer to undergo treatment by acupuncture for your congested sinuses than to visit another factory; in which case you should try and persuade your interpreter to take you to hospital.

Chinese brands of cold cream and hand cream give good

protection against the dry and cold winter winds, but you will have to bring just about all other toilet items with you: toothpaste, shampoo, hair conditioner, shaving cream, razor blades, tissues and cotton wool. You can bring an electric shaver and hair-dryer, but even with a multiple adaptor you may find that you cannot use them everywhere (voltage in China is 220 V, 50 c/s, with sockets for two- or three-flat-pin plugs).

China Travel Service (CTS). Known in Chinese as *Luxingshe* (pronounced 'Lusingsher'), the official travel agency has complete control over the tourist trade with China. It has permanent representatives stationed in all the cities frequently visited by tourists and controls the passenger traffic across the Hong Kong border to and from Kowloon railway station. Passengers entering China from Hong Kong have to purchase their air, rail or Hovercraft tickets from one of its local offices (Hong Kong Central address: China Travel Service (H.K.) Ltd., 77 Queen's Road Central, Hong Kong). CTS (H.K.) also processes visa applications from local residents or from foreigners who, having received an official invitation to visit China (from a Foreign Trade Corporation, for instance), have not been issued a visa in their country of origin.

CTS representatives will be your guardian angels from the time you arrive until you leave China. They will organize your life entirely: your interpreter will book hotel rooms, buy train, plane, opera tickets, tell you when you should rest, take you to a doctor should you fall ill, and accompany you shopping.

Your interpreter will also act as your tutor and political adviser. A visit to a factory, a commune, or a museum, etc., in the company of a CTS representative follows a set pattern. The foreign visitor is received by a few leading members of the organization or a guide (in a museum) and taken to a parlour for a 'brief introduction', translated by the interpreter. The history of each organization is presented in the context of the major political campaigns since Liberation (1949), and you will soon become familiar with such leitmotivs as 'Since the beginning of the Cultural Revolution' and 'Since the smashing of the Gang of Four'. After some questions and answers, the visit proper begins.

If you manage to escape the attentions of your interpreter — for instance during the siesta — this guidebook will enable you to explore on your own. Its aim is to give you a more complete picture of what each city has to offer than the CTS programme presents, and to make up for the shortcomings of interpreters. I remember a CTS representative in Beijing who when asked where the Old Legation Quarter was, declared that there was no such thing. Some interpreters, however, combine a good command of a foreign language with extensive knowledge of the town in which they work (not often their home town).

Transportation and accommodation. Air travel within China is safe, but often frustrating because flights may be delayed or cancelled without any warning on account of the weather. Food on internal flights, when any is served, consists of an unappetizing tray of cold bits and drinks of tea or fizzy orange, poured from a battered aluminium kettle.

Trains are fairly comfortable, although heating or ventilation are dispensed sparingly and radio broadcasts over-generously. You can turn the sound volume down in your compartment, but it may still be blasting away in the corridor. You can appeal to your carriage steward (he is the one who took your ticket and kept it) if you are unhappy with the other occupant(s) of your compartment, or if you want the fan to be switched on. The food in the restaurant car is usually simple but good, and if you order a Western-style breakfast and Chinese-style lunch and dinner, without expecting all the dishes listed on the menu to be available, you will be satisfied. Drinks can be obtained from the restaurant car at any time.

The Chinese railway network is split up among different regional companies, and you may discover that the standard of cleanliness and service varies. You can often tell from the beer, as the regional companies each serve a different, local brand of beer in their restaurant cars.

In cities, unless one is with a group, one is expected to travel by taxi, even for long distances. Should you want to cut down the cost of an excursion out of town when travelling privately, you can ask to join a tourist group or share a taxi with another lone traveller (maximum four persons per taxi). Interpreters believe that all foreigners are millionaires, so don't be afraid to tell yours that you are spending your life's savings on this trip; keep a sharp eye on the mileage gauge, and always ask the distance to a place you are proposing to visit.

Taxis are available at the main hotels or outside railway stations. They can be booked, by you or your interpreter, at the transport desk in the lobby of your hotel. When you go out to dinner, order a taxi to bring you back before leaving the hotel. On an excursion, always keep your taxi waiting.

Hotels for foreigners traditionally fall into two categories: those built for the Soviet experts in the 1950s, sometimes with palatial dimensions, but ageing plumbing, and tourist hotels, usually more comfortable. In either category, the rooms are gloomy with dim lighting and unattractive furniture. There are usually two large single beds and an adjoining bathroom. The standard of cleanliness, while not shocking, often leaves a lot to be desired. More tourist hotels are now being built with Chinese funds, as well as some foreign-designed and -built hotels.

Hotel services available include lobby shop, hairdresser, bank, post office, laundry (no dry cleaning). As yet there is very rarely room service, but a thermos of hot water is available in every room. The Chinese could not live without hot water and you wonder how you have been able to survive without a thermos for so long. It is safe to drink the water everywhere.

Tipping is not accepted anywhere, but you can show your appreciation by offering small things like sweets or cigarettes or leaving your books and magazines behind. Your room boy or girl will probably walk into your room unannounced but be nowhere to be found when you want something.

Western-style food is only available in the larger hotels, but neither Chinese nor Western-style food is very good in the dining rooms of hotels for foreigners, except in Shanghai. Chinese food is often the only kind available (except at breakfast) and can be very bad in a small provincial hotel in the North. To have a good meal, one should book a table in a restaurant in town, stating a maximum price per head. But there again, it is only in the large and relatively modern cities (Beijing, Shanghai, Guangzhou and a few others) that you can hope to find a good restaurant. Because China is a poor country, good food is rare in many provinces. If your interpreter says that he cannot book a table for you in a restaurant, take it to mean that there is no decent restaurant in town.

Shopping. China is killing the golden goose, not so slowly and very surely. Don't expect to find bargains any more in the antique shops; sometimes prices are higher than in auction rooms in the West, and quality is poor. Unless you are an expert in Chinese ceramics or paintings and can spot the piece which by chance has been priced below its market value, buy what you like and can afford, knowing that you have probably paid a high price.

Tourists are usually taken to Friendship Stores to buy handicrafts. These are department stores, found in most of the larger cities open to foreign tourists, which sell goods destined for the export market. The Chinese themselves cannot shop there without special authorization, granted only to those in managerial positions. The selection is good in the larger Friendship Stores and poor in smaller ones, but it is seldom representative of the local handicrafts. You will see a bit of the same in every province and would be well advised to buy in the larger stores where the quality is likely to be better. There are very few bargains to be had in Friendship Stores. Most of what they sell is available cheaper in the Chinese emporiums in Hong Kong, where the choice is far greater and better suited to the taste of foreign tourists.

So, what can you buy? Silk by the metre and silk goods (beware, most brocade is made of rayon; ask the salesperson), cashmere by the metre and knitwear, cloisonné and other inexpensive jewellery, basketware, paper goods, silk flowers and furs. Stone rubbings make particularly cheap and easy-to-pack presents; reproduction Han and Tang pottery figures are very attractive, furniture (if you don't mind the trouble of shipping it) is both beautiful and good value. It can be bought in second-hand shops or antique shops. Canvas bags, caps, T-shirts, ordinary ceramic pots and baskets can be bought in department stores and hardware stores, always interesting to look around.

Remember two things: have plenty of cash with you (you always have to pay cash and can only change your Travellers' Cheques in a bank); and if you see something you like, buy it straight away, there will probably not be another chance.

GEOGRAPHY

China is a country of great physical contrasts with a relatively small percentage of arable land. It covers an area (3,650,000 square miles) about equal to that of the USA, between roughly the same latitudes. For more than two thousand years, the Chinese have made a distinction between China proper, also known in the past as the Eighteen Provinces, and the empty desert highlands to the north, west and south-west which were populated by 'barbarians' who paid tribute to the Chinese empire. Bounded on three sides by these semi-desert highlands, or by jungle, and on the fourth by the Pacific Ocean, China has been largely cut off from the rest of the world until modern times. Trading contacts with India and Persia were maintained only when the Chinese empire controlled the famous Silk Route.

China can be divided into six major geographical areas: the Northeast, the North, the South, the Southwest, Xinjiang (Chinese Turkestan) and Inner Mongolia, and Tibet.

The *Northeast* comprises the provinces of Heilongjiang, Jilin (Kirin) and Liaoning. The area is almost totally encircled by mountains but is open to the sea on the south. The climate is very hard, characterized by long, cold and very dry winters, spring droughts, and a short summer season during which most of the yearly precipitation falls.* Lying as it does north of the 40th Parallel, the area has a relatively short growing season (four months). The Northeast contains rich deposits of coal, iron ore, non-ferrous metals and oil (offshore), first exploited during the periods of Russian and Japanese occupation in the nineteenth and twentieth centuries. It has the most extensive railway system in the country, and is the most important industrial region of China.

The *North* includes the densely populated and intensively

THE GEOGRAPHICAL REGIONS OF CHINA

	XINJIANG–INNER MONGOLIA		THE NORTHEAST
	TIBET		THE NORTH
	THE SOUTHWEST		THE SOUTH

---

*See Appendix for tables of average temperatures and precipitation in the various regions of China.

cultivated North China plain, the loess* or dust plateaux of Shanxi and Shaanxi, and the provinces of Hebei and Shandong. The landscape is generally monotonous and somewhat desolate, with almost no natural ground cover. The climate is similar to that of the Northeast: bitterly cold winters, strong dust-laden winds and almost no snowfall; and hot and humid summers, the contrast between winter and summer being even greater in areas removed from the coast. This area, watered by the middle and lower Yellow River and its tributaries, is the cradle of Chinese civilization.

North of the Great Wall begin the steppes of Inner Mongolia, which are grazing lands for sheep and ponies. The North is a fairly rich agricultural area and the taming of the Yellow River (sometimes called the Sorrow of China) has helped greatly to diversify and increase agricultural production. It is now also a very active industrial area of coal mines, steel and cotton mills, chemical plants and factories centred around the large cities of Beijing, Tianjin, Xi'an, Taiyuan, and elsewhere.

The *South* comprises the middle and lower Yangzi (Yangtze) River basin, the southern provinces of Guangdong and Guangxi, and the coastal provinces of Fujian and Zhejiang. The natural ground cover gets thicker, to become sub-tropical in the hills of Guangxi. The climate ranges from temperate to tropical. The population is concentrated in the valleys, which comprise only 20 per cent of the area. Here the land is cultivated almost like a garden, with the lower hills terraced and irrigated. Rice (two to three crops a year) and tea are grown. Navigable waterways and canals are extensively used.

The Yangzi valley contains nearly half the industry of the region, concentrated around the large metropolises of Shanghai, Wuhan and Changsha. Guangzhou (Canton), which is also an important industrial centre, lies in a delta where the density of population is the highest in the South. Industry includes such traditional crafts as silk weaving, embroidery, lacquer work and carving.

The *Southwest* includes the province of Sichuan, with its fertile and densely populated basin, and the Yunnan and Guizhou uplands. The Sichuan basin is surrounded by high mountains and drained by the upper Yangzi and its tributaries. It has a long tradition of independence, being naturally self-sufficient and somewhat inaccessible. Thirty-five per cent of the area is under cultivation. It is now also an important industrial region, whose development dates from the Japanese occupation of other parts of

---

*Fine yellowish soil brought by the wind and deposited in a thick layer varying in depth from a few feet to over 250 feet.

the country. The Yunnan-Guizhou mountains, by contrast, are sparsely populated with non-Chinese minorities, mostly scattered in the valleys, and has as yet little industry. The climate of the region is generally temperate to subtropical.

Xinjiang-Inner Mongolia is a vast area (one-fifth of China) of desert land, high mountains and steppes and has only 2 per cent of the total population. The climate is very dry. A string of oases mark the ancient Silk Route which was for many centuries the only and tenuous link with the rest of the world. The industrial development of the area — nuclear installations, oil fields, coal mines, textile mills, etc. — is recent. The native population in Xinjiang and Inner Mongolia, as in all the other 'autonomous regions' of China, is in the process of becoming a minority in its own region.

Tibet comprises one-quarter of the area of China and less than 1 per cent of the population. Its very high mountains are the source of great rivers: the Yellow River, Yangzi, Mekong, Indus, Brahmaputra. Unchanged in the centuries before 1951, Tibet is now developing its own agriculture and industry. The population is mainly concentrated in valleys below 4,000 m (12,000 ft).

Population. As everyone knows, China is the most highly populated country in the world. The 1979 census may reveal that the population is actually greater than the estimated figure of 900 million. The density varies from an average of 130 persons per square mile to over 520 per square mile in the Guangzhou delta. Travelling in China brings this fact home to you very quickly: you realize there is nowhere you can be alone.

The population is currently estimated to be growing at an annual rate of 1.2 per cent. Sixteen cities have more than one million inhabitants. Almost the entire population is of Mongolian stock, ethnic distinctions being largely linguistic and cultural. The population comprises 95 per cent 'Han' Chinese and 5 per cent minority nationalities, including Manchu, Mongol, Turk, Tibetan and Korean people in the North and West, and Miao people in the South and Southwest, related to the South Asians and Indo-Chinese.

HISTORY

Prehistory. There is evidence of life in China from the palaeolithic period onwards. The 'Peking Man' whose remains were discovered in a cave 40 km south-west of Beijing is presumed to have lived between 600,000 and 300,000 B.C. The neolithic period has been well documented, with the discovery of important sites in Henan and Shandong of the Grey Pottery Culture, in Gansu, Shanxi,

Shaanxi and Henan of the Painted Pottery Culture (Yangshao Culture), and in Shaanxi and Henan of the Black Pottery Culture.

Feudal China. For the Chinese, the history of the dynasties traditionally begins with the Xia dynasty (2205-1766 B.C.), whose founder, Yu the Great, is credited with draining the flood waters and building canals. The remains of a Xia dynasty palace dating from *c*. 2100 to 1475 B.C. have been found in a suburb of Luoyang in Henan province. Sericulture (the growing of silkworms) and a system of writing date from this period. During the Shang dynasty (1766-1122 B.C.) bronze casting attained a level of perfection never again seen in the world, except perhaps in the West during the Renaissance. Bronze was reserved for making weapons and sacrificial vessels; agricultural tools were made of wood and stone. The Shang rulers were frequently at war and ancestor worship began. Remains of former Shang dynasty capitals have been found near Anyang and Zhengzhou, in Henan province. The last of these capitals, Yin, near Anyang, was razed to the ground and its population transplanted when the dynasty fell in the eleventh century B.C.

The kings of the next dynasty, the Zhou, ruled through their vassals and the empire was a collection of rival city-states, under constant threat of invasion and pillage from barbarian peoples to the north and west. In 771 B.C., the first Zhou capital, near modern Xi'an in Shaanxi province, was raided and the Zhou moved eastward to modern Luoyang; the dynasty is known thereafter as Eastern Zhou. Over the next five centuries under the Zhou agriculture was revolutionized by the discovery of iron casting and the introduction of irrigation on a large scale; at the same time new philosophies emerged which were to influence Chinese thinking for nearly two thousand years: Confucianism, Taoism, the school of Mencius and the Legalists. The period known as 'Spring and Autumn' was succeeded by that of the 'Warring States', and in the second century B.C., the protracted quarrels among the rival vassal states ended with the supremacy of the state of Qin, where a new dynasty was founded and a centralized empire emerged for the first time.

Imperial China. Qin Shihuangdi, the first August Sovereign of the Qin dynasty (221-210 B.C.), broke up the power of the rival noble families by moving them out of their fiefs to his new capital, again near Xi'an in Shaanxi province. He burned the classics and buried the Confucian scholars alive, but he also standardized weights and measures, the money, the system of writing and the length of the axles of carts, linked up and extended the Great Wall, built a network of roads and many palaces. His dynasty only outlasted him by six years, but the centralized empire was to remain until 1912.

The basic administrative and social structures of the empire were laid down by the succeeding dynasty, the Han. The Western Han (206 B.C.-A.D. 8) ruled from Xi'an and sought the support of the scholars and the land-owning gentry. A pattern of society emerged which was to last two thousand years: below the Imperial Clan and a small aristocracy were the land-owners and bureaucrats, the merchants, the peasantry, the domestic slaves, and a class of mercenary soldiers. Civil servants were recruited by imperial examinations open to all.

The Han emperor Wu Di sent envoys to western Asia and conquered territories in the west, south, north-east and along the east coast, extending the empire to roughly its modern limits. His expansionist policies caused his ruin and the empire was lost for a time to Wang Mang, who created his own dynasty. But in A.D. 23, the Han dynasty, known thereafter as the Eastern Han, was restored and the capital moved east to Luoyang, in Henan province. The emperor now gained control of even greater territories, including parts of Korea, Manchuria and North Annam (Vietnam) which remained under Chinese rule for nine centuries.

As long as they were able to keep the barbarian* tribes at war with each other, the Han controlled the Silk Route and stayed in power. But after the fall of their dynasty in A.D. 220 the empire broke up, and three and a half centuries of anarchy followed. Buddhism spread into North China during this period of division (known as the 'Southern and Northern Dynasties'), becoming the official religion in some of the northern barbarian empires (e.g. the Wei, A.D. 386-550). In A.D. 589 the Sui restored the empire, regaining tight control at the expense of heavy taxes. The dynasty lasted only a few decades (590-628), but the next rulers, the Tang (618-907), further improved the old administrative system, and were able to build a strong empire, stretching far west into what is now Russian Turkestan.

The Tang dynasty is famous for its refined civilization, its artists and craftsmen, and most of all its poets. While the official religion was Confucianism, tolerance prevailed and the capital, Chang'an

---

*The word used traditionally for the nomadic people living in Manchuria, Mongolia and Turkestan.

(modern Xi'an), became a great cosmopolitan city where Arabs, Persians, Tartars, Tibetans and Chinese lived and practised their various religions. The Tang emperor Xuan Zong was a great patron of the arts, and Empress Wu, an ambitious and devout woman, had some beautiful cave-temples carved. But she allowed the Buddhist monasteries to become the greatest land-owners in the country, and ruled by intrigue, precipitating the end of the dynasty.

After a few decades of anarchy during which the barbarian people in the north and east regained control over large portions of the empire, a new dynasty came into power, the Song (960-1276), who established their capital in Kaifeng, Henan province, further east than ever before in history, thereby acknowledging that the West was outside China's control. The threat from the barbarians within the empire, the Liao, and later the Jin, was permanent, however, and in 1126 Kaifeng was overrun and the court fled to Hangzhou in Zhejiang province. Life at the court in Hangzhou became a perpetual garden-party. The art of ceramics, in particular the making of monochrome glazed wares, reached a peak in design and quality in this period, and paper money and printing were developed. But when the Yuan overthrew the Jin in 1215 and headed for the rich southern provinces, there was little resistance.

The Yuan (1276-1368) was a foreign dynasty. Genghis Khan, who completed the conquest of Mongolia and of the Jin empire, was succeeded by his grandson Kublai Khan, who brought the Chinese empire under his rule. Beijing, then known as Khanbalik (Cambaluc), became for the first time the capital of the empire. During the Yuan dynasty, the Silk Route was again reopened and China's suzerainty established over Tibet and Yunnan. A powerful class of merchants prospered, Christianity penetrated, but the Yuan rulers never really controlled the Chinese population.

After a century of rule, the Yuan were driven north of the Great Wall and a Chinese dynasty, the Ming (1368-1644), came to power with the help of a Buddhist secret society. The first capital was Nanjing, but Emperor Yong Le* reconquered the northern provinces and moved his capital to Beijing. He showed an interest in the world, admitting Jesuits to his court and sending expeditions to the South Seas, but after his death in 1425, China stood still.

Once more, the dynasty was terminated by a combination of revolt from within and a barbarian invasion, and for the second time a foreign dynasty replaced it. The Qing (1644-1912) came from

---

*Correctly, the Yong Le emperor; the Ming and Qing emperors chose titles for their reigns by which they are commonly (and throughout this book) referred to rather than by their personal names.

Manchuria and modelled their administration on the Chinese pattern. Under the two powerful emperors Kang Xi and Qian Long,

THE DYNASTIES

XIA (Hsia)	B.C. 2205-1766
SHANG (Shang)	1766-1122
ZHOU (Chou)	1122-770
SPRING AND AUTUMN	770-476
WARRING STATES	476-221
QIN (Chin)	221-206
HAN (Han)	B.C. 206- A.D. 220
THREE KINGDOMS	A.D. 220-265
JIN (Tsin)	265-420
SOUTHERN AND NORTHERN DYNASTIES	420-589
Northern Wei (Wei)	386-534
SUI (Sui)	589-618
TANG (Tang)	618-907
FIVE DYNASTIES AND TEN KINGDOMS	907-960
Liao (Liao)	907-1125
Jin (Chin)	1115-1234
SONG (Sung)	960-1280
YUAN (Yuan)	1280-1368
MING (Ming)	1368-1644
Hong Wu (Hung Wu)	1368-1399
Jian Wen (Chien Wen)	1399-1403
Yong Le (Yung Lo)	1403-1425
Hong Xi (Hung Hsi)	1425-1426
Xuan De (Hsuan Teh)	1426-1436
Zheng Tong (Cheng T'ung)	1436-1450*
Jing Tai (Ching Tai)	1450-1457
Tian Shun (Tien Shun)	1457-1465*
Cheng Hua (Cheng Hua)	1465-1488
Hong Zhi (Hong Chih)	1488-1506
Cheng De (Cheng Teh)	1506-1522
Jia Jiang (Chia Ching)	1522-1567
Long Qing (Lung Ching)	1567-1573
Wang Li (Wan Li)	1573-1620
Tai Chang (Tai Chang)	1620-1621
Tian Qi (Tien Chi)	1621-1628
Chong Zhen (Chung Chen)	1628-1644
QING (Ching)	1644-1911
Shun Zhi (Shun Chih)	1644-1662
Kang Xi (Kang Hsi)	1662-1723
Yong Zheng (Yung Cheng)	1723-1736
Qian Long (Chien Long)	1736-1796
Jia Qing (Chia Ching)	1796-1821
Dao Guang (Tao Kuang)	1821-1851
Xian Feng (Hsien Feng)	1851-1862
Tong Zhi (Tung Chih)	1862-1875
Guang Xu (Kuang Hsu)	1875-1908
Xuan Tong (Hsuan Tung)	1908-1911+

* (resumed rule)
+ (abdicated)

the empire recovered its prosperity, but at the end of the eighteenth century the authority of the emperor diminished and corruption spread. China's refusal to enter into diplomatic relations with the Western powers, and Britain's refusal to stop exporting opium to China in exchange for tea, led to the Opium Wars (1839-62), easily won by the British who gained the island of Hong Kong and the opening of so-called 'free ports' to trade. Other nations obtained similar concessions, and legations were opened in Beijing.

The Taiping rebellion nearly brought the Qing dynasty to an end in the middle of the nineteenth century. There were short-lived attempts at reform, but in 1900 the autocratic Dowager Empress Ci Xi suffered the humiliation of having to flee from Beijing, besieged by the Boxers, a secret society whose members rose against the Manchus and foreigners alike. The Boxer Rebellion was crushed with the help of the foreign powers but the Qing dynasty was doomed. The Dowager Empress died in 1908 and a democratic revolution, led by a southerner, Sun Yatsen, overthrew the dynasty in 1911.

The Republic. A provisional republican government was established in Nanjing, then Sun Yatsen stepped down to let Yuan Shikai, a former Qing minister, become the first President of the Republic, convinced that Yuan had a greater following in the North than he. Yuan tried unsuccessfully to make himself emperor. The Japanese, who were by then occupying the Northeast, seized the former German concessions in Shandong. In 1917, China entered the war on the side of the Allies, but the Treaty of Versailles confirmed the Japanese possession of Shandong. A revolt led by intellectuals broke out in Beijing on the 4th of May 1919. By 1921, however, the North had become a prey to warlords and Sun Yatsen had to retreat to his home base, Guangzhou, where he established a republican government. The Chinese Communist Party, founded in Shanghai in 1921, was organized under Soviet guidance and pressed by the Soviets to join the Nationalist party, the Kuomintang (KMT), in the fight against the warlords.

In 1925, Sun Yatsen died and the leadership of the KMT went to Chiang Kaishek, who made war on the Communists in Shanghai in 1927 and forced the survivors underground. In 1928, he captured Beijing, declared the country unified and established a government in Nanjing. Some of the Communists, under the leadership of Mao Zedong (Mao Tse-tung), regrouped in Jiangxi province and organized their own Red Army. The KMT mounted an offensive against their bases in Jiangxi, and in 1934 drove the Communists on the Long March, which ended in Yenan, Shaanxi province, in 1935. At the end of 1936 Chiang Kaishek agreed to a truce with Mao's forces in order to repulse the Japanese who, having secured Manchuria in 1932, were marching south towards Nanjing. By 1939, however, the KMT had resumed its attacks on the Communist bases in Shaanxi.

At the onset of World War II China was divided into three zones: the Northeast and Eastern provinces under Japanese occupation, the Northwest run by the Communists from Yenan, and the South and Southwest administered from Chongqing (Chungking), in Sichuan province, by the Nationalists. After the Japanese surrender in 1945, the Communists and the Nationalists scrambled to reconquer the national territory. The Communists won out and the People's Republic was proclaimed in Beijing in 1949, while the Nationalists retreated to the island of Taiwan.

The People's Republic. Beginning in 1949, the new leaders redistributed the land among the peasants, attacked corruption and tried to win the support of the whole population. A Friendship Pact with the Soviet Union was signed in 1950. The First Five-Year Plan, begun in 1953, as soon as the Korean war ended, created agricultural co-operatives, followed in 1956 by the collectivization of ownership of the means of production. In 1957, the Hundred Flowers Campaign launched a national debate which ended in severe repressive measures against intellectuals and liberals who did not fit the socialist pattern imposed by the Communist Party. The following year, China launched the Second Five-Year Plan, and the Great Leap Forward which was to give impetus to the country's economic growth. But by that time China had fallen out of favour with its only friend, the Soviet Union, and by 1960, all economic aid and all Soviet personnel had been withdrawn.

From 1961 to 1966, a return to more pragmatic economic policies brought a measure of relaxation. China began to open up to the world: it made friends, within the Communist bloc, not only with little Albania but with Romania and Yugoslavia; in 1964 France, followed by a number of Francophone African countries, recognized the People's Republic. But Mao Zedong, the old revolutionary, was not prepared to relinquish ideological purity; late in 1965 he launched the so-called Cultural Revolution to regain control of the party and realize his socialist dream. Young members of the Red Guards were set to tracking down counter-revolutionaries among the party cadres (those in managerial positions), in their schools, their neighbourhoods and even among their own families, in order to destroy the 'Four Olds' (old ideas, culture, customs and habits). The result was a cultural stasis lasting ten years, while higher education broke down, progress in agricultural and industrial production was impeded and the cult of Mao Zedong's personality rose to extreme heights. In the end the Army stepped in, and the Red Guards were banished to distant provinces. Still, a majority of radicals, including Mao's wife, Jiang Qing (Chiang Ching), were given key posts at the Ninth Party Congress (1969) and the witch-hunt continued into the Seventies.

1970-1980. The first half of the 1970s saw a gradual rebuilding of the Communist Party and the machinery of government in the wake of the Cultural Revolution. A key political development was the elimination in 1971 of Marshal Lin Biao, Minister of Defence and formally-designated successor to Mao. This opened the way to friendship with the USA, a policy Lin had allegedly opposed, and also made possible the reassertion of the Party's civil authority over the military.

The Premier, Zhou Enlai (Chou En-lai), asserted himself discreetly as leader of those who favoured a pragmatic, rational government and wanted China to be opened to the world. He faced opposition from a leftist faction which enjoyed considerable support from Chairman Mao Zedong, and in which Mao's wife, Jiang Qing, was prominent.

Nevertheless, many of the most prominent victims of the Cultural Revolution were restored to honour and power, the most important being Deng Xiaoping, who had been a leading target of Maoist attacks, and the new diplomacy resulted in 1971 in the People's Republic of China being accepted, rather than the increasingly isolated Nationalist regime on Taiwan, as the rightful occupant of the China seat at the UN.

In 1973-4, China launched a programme of importing foreign plant and equipment in areas of sophisticated technology such as the manufacture of chemical fertilizers and aircraft. A very modest start was also made on a new programme of scientific, educational and cultural exchanges with the West, though all such initiatives were opposed by the Maoists, who had the power to block most of the reforms the pragmatists would have wished to introduce.

In the last two years of his life, Zhou Enlai used his prestige to influence China's course for the future. He established the 'Four Modernizations' (in industry, agriculture, science and technology, and national defence) as China's goal to be attained by the year 2000. When he died in January 1976, the leftists attacked Deng Xiaoping, who had been expected to succeed Zhou as Premier, and the modernization policies which he and other pragmatist reformers had been developing.

In April 1976, popular demonstrations of loyalty to Zhou Enlai and the 'Four Modernizations', and against Jiang Qing and her leftist associates, took place in Tiananmen Square in Beijing and in dozens of other cities, of a size and character not seen in China since the May Fourth demonstrations of 1919.

Mao Zedong died in September 1976 and within a month of his death, his widow, her three major allies and thirty other prominent leftists were arrested. The fall of the 'Gang of Four' was greeted with intense public rejoicing. Since Mao's death, there has been collective leadership by a few powerful men. Hua Guofeng became Chairman of the Party as well as Prime Minister, with the support of the Minister of Defence, Ye Jianying. In July 1977, eleven months after Mao's death, Deng Xiaoping was restored to all his former posts, and although he had not been made Premier, he did become the most powerful figure in the leadership.

The most important issue after Mao's death was whether the Communist Party should maintain that Mao was infallible. Deng and his followers had great respect for Mao's leadership in the years before 1949, when the Communists were fighting to gain power in the country, but they thought he had made some disastrous mistakes after 1949 — a view that was widely shared by ordinary citizens. Eventually, Mao's fallibility was publicly acknowledged and this gave the new leadership greater freedom in charting a fresh course for China.

The reforms introduced included the implementation of the rather full civil and criminal code of law already in force. An ambitious programme for sending students abroad was announced as well as cultural and scientific exchanges. In the economy greater reliance was placed on material incentives and on the autonomy of enterprises. The press was given greater freedom, and hundreds of thousands of intellectuals and cadres were rehabilitated. The official policy of liberalization and the redress of past injustices encouraged young people to appeal for democracy and human rights.

In foreign policy a new self-confidence and energy was also evident. For the first time since 1949, China launched a really vigorous attempt to tap the economic resources of the outside world: foreign loans, foreign direct investment and partners for joint ventures were sought. China's opening to the world was dramatically emphasized by the establishment in 1979 of full diplomatic relations with the USA.

The difficulties facing the new leadership of this nation of almost one billion people were enormous. The standard of living for most people had not risen dramatically under the People's Republic, and there was opposition to reform by many conservative-minded cadres. But as China entered the 1980s, there was greater optimism about the prospects than for the past twenty years.

The present political system. Political power in China today is held by the Communist Party, the state (i.e. the machinery of government) and the Army. The Party decides policies and controls the state and the Army. The Party is headed by a Chairman who presides at meetings of the Politburo (23 members and 3 alternate members) and its very important Standing Committee (consisting, in 1979, of the Chairman plus 5 members). Under these come the Central Committee with 201 full members and 132 alternate members, and the provincial Party organizations. The Party has 37 million card-holding members. The highest organization within the state is the National People's Congress, which does little more than ratify the decisions of the Party leadership. Its members include representatives of non-Communist parties and religious leaders. The main organ of government is the State Council whose members are Party members and who are nominated by the NPC on the recommendation of the Party. The State Council is made up of the Premier, about 12 vice-premiers, ministers and heads of bureaux and commissions. The Party leadership lays down policies for the Army and makes key appointments in it. There is some overlap in the upper echelons of leadership of the Party and the Army.

CULTURE

Language and system of writing. Chinese is the mother tongue of more people than any other language in the world, but the number of non-Chinese who speak the language is extremely small; and within China itself, there are many spoken dialects which are mutually unintelligible. However, the written language, with its elaborate system of ideograms, is intelligible to every literate person. It is as if, in Europe, Latin had remained the common written language while French, Spanish and Italian were the spoken forms.

Spoken Chinese is characterized by its limited range of sounds, which is compensated for to some extent by the use of four different 'tones' (variations in pitch). For example, the syllable *mao*, pronounced in the first tone, means 'cat'; in the second tone, 'hair' (which is also Chairman Mao's family name); in the third tone, 'still water'; and in the fourth tone, 'to rush out' or 'a hat'. Each of these different meanings is expressed in writing by a different ideogram, or character, and there is a separate ideogram for each syllable of a word.* Thus, the word *maobi*, 'a brush', will have two characters, the second of which is made up of the radical for 'bamboo' and the element which means 'hair'; but the syllable *bi* on its own means 'pen', or any instrument for writing. The characters give no phonetic clue to the pronunciation; nor do they make any allowance for indicating number, gender, tense, etc. — changes which are conveyed by the addition of separate characters or particles.

Since the beginning of the century, and particularly since 1949, the Chinese have been attempting to modernize their system of writing and render it usable by a larger part of the population, by making spoken 'mandarin' Chinese the basis for a standard form of phonetic transcription. In 1979 the Chinese government made official the system known as Pinyin, based on the Northern pronunciation (Beijing dialect), for the phonetic transcription of proper names. The Pinyin spellings are therefore used in this guidebook for names of persons and places rather than the older Wade-Giles forms of romanization (i.e. transcription of Chinese characters into the roman alphabet) until recently in widespread use in the West. The replacement of all the ideograms by the Pinyin phonetic forms is a long-term goal for the Chinese, for which no date has been fixed.

Arts and crafts. Bronze vessels cast during the Shang and Zhou dynasties (seventeenth to third centuries B.C.) are almost certainly the finest in the world in design and technical perfection. The technique employed is the *cire perdue* process: a model of the vessel is made of wax, which is then coated with clay and baked; the wax melts and runs out, and bronze is poured in, allowed to harden, and the clay mould removed.

Ceramics is a very ancient art, the earliest examples dating back to the neolithic period. The first glazed stoneware appeared about the eleventh century B.C. It was the ancestor of porcelain and required firing temperatures of about 1100°C. True porcelain was first made at the beginning of the Tang dynasty. The coloured glaze ceramics of the Song and Yuan dynasties are among the most highly valued by collectors. At the end of the Yuan dynasty appeared another celebrated ceramic: the blue and white underglaze wares. The best examples date from the fourteenth and fifteenth centuries. The overglaze enamel decorations (requiring a second firing) were first made in the fifteenth century and mark the beginning of the

---

*The list of Chinese phrases in the Appendix gives a fuller account of the different tones and the principles of pronunciation of spoken Chinese.

richly decorated polychrome ceramics of the Ming dynasty. In the eighteenth century, new types of high-fired monochrome glazes such as the *'sang de boeuf'* appeared, as well as new types of enamel decorations such as the *'famille rose'*.

Excavations of tombs of the fourth and third centuries B.C. have brought to light some paintings executed on silk with brush and ink. Silk is still used today but has been largely replaced by highly absorbent thin paper which is then mounted on thick paper and set in a silk background. Because they cannot be touched up, the brush strokes have to be light and quick; the artist's mind must be calm and his hand steady. The art of calligraphy is also inseparable from the art of painting.

Few examples of painting from the Han to the Tang dynasties have survived. Murals and paintings on silk, found in tombs and caves, evolved from abstract designs to figures and landscapes of great realism. With the Song dynasty, romantic landscapes, 'bird and flower' paintings academic in style, and free-style bamboo and blossom paintings all developed concurrently. The individualistic, subjective and impressionistic painting practised by Chan (Zen) Buddhists from the seventh century onwards is the basis of a 'modern' style of painting developed in the late nineteenth and early twentieth centuries, but which continued to exist alongside the increasingly academic style of the Ming and Qing paintings of landscapes and 'birds and flowers'. The art of large-scale landscape painting reached its height in the Yuan and early Ming dynasties.

China is also deservedly appreciated for its handicrafts: silk brocades, embroidery, basketware, lacquer work, hard stone and ivory carvings, etc.

Among the musical arts, Chinese opera is a complex mixture of acting, acrobatics, music and mime, built round themes borrowed from history and mythology, and has traditionally been enjoyed by the educated gentry and the mass of the people alike. For a westerner, its most striking features are the richness of the costumes and make-up, the large repertoire of conventional gestures and facial expressions, and the high-pitched — and to our ears, discord-ant — music. In recent years, the impoverished 'revolutionary opera' has lost ground in favour of a revival of classical opera.

Chinese cuisine is without doubt an art. There are four main styles of cuisine: the Northern cuisine (Beijing and the North China plain), with such well-known dishes as Peking Duck and Mongolian Hot Pot; the cuisine of the coastal provinces (Jiangsu, Shandong, Zhejiang, Fujian) with its soups and seafood; the spicy and peppery cuisine of the central provinces (Sichuan and Hunan); and the Cantonese cuisine, perhaps the most delicate and varied and also the best known outside China. The cuisine has declined since the 1950s in the People's Republic, where only the largest cities now have restaurants which maintain high standards of cooking.

Philosophy and religion. Confucianism is a code of morals rather than a religion. Its essence is the defining of proper relationships within society, beginning in the home with the relationship between old and young, men and women. The son must respect his father, the wife must respect her husband, everyone must respect their superiors. In turn, the prince must behave in a respectable way if he wants the respect of his inferiors. The prince ultimately gets the blame for unrest in his kingdom and must answer to Heaven for it. There were temples of Confucius in every town and its 'priests' were the local officials.

The doctrine of Taoism was first devised by Laozi (Lao-tsze), a contemporary of Confucius, who emphasized the place of man in nature, as opposed to society. A Taoist does not try to fight against nature, but lives in harmony with it. Taoism is a return to the sources, an antithesis to Confucianism which wants to create the perfect 'society man'. Taoist monks were in search of immortality and practised magic. Taoist temples contain shrines dedicated to the spirits of mountains, springs, lakes, etc.

The Buddhist religion was brought to China from India, along the Silk Route, at the beginning of the Christian era. It implanted itself first in western and northern China among the non-Chinese nomadic people, but by the seventh century had reached the peasant population almost everywhere. A lamaic form of Buddhism which originated in Tibet is found only in North China and was practised by the Manchus and the Mongols. Chinese Buddhism belongs to the Mahayana (Great Vehicle) tradition which holds Buddha to be the supreme Truth and Wisdom and says that men can attain nirvana (enlightenment) by searching for Truth and Wisdom. Chan (Zen) Buddhism rejects the scriptures as a means of teaching. The most beautiful stone sculptures in China were inspired by the Buddhist faith.

The influence of the Islamic faith was particularly strong during the Tang dynasty and the religion is still practised today. There are Hui (Moslem) communities in many cities in China, in particular in the northern provinces.

The Christian faith did not make many converts in China, though the Jesuits at the imperial court were instrumental in spreading scientific knowledge, and the presence of Christian missionaries in the country helped to foster Chinese understanding of European social values. Confucianism, Taoism, Buddhism and the cult of ancestors were in the past often practised simultaneously by the Chinese. Monotheistic faiths like Islam and Christianity failed to gain much ground because of their uncompromising and exclusive nature.

Chinese temples, and in particular Buddhist temples, are not always easily distinguishable from the neighbouring houses. Those patronized by the emperor had the privilege of being roofed with glazed tiles, and their walls were painted brick red. Mosques are indistinguishable, at least on the outside, from other temples, which was one of the conditions of their survival; unlike other temples, however, they do not face south, but west, towards Mecca. There are now few active temples in China, and only of the Buddhist or Islamic faiths. Only the larger Buddhist temples, which in the past had large communities, still have monks.

Among the figures most commonly represented in Buddhist temples are Sakyamuni Buddha, the supreme Buddha, the Buddha of the throne of diamond, often shown seated on a lotus, with three fingers of the right hand raised. Amitabha Buddha (Buddha of Boundless Light) is the saviour who will guide the faithful to the 'pure land' (or Western Heaven), and is often represented with Sakyamuni. Maitreya Buddha, the 'laughing Buddha', will be Buddha in five thousand years, waiting in Tushita (Heaven) to succeed Sakyamuni. Represented seated, fat, smiling and holding a rosary, he does not have a *usnisa*, or bun — the sign by which Buddhas are customarily recognized — on top of his balding head.

Below the rank of Buddha, there are the Bodhisattvas, in their last incarnation before attaining Buddhahood (*pusa* in Chinese). The most famous are the Three Great Beings: Puxian, Wenshu and Guanyin (Kuanyin). Puxian (Samantabhadra) symbolizes love; he is the patron of the sacred Mount Omei in Sichuan province and is represented riding an elephant. Wenshu (Manjusri) symbolizes wisdom. Patron of the sacred Wutaishan in Shanxi province, he is represented riding a lion, holding a lotus, supporting a book in his left hand. Guanyin (Avalokitesvara), who symbolizes compassion, is the most popular. Bodhisattvas are recognizable by their elaborate headdress, their floating gowns with sashes and jewels, and their feminine looks.

The two disciples found one on either side of a main Buddha figure are Ananda on the left, looking young, and Kassapa (Kasyapa) on the right, looking old. They are always represented dressed in Chinese monks' robes but with Indian features. Lohans (disciples) can be represented in very large groups (up to 500).

Two groups of fierce and oversized figures, the two gate guardians (*dvarapala*) and the four celestial kings (*devaraja*), are found at the entrance of a Buddhist temple. *Apsarah* (pl.; *apsara*, sg.), the equivalent of our angels, are represented flying in the air with their robes floating around them. (See plan of a Buddhist temple, p. 130.)

Everyday life. China is a poor country, where the average per capita income is the equivalent of US $400 per year. Workers in large factories fare best as to fringe benefits (housing, canteen, crêche, virtually free clinic), but the salary scale depends more on the length of employment than on skills, which are usually acquired on the job. Political education at the worker's unit (place of employment) is compulsory. There are often two two-hour sessions per week, and sometimes during working hours.

Farm workers, who are organized into brigades, receive a very small amount of their income in cash. Real income varies according to the prosperity of the brigade, but on the whole, market-garden brigades situated near urban centres fare best; brigades in remote parts of the country where the growing season is short may live at barely subsistence level.

The cadres, those in managerial positions, enjoy a great measure of privileges: good housing, a chance to send their children to good schools, occasionally the use of a car with a chauffeur (which can be the same as if not better than owning one), the privilege of shopping in special 'cadre stores' or in Friendship Stores, domestic staff, and of course, a higher income. High cadres in the Army are, along with cooks, the fattest people in China.

Medical care is not free, although it is not expensive, but the availability and cost of such care varies from one employment unit to another. Pensions also vary in the different employment units. Overmanning is used as a remedy against unemployment.

The Chinese are not free to choose where they will work or live, and families are too often broken up. Most of China's housing whether in the cities or in the countryside, is old, inadequate and in bad repair, though an immense effort at modernizing it has been made. Farmers, who often own their houses and can leave them to their children, fare best as to space, but live in extremely primitive conditions. In the cities, most families live in no more than two rooms, cook outdoors almost all the year round, get water from a tap in the yard and often have, even now, to use a public lavatory. To bathe, they go to the public baths or the showers at work. Blocks of flats are still not very common in China, and those built before 1949 have not been properly maintained. Heating in such blocks is available only during certain times of the day (morning and evening).

Rents are very low; the bulk of the family income is spent on food. In principle, education is available to all, up to the age of fourteen, but again, the quality and availability of education at higher levels depends on the area. There are only about 500,000 places in universities and colleges and about 10 million apply to get in. Academic curricula have been enlarged since 1978 to include subjects once taboo and foreign languages are taught increasingly, using foreign texts; science students can again have access to foreign scientific publications. Admission to universities is once again on merit and not on political record.

Young people find courting very difficult. They live with their parents or in dormitories for unmarried people. Winter is long and cold in the North and love in the parks can be very uncomfortable. Couples are urged to wait until their combined age is fifty-three before they marry, and even then, if they cannot move in with their parents, they have to live apart while they wait to be allocated a flat or a house.

Birth control is achieved through many means besides contraceptives. A quota of children is assigned to each unit and if Mrs Zhu is expecting her third child and Mrs Ma is expecting her first when the quota is nearly reached, pressure will be put on Mrs Zhu to have an abortion; she may even lose work points or be demoted if she goes ahead against her unit's advice.

Law and order in China is, by our standards, very good, largely thanks to the network of units which ensures that little is left unwitnessed and unreported. This does not mean that there is no crime in China; stealing bicycles is extremely common. But you, as a foreigner, will be very safe. A Chinese would not like to be caught stealing from a foreigner and he would have trouble reselling foreign-made goods without attracting notice.

Since 1977, cultural policies have been relaxed considerably and queues are growing longer outside cinemas and theatres. Not many new Chinese films have been produced, but some old favourites, including foreign films, are being shown. A major breakthrough is the revival of traditional opera. Cinema or opera tickets are seldom sold at the theatre; they are allocated to the units who in turn sell them to their members. People think little of leaving work to go and see a film. There are several showings a day, beginning at 8 a.m.

II
THE NORTHEAST
AND
THE NORTH

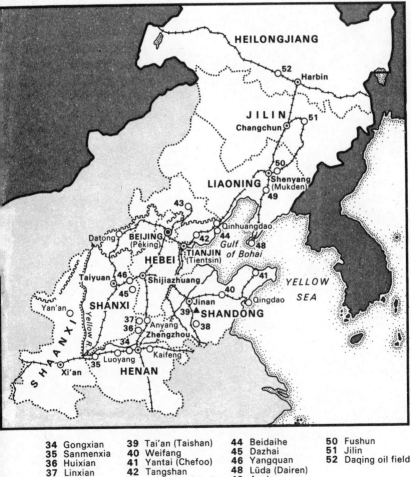

34 Gongxian	**39** Tai'an (Taishan)	**44** Beidaihe	**50** Fushun
35 Sanmenxia	**40** Weifang	**45** Dazhai	**51** Jilin
36 Huixian	**41** Yantai (Chefoo)	**46** Yangquan	**52** Daqing oil field
37 Linxian	**42** Tangshan	**48** Lüda (Dairen)	
38 Qufu	**43** Chengde (Jehol)	**49** Anshan	

1 Beijing (Peking) and its environs

Beijing (the Northern Capital) lies within Hebei province, but is a municipality directly under the control of the central government. It is about 15 km south of the foothills of the Yanshan which mark the border with Mongolia. The Western Hills can be seen from the city on a few rare days when the air is free of pollution. Beijing is almost perfectly flat, and a paradise for cyclists.

In winter, the Siberian anticyclone moves south, keeping the temperatures between zero and −30°C. for the best part of December, January and February. Spring is short, subject to sudden changes in atmospheric pressure, and brings powerful and cold winds laden with dust from the Gobi desert and the loess plateaus. By May, summer has come, the humidity rises and the temperature remains around 30°C. Forty per cent of the yearly rainfall occurs in July. Autumn begins gradually, after the middle of August, and is by far the most pleasant season.

The municipality of Beijing has a population of about 8 million. Though the city is the seat of the national government, its position as a cultural and business centre is challenged by Shanghai. In form, it consists of three concentric cities − the Forbidden City, the Imperial City, the Inner or Tartar City − with a fourth or Outer City to the south. Although Beijing was almost entirely rebuilt in the fifteenth century, the basic layout has remained unchanged since the thirteenth century. The four cities originally all had their own walls; although only the grey crenellated wall of the Forbidden City remains intact today, the outline of old Beijing is still discernible, and portions of the brick-coloured walls of the Imperial City can be seen in Changan Avenue. But the walls of the Inner City and its moat have gone, to make way for the subway in the north, the railway in the south, and motorways to the east and west. Qianmen, the Front Gate, with its two gate houses due south of Tiananmen Square, marks the border of the Inner City, and a new 'wall' of tall modern buildings has gone up between it and the Outer City.

The Chinese or Outer City, with its busy shopping streets and the Red Lantern (entertainment) district of the Bridge of Heaven, has always had a lively and popular character. The Old Legation Quarter (7), in the south-east of the Inner City, is easily distinguished from other districts by its European architecture. In the eighteenth century affluent Chinese families built houses in the Inner City,

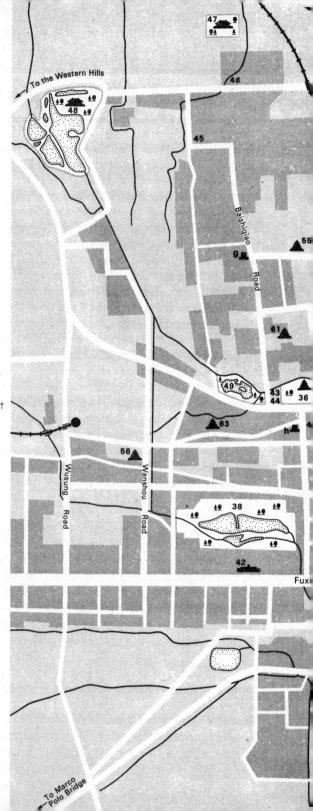

Hotels and amenities

a   Peking Hotel
b   Xinqiao Hotel
c   Minzu Hotel
d   Qianmen Hotel
e   Heping Hotel
f   Huaqiao Hotel
g   Friendship Guesthouse
h   Xiyuan Hotel
i   Capital Hospital
j   International Club
k   Friendship Store
l   Liulichang antique shops
m   New Theatre Shop
n   Baihuodalou Department Store

Places of interest

1   Forbidden City
2   Zhongshan Park
3   Cultural Park of the Working People
4   Monument to the People's Heroes
5   Great Hall of the People
6   Museum of National History
7   Old Legation Quarter†
8   Ritan Park
9   Yuetan Park
10 Ditan Park
11 Temple of Agriculture
12 Temple of Heaven
13 Joyous Pavilion Park
14 Southern Cathedral
15 Protestant church
16 Dongsi Mosque
*17 Old Mosque
*18 Eastern Cathedral
*19 Northern Cathedral
*20 Western Cathedral
21 Lake of the Ten Monasteries
22 Beihai (North Lake) Park
23 Coal Hill
24 National Library
25 Zhongnanhai (Middle and South Lake)
26 Jianguomenwai Foreigners Compounds†
27 Sanlitun Foreigners Compounds†
28 Agricultural Exhibition Hall
29 Workers' Stadium and Gymnasium
30 Eastern Market
31 Xidan Market
32 People's Market
33 Museum of Fine Arts
34 Natural History Museum
35 Lu Xun Museum
36 Zoo
37 Beijing Exhibition Centre
38 Yuyuantan
39 Five Stupas Temple
40 Planetarium
41 Observatory
42 Museum of the People's Revolutionary Army
43 Capital Gymnasium
44 White Stone Bridge
45 Beijing University
46 Qinghua University
47 Old Summer Palace
48 Summer Palace
49 Purple Bamboo Park
50 Drum Tower
51 Bell Tower
52 Lama Temple
53 Temple of Confucius
54 Yellow Temple
55 Big Bell Temple
56 Pagoda of the Eight Li Village
57 Temple of the White Cloud
58 Pagoda of the Temple of Heavenly Repose
59 Temple of the Eastern Peak
60 Temple of the White Dagoba
61 Big Buddha Temple
62 Temple of the Transformation of the Intellect
63 Temple of the Sea of the Law
64 Temple of Universal Rescue

* closed

† see Appendix for plan

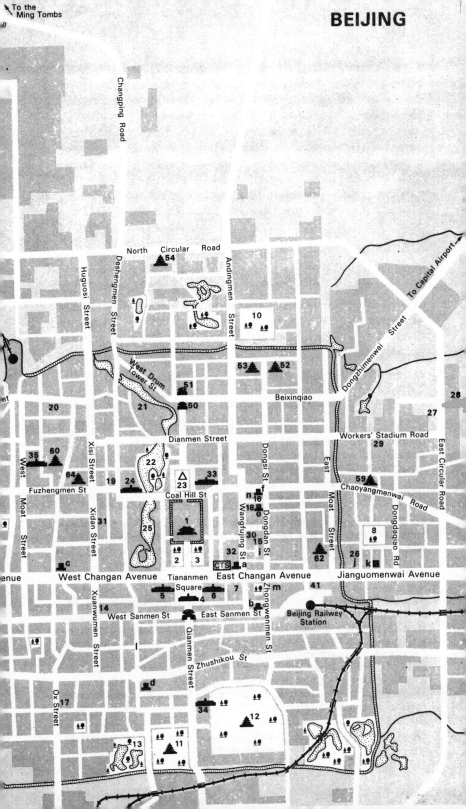

BEIJING

To the
Ming Tombs

Changping Road

North Circular Road

To Capital Airport

Huguosi Street

Deshengmen Street

Andingmen Street

Dongzhimenwai Street

54

10

West Drum Tower St

53 52

Beixinqiao

51

20 21 50

Dianmen Street

Workers' Stadium Road

27

28

29

East Circular Road

35 60

Xisi Street

Fuzhengmen St

64

19 24

22

23

33

Coal Hill St

Dongsi St

59

Chaoyangmenwai Road

Dongdaqiao Rd

East Moat Street

f

n 16

31

25

1

Wangfujing St

18
6

30
15

i

8

West Moat Street

c

2 3

32

CTS

a

62

26

j k

West Changan Avenue

Tiananmen Square

East Changan Avenue

Jianguomenwai Avenue

5 4 6 7

b

m

41

14

West Sanmen St

East Sanmen St

Zhongwenmen St

Beijing Railway Station

Xuanwumen Street

l

Qianmen Street

Zhushikou St

d

Ox Street

17

34

12

13 11

formerly reserved for the Manchu Bannermen whose loyalty to the emperor could not be questioned. But the most beautiful houses in Beijing are in the areas around the Forbidden City (1), where they are difficult to spot because their entrances are discreet, and in a state of neglect. Most of Beijing's downtown residents still live in *hutong* (alleys) with their compounds of single-storey houses arranged around inner courtyards. An imperial edict forbade houses of more than two storeys which would be visible from within the Forbidden City and would overlook it. Moreover no house could be higher than a temple; and a man who built a house taller than his neighbour's could be taken to court for depriving the other man of sunlight.

PRACTICAL INFORMATION

Hotels. If you come to Beijing as a tourist your hotel will probably be chosen for you by the China Travel Service; but following are details on a range of hotels into which foreigner visitors are presently booked:

Peking Hotel (Beijing Fandian), East Changan Avenue (a), tel. 552231, 556531, 558331. Built in 1975, this is the most modern, but also the most expensive hotel in the city. It is conveniently located near the Imperial City, Tiananmen Square and Wangfujing Street, nicknamed 'Oxford Street' by the British and 'le Faubourg Saint Honoré' by the French. Rooms on the west side overlook the Forbidden City. They all have private baths and are spacious and comfortable, but the décor is unfortunately dull and grand; in the suites the curtains are electrically operated but there is no way of controlling the heating or air-conditioning, both of which are overgenerous. Peking Hotel waiters and roomboys are notorious for their revolutionary spirit and their indifference to customers. Facilities and services include bar, lobby shop, post and telegraph office, barber and hairdresser, laundry, massage parlour, dining hall, private dining rooms and conference rooms. The restaurants serve Chinese, European and Japanese food (this last not available anywhere else in town) — if the waiters approve of you and if you arrive in good time. The food is of reasonable quality. Taxis can be ordered in the lobby.

Xinqiao Hotel (New Expatriates Hotel), East Jiaomin Street (b), tel. 557731. Built in the early 1950s next to the old Belgian legation, the Xinqiao Hotel is centrally located and enjoys a much better reputation for its service than the Peking Hotel. The rooms are old-fashioned, with private baths, and are not air-conditioned. The facilities and services are the same as at the Peking Hotel and the central taxi pool is located there (tel. 557461). There is a Chinese restaurant on the lower ground floor and a Western restaurant on the seventh floor* with a terrace and a view over the roofs to Tiananmen Square; the food is good in both.

---

*The Chinese follow the American system of numbering floors, i.e. the ground floor is called the first floor, and from thence upwards.

Minzu Hotel (Minorities Hotel), West Changan Boulevard (c), tel. 668541. Still in downtown Beijing, but far from the most favourite haunts of foreigners, the Minzu is increasingly used to receive tourists and other delegations. The hotel was built in the '50s but to lower standards than the Xinqiao Hotel. The rooms are small and the beds typically Chinese, i.e. very hard. There are both a Chinese and a Western restaurant on the ground floor; the food is fair.

Qianmen Hotel (Front Gate Hotel), Yongan Lu (d), tel. 338731. Situated in the Outer City, about 1 km south of Liulichang, the street of the antique shops, the Qianmen is a second-class hotel, hastily brought up to standard with a coat of paint to accommodate the influx of foreign visitors. Not all the rooms have telephones or private baths. The lobby shop has a limited range of goods. The food is passable.

Heping Hotel (Peace Hotel), off Dongdan Street (e), tel. 558841. Centrally located, in the compound of a former Qing dynasty prince — the entrance is on Jinyu Hutong (Goldfish Alley) — the hotel itself is a rather poorly constructed tall block; the rooms are small and not very comfortable. Foreigners are put up there only when the China Travel Service cannot find space anywhere else. The Heping has the best 'European' cooks in the city, and large parties are entertained in the formal rooms in the old compound which is kept in beautiful condition.

Huaqiao Hotel (Overseas Chinese Hotel), Wangfujing and East Dongsi Streets (f), tel. 558851. Reserved, as its name indicates, for overseas Chinese visitors.

Youyi Binguan (Friendship Guest House), North Circular and Baishiqiao Roads (g), tel. 890621. This vast complex of hotel blocks, blocks of flats, shops, an outpatient clinic, meeting halls, swimming pool, etc., built in the '50s to house Russian experts and their families, lies in the suburbs, on the way to the Summer Palace. One building has been set aside for foreign tourists and other groups, but most guests complain that it is too far from downtown Beijing.

Xiyuan Hotel (Western Garden Hotel), Xizhimenwai Road (h), tel. 890721. Just at the city limits, near the Zoo and the Planetarium, the Xiyuan has recently been receiving foreign tourists. It is quiet and simple, very much a second-class hotel.

Jade Fountain Hotel, near the Summer Palace (48), is an old country estate recently converted into a hotel for foreign guests. It is not the most convenient, being far from the city, but the most romantic and restful.

A new hotel is being built outside Beijing which is to be completed by 1980 and should meet international standards.

Restaurants. Eating out is one of the few forms of evening entertainment in Beijing, and there are a number of good restaurants, serving food from all the Chinese provinces, though Cantonese food is under-represented. Those listed below all have private dining rooms where foreigners are supposed to eat. Dinner starts early (7 p.m. at the latest) and the staff will expect you to leave promptly at the end of the meal. (As elsewhere, tipping is not allowed.) It is wise to book at least a day in advance, and when ordering a meal to set a cash limit per head, excluding drinks. But remember that the more money you spend, the more likely it is that you will be served exotic dishes, highly appreciated by the Chinese, like sea slugs, fish lips or tripes, 'thousand-year-old' eggs, caterpillar fungus, eels (water snake), etc.

If you prefer simple cooking, try one of the numerous 'masses' restaurants, i.e. one without a private dining room, but go accompanied by a Chinese speaker, and with a small party (four or five). Arrive early (11 a.m. or 5.30 p.m.) and don't lose your nerve when the staff try to discourage you by ignoring you, or make a fuss and clear a whole table with much gesturing and shouting, leaving you embarrassed at having dislodged an unfortunate party. The reward can be a delicious meal for a small amount of money, and conversation with people you would not otherwise have met. Some 'masses' restaurants will maintain that they cannot serve you because you do not have ration coupons for grain, oil and meat, and if this happens, you should not insist, or try to force your way in.

The décor of Chinese restaurants is usually extremely drab, but Beijing boasts a few beautiful ones. The Sichuan Restaurant is in a nine-courtyard house said to have been built by a rich businessman for his family, who then 'donated' it to General Yuan Shikai for one of his mistresses; and the Beihai or Fangshan Restaurant (Tradition of the Empress Cuisine) is situated on Hortensia Island in Beihai (North Lake) Park (22). In the past some cooks began their training in the Palace; a restaurant which also follows the tradition of the 'Empress cuisine', the Tingliguan, is in the Summer Palace (48), in a small compound called the Pavilion for Listening to the Orioles (Tingliguan). The Pavilion was once a private theatre, for the Dowager Empress Ci Xi was very fond of theatrical entertainment, particularly of the vulgar kind popular in the district of the Bridge of Heaven, the 'Pigalle' of Old Beijing.

Drinks served in restaurants include beer, fizzy orange, mineral water, sweet red wine (to be avoided), the fiery *maotai,* a white or brown spirit made from sorghum and seemingly indispensable for giving toasts, and the delicious yellow wine — a rice wine similar to the Japanese *sake,* served warm in small cups — the best of which comes from the region of Shaoxing in Zhejiang province. You will be amazed at the number of bottles of beer a large party can drink, until you look in the crates and see that most have been discarded one-third full.

RESTAURANTS *Central Beijing*

Name	Specialities/Comment	Address/Location*	Tel. no.
BEIJING — NORTHERN CHINESE COOKING			
Beijing Kaoyadian (nicknamed Sick Duck)	Peking duck	Shaifuyuan, Santiao Hutong, No. 13. Off Wangfujing, on the left in the road leading to the Capital Hospital (**1**).	55-3310
Beijing Kaoyadian (nicknamed Big Duck)	Peking duck	Qianmen, No. 24. On the east side, opposite small car park.	75-1379
Zhongwen-menwai Kaoyadian	Peking duck	Zhongwenmen, No. 2. In the new Zhongwenmenwai Hotel, on the left south of East Sanmen/ Zhongwenmen (Hatamen) intersection; enter by the south entrance.	75-0505
Hepingmen Kaoyadian	Peking duck. New premises, clean but without charm.	Xinsanmen (Sanmenjie) at Hepingmen; entrance on Nan Xinhuajie which leads to Liulichang.	
Jinyang Fanzhuang	Salted roast duck; Shanxi specialities	Zhushikou West, No. 241. 400 yards west of Qianmen; bright red gate.	33-1669
Beihai or Fangshan (The Tradition of the Empress Cuisine)	Imperial specialities including minced pork with sesame seed cakes; also duck	In Beihai Park (**22**), on Hortensia Island	44-3573
CENTRAL CHINESE COOKING			
Xiangjiang Fanzhuang	(Hunan) Peppery Dongan chicken; dog (not obligatory)	Xidan, No. 133. On the west side opposite covered market (**31**).	66-1414
Sichuan Restaurant	Excellent hot peppery dishes (including Sichuan duck). Beautiful décor; fairly expensive.	Rongxian Hutong, No. 51. Turn left at first lights south of Changan/Xidan intersection.	33-6356
EASTERN CHINESE COOKING			
Fengzeyuan	(Shandong) Fine seafood, chicken. Expensive; prestigious.	Zhushikou, No. 83. On the right, 100 yards west of Qianmen.	33-2828

*All directions take Changan Avenue, East or West, as a starting point.

Name	Specialities/Comment	Address/Location	Tel. no.
EASTERN CHINESE COOKING (contd.)			
Huaiyang Fanzhuang	(Jiangsu) Good rich seafood: crabs, prawns, eels, etc.	Xidan North, No. 217. On the west side, close to the Changan/Xidan intersection.	66-0521
Kangle Canguan	(Fujian) Wide variety: crispy rice and shrimp, Yunnan steamed chicken	Andingmen Dajie, No. 259. On the west side.	44-3884
Shoudu Fanzhuang	(Shandong) Seafood, crispy rice with shrimps	Wangfujing, No. 60. On the east side, after the first lights.	55-4581 55-2591
Tongheju	(Shandong) Seafood, dessert called Sanbuzhan (3 non stick)	Xisi South, No. 3. On the west side, two doors before the second lights (i.e. Xisi intersection).	66-0925
Zhenjiang Fanzhuang	(Jiangsu) Excellent seafood	Changan/Xidan intersection, south-west corner.	66-2115 66-1289
Hongyun Jiudian	(Jiangsu) Suzhou cuisine. Seafood. Freshwater shrimps and hairy crabs in season	Fuzhoulu, No. 556	
MANCHU COOKING			
Shaguo Ju	Pork in many forms, some cooked in ceramic pots. Oldest restaurant in Beijing, 300 years old.	Xisi Dajie, No. 60. On the east side.	66-1126 66-3026
NORTH — WESTERN CHINESE COOKING			
Qinghai Canting	Spring rolls, lamb kebabs, garlic lamb chops, chicken with 'caterpillars'	Dongsi Beidajie, No. 555. On the west side, close to the intersection.	44-2947
MINORITIES COOKING			
Hongbinlou	(Hebei, Mohammedan) Shashlik, seafood, hot pot, sheep's eyes	West Changan Avenue, No. 82. On the south side, close to the intersection with Xidan.	33-0967
Shoufeng Huimen Kaorou	(Mongolian) You cook your meat on barbecue irons. Northern dishes available. Old, charming.	Xuanwumennei, No. 102. On the east side.	33-0700
Minzu Fanzhuang	(Mongolian) Hot pot, shashlik	Donghuamen, No. 16. East off Wangfujing at the north entrance of the Eastern Market (o); upstairs.	55-0069

Name	Specialities/Comment	Address/Location	Tel. no.

Name	Specialities/Comment	Address/Location	Tel. no.
Shoudu Kaorou Canting (also called Kaorouji)	(Mongolian) Barbecue. Beautiful setting; you eat on a balcony in the summer.	Near the Drum Tower (50). Turn left at the Tower, on the Gulou Xidajie, left again into the *hutong* across from the market on the right-hand side. Follow to the lake, where you turn left along the lake and past a bridge. The restaurant is on the left, at No. 14. (This is a hard one to find — go with a friend who's been there before.)	44-5921
Xinjiang Canting	Spicy shashlik	Sanlihe Road. Low grey building on the left side, almost at the intersection by the Zoo (36).	89-0721

VEGETARIAN

Name	Specialities/Comment	Address/Location	Tel. no.
Beijing Shucai Canting	Flavourful, skillfully prepared. Good for a change.	Xuanwumennei, No. 74. On the left, just past the first lights.	33-4296

WESTERN FOOD

Name	Specialities/Comment	Address/Location	Tel. no.
Peace Restaurant	Banquets (vol-au-vent, roast leg of lamb)	Jinyu Hutong (Goldfish Alley), off Wangfujing, at the south entrance to the Eastern Market, on the right-hand side.	55-4552
Xinqiao Hotel	Western food on 7th floor and Chinese food on lower ground floor.	East Jiaomin Street (b).	55-7731
International Club	Western and Chinese	Jianguomenwai Avenue/West Ritan Street (j).	52-2188
Peking Hotel	Western and Chinese. Orders taken until 8.30 p.m.	East Changan Avenue (a).	55-8331 55-2231
The Russian Restaurant		In the Exhibition Centre (37) near the Zoo, in Xizhimenwai Street.	89-3713

OTHER RESTAURANTS

Name	Specialities/Comment	Address/Location	Tel. no.
Ritan Park Restaurant	*Jiaozi* (dumplings); hot dogs.	In the centre of the park (8) near the British Embassy. Open to foreigners only, 4 p.m. to 9 p.m.	
Jiangsu Restaurant	Spring rolls	Dongsi North, No. 12. On the east side, one door north of the commission shop.	

Name	Specialities/Comment	Address/Location	Tel. no.
OTHER RESTAURANTS (contd.)			
Yanji Lengmianguan	Noodles	Xisi Dajie, No. 181. On the west side of the street.	66-2984
Xiaochidian	Chinese snacks.	Qianmen, just south of the Big Duck.	
Songhu Canting	Chinese snacks.	Qianmen, just south of the above.	
Jinfeng Baozi	*Baozi* dumplings.	Qianmen, No. 157. On the right-hand side.	
ENVIRONS OF BEIJING			
Tingliguan (Pavilion for Listening to the Orioles)	Lake fish, Velvet chicken, imperial dishes. In a former private theatre.	At the Summer Palace (**48**), on the north shore near the Marble Boat.	28-1276
Xiangshan Fandian	General/Northern cuisine: Excellent soft fried duck liver, spring rolls, fried noodles. Reasonable Prices.	In the Western Hills. Enter the Hunting Park by the main (i.e. east) gate, turn left and 75 yards on turn right up the hill. Restaurant is on the left.	81-9244

Transport. Taxis are available at all the main hotels and can be ordered at the reception desk. There are no taxi stands in the streets, except outside the railway station, where an old bus permanently parked at the east end of the station car park serves as a dispatching office. The International Club (**j**) in the Jianguomenwai district also has a fleet of taxis which can be ordered from the gate house. The only number for ordering taxis by telephone is 55-7461 and you have to state your location, destination and nationality, in Chinese or English. Beijing taxis have no meter and the price can vary slightly for the same run, depending on the vehicle. The driver will give you tickets with a yuan value printed as a receipt.

Buses run frequently and serve many routes, but are crowded. Two routes are particularly useful: the No. 1 route which serves the long east-west stretch on Changan Avenue (the Avenue of Eternal Peace), stopping among other places at the Minzu Hotel (**c**), Tiananmen Square, the Peking Hotel (**a**), the International Club, the Friendship Store (**k**) and the Jianguomenwai and Qijiayuan foreign compounds (**26**); and the No. 7 route, which will take you from the south-west of Tiananmen Square to the Zoo (**36**). A suburban route, No. 32, runs from the Zoo to Beida (Beijing

University) (**45**) and the Summer Palace (**48**).

The subway, completed in 1969 but opened to commuters only four years later, is not really a mass transit system. If you are with a group you can be treated to a ride in a special convoy, which bypasses all the stations between the Museum of the Army (**42**) and Qianmen and brings traffic to a standstill — by special arrangement with the China Travel Service.

Shopping. The Friendship Store (**k**), on Jianguomenwai near the International Club, sells a variety of goods intended for export. You can ask at the 'Suggestions' counter in the lobby for an interpreter to help you shop. Following is a list of some of the things you can buy:

Ground floor: Foodstuff, caviar (coarse but relatively cheap), tea, Chinese wine and spirits, dried fruit (delicious and easy to pack), sweets, cigarettes, fresh fruit, vegetables, meat, fish and flowers, drugs (but not things you may need, like aspirin or vitamins), bicycles. *First floor:* Cloth (you do not have to give cotton coupons if you are a visitor), knitted goods, scarves, shoes, suitcases, furs, sewing-machines, toys, pots and pans, tableware, haberdashery, shoe polish, mosquito coils and cockroach pills (ineffective), cosmetics and electrical goods. There are two tailors: a ladies' tailor at the end of the cotton counter near the back stairs, and, in a room off the back stairs, the general tailor, the only one who makes traditional Chinese clothes (for the foreigners) and also works fur. Delays are long (two to three weeks) but you can ask for fast service if you are a visitor. Prices are lower than in Hong Kong but the results not guaranteed. *Second floor:* Handicrafts and antiques, basketware, embroidered linen, cloisonné ware; china, jewellery, jade, ivory (old and new); silk flowers, birds and dolls, brocade, scroll paintings (secondrate). The carpet shop is in a room off the back stairs. The carpets are mostly new and you can also buy old and new silk embroidery and silk boxes.

The Friendship Store branch of the Bank of China is to the left of the main entrance. In a separate side courtyard of the store, to the left, there is also a Purchasing Shop which will buy your old clothes, transistor radio, etc.; a laundry and drycleaner (results not guaranteed); a very good watch-repair shop; a transport shop where you can arrange packing and shipping of goods abroad.

Small antiques can as I have said be bought at the Friendship Store, but most of the antique stores are in the Liulichang area (**l**), in the Outer City. From Changan Avenue, go past the Zhongnanhai (**25**), and take the first left at the traffic lights. Continue south through the intersection with the new Sanmenjie (Three Gates Street) for about 600 yards to a small square (on your left). Parking is allowed at the entrance to both the eastern and western sections of Liulichang. *Liuli* means lapis lazuli, and is also the poetic name for glazed tiles; there was once a glazed-tile factory here, supplying the Palace.

Western section: No. 17 — Small antique ceramic shop. No. 19 — The Rongbaozhai (Studio of Glorious Treasures), known in the Ming dynasty as the Songzhuzhai (Pine and Bamboo Studio), specializes in woodblock printing, and the workshop at the back is worth a visit (make prior application). Apart from woodblock prints, the shop sells artists' materials, seals, and is the best place for buying contemporary paintings (the best and the worst, expensive). There is a wide choice of cards: and you can have your chops* engraved (except bronze ones), scroll paintings mounted, remounted and repaired, and stone rubbings backed. No. 31 — Also a studio for mounting paintings. No. 24 — Bank of China, Liulichang Branch. No. 20 — Old inkstone and rubbing shop.

Eastern section: On the north side of the square, an old book shop (mostly in Chinese). No. 136 — The Han and Tang Reproduction Shop sells stone and brick rubbings (alas, no rubbings made from old carvings any more) and reproductions of pottery funerary figures, both of which make inexpensive and attractive presents. No. 92 — The Lantern Shop sells lanterns, scroll paintings and makes lampshades. No. 80 — Antique shop selling ceramics. It is to date the largest old ceramic shop, but expect no bargains. No. 70 — Antique shop selling small tables, leather chests, bronzes, carvings, mandarin hat buttons, mirror paintings. No. 63 — The Scroll Shop was for a long time the best place to buy paintings of the nineteenth and early twentieth centuries. It carries paintings by the best Chinese painters of the period, but nowadays seldom any major work, and at prohibitive prices. Album leaves are sold by the piece or in complete albums. There are also fan paintings and old embroidery. No. 60 — A newly-opened Chop Shop; engraves seals made of any material, including bronze and brass. No. 89 — An art supply shop; it is a delight for tourists to see the enormous variety of brushes sold here. No. 58 — A painting shop selling contemporary paintings.

There are two other antique shops in Beijing, along with the many second-hand shops. At Zhongwenmennei Dajie (formerly known as Hatamen Street), No. 12, near the Xinqiao Hotel, is the New Theatre Shop (**m**), so called by foreign residents because it used to be in a theatre-like building in the Outer City and had a big department selling opera costumes. It still sells a few and also some hardwood furniture (the black stain often camouflages extensive repairs), embroidered linen (seconds), furs (second-hand), old clocks, cut glass, pewter, silver plate and Japanese-style ceramics. The Antique Furniture Store at Wangfujing No. 56 (near the Shoudu or Capital restaurant) sells the best hardwood furniture in Beijing. Prices are high. All items sold in the antique shops carry the red wax seal to show that they were made after 1840, without which they cannot be exported.

---

*Seals made of stone, ivory or bronze, used instead of a signature.

Finally a list of articles, or categories of articles, you may want to buy, with suggestions as to where in Beijing you can obtain them:

Handicrafts: Wangfujing, No. 200, the Arts and Crafts Department Store; the Friendship Store; any hardware store for baskets and pots.

Furs: Wangfujing, No. 192, the Fur Shop; Zhongwenmennei Dajie, No. 12, the New Theatre Shop (second-hand furs); the Friendship Store; Dazhalan, No. 9 (Qianmen district), the Minority Hat Shop (fur hats).

Carpets: Qianmenwai Dajie, No. 208, the Carpet Shop (mostly new carpets); you can also try your luck in a second-hand shop.

Stamps: Any post office; Donghuamen Jie, No. 28 (off Wangfujing), the China Stamp Export Company.

Chops: Many shops in the city sell chops, including those in Liulichang, in the Dongfang (Eastern) Market and at Wangfujing, No. 261, and Qianmenwai Dajie, No. 28.

Everyday shopping: Wangfujing, No. 255, the Baihuodalou (n), department store; Wangfujing, the Eastern Market; Longfusi Hutong, the People's Market (32) (the last remains of the temple which gives its name to the alley were razed in 1977).

Books: Liulichang and the Eastern Market for old books; Wangfujing, No. 235, the Foreign Language Bookstore, for maps and old books; Wangfujing, No. 214, the Xinhua Bookstore, for new Chinese books.

HISTORY

The area around Beijing has been inhabited for about 500,000 years, since the palaeolithic period, as remains of the Peking Man, found 40 km south-west of the city, attest. Beijing was no more than a large village until the Qin dynasty, and then it becáme a centre for trade among Mongolia, Korea and the regions of the middle basin of the Yellow River and Shandong province. After the fall of the Tang in 936, it became the capital of the Liao dynasty and was called Yanjing. When the Jin overran the Liao in 1115, they made Beijing their capital, renamed it Zhongdu, and enlarged it. Then they took Kaifeng (Bianjing), the capital of the Song empire, and in 1127 brought back Chinese craftsmen and spoils which were used further to beautify Zhongdu.

The city was almost totally destroyed during the Mongol invasion, and was rebuilt on a truly imperial scale by the Yuan in 1261. Under Mongol rule, for the first time in its history, Beijing became the capital of the Chinese empire and was renamed Dadu (the Great Capital). The Yuan capital was slightly to the north of the present Inner City, and the remains of the north wall — an elevation of mud, not faced with bricks — can be seen about 3 km north of the North Circular Road, intersected by the Changping Road on the way to the Ming Tombs. Marco Polo visited the city at the end of the thirteenth century, calling it Khanbalik or Cambaluc (the Khan's Town).

For the first thirty-five years of the Ming dynasty, the capital was in Nanjing, until the third emperor, Yong Le, decided to move it north again. He gave the city the name of Beijing (the Northern Capital), and enlarged and embellished it considerably. The

OLD BEIJING: THE WALLED CITIES

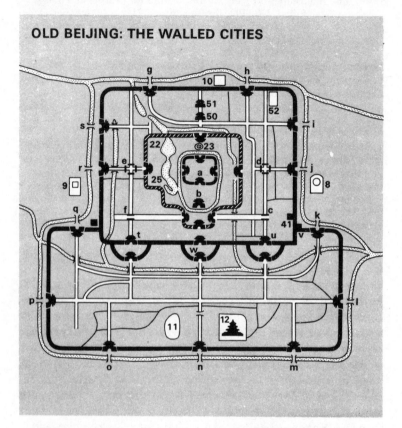

Numbered locations correspond to general map of Beijing, pp. 34-5

a	Wumen (Meridian Gate)
b	Tiananmen (Gate of Heavenly Peace)
•c	Dongdan
•d	Dongsi
•e	Xisi
•f	Xidan
g	Deshengmen
h	Andingmen
•i	Dongzhimen
•j	Chaoyangmen
•k	Dongbianmen
•l	Guangqumen
•m	Zuoanmen
•n	Yongdingmen
•o	Yuoanmen
•p	Guanganmen
•q	Xibianmen
•r	Fuzhengmen

•s	Xizhimen
•t	Shunzhimen
•u	Zhongwenmen (Hatamen)
v	Fox Tower
w	Qianmen (Front Gate)
8	Altar of the Sun
9	Altar of the Moon
10	Altar of the Earth
11	Altar (Temple) of Agriculture
12	Altar (Temple) of Heaven
22	Beihai (North Lake)
23	Coal Hill
25	Zhongnanhai (Middle and South Lake)
41	Observatory
50	Drum Tower
51	Bell Tower
52	Lama Temple

*demolished gates and archways

Imperial City remained where it was, the Inner City was moved south and a new Outer City was built to the south. It was only in 1535 that the city walls were faced with bricks.

In 1644, the last Ming emperor hung himself from a tree on Coal Hill when the rebels, led by Li Zicheng, entered the city and the defences against the advancing Manchu armies broke down. Extensive rebuilding was carried out during the reign of two Qing emperors, Kang Xi and Qian Long, but the basic plan of the city was left unchanged. Beijing was besieged during the Boxer Rebellion in 1900 and many buildings were burned down.

THE INNER CITY

Tiananmen Square.   Tiananmen, the Gate of Heavenly Peace, on the north side of the square, commands the entrance to the Imperial City. Two marble lions and two 'Celestial Pillars' stand in front of the five marble bridges spanning the Golden Stream and leading to the five openings in the gate. Actually the lions are more like large Pekingese dogs, which the Chinese call lion-dogs. As for the pillars, legend has it that they were ordered by Emperor Yao — one of the five legendary emperors — to be erected outside his palace for the citizens to write their opinion of the sovereign, or their suggestions. Imperial edicts used to be lowered from the gate and read out.

Tiananmen Square, now twice its original size and otherwise greatly transformed, has often been the scene of political rallies. On 1 October 1949 Mao Zedong (Mao Tse-tung) proclaimed the People's Republic here and hoisted the national flag for the first time on the flagpole to the south of the gate. The first portrait to be hung above the main archway was Sun Yatsen's. Now Mao's portrait faces the giant hairy images of the four founding fathers of communism: Marx, Engels, Lenin and Stalin.

The Great Hall of the People (5), on the west side of the square, was built in 1959, and completed in less than a year. This is where the National People's Congress meets, where formal meetings and receptions for visiting heads of state and government take place, and where Mao Zedong's body lay in state. In addition to a banquet hall for 5,000 people and a concert hall for 10,000, it has many reception rooms, and offices on the top floor. The building has recently been opened again to the public, having been closed since the late 1950s.

The Museum of National History (6), also completed in 1959, is on the east side of Tiananmen Square. Its exhibits cover Chinese history from primitive society to the Opium Wars in 1840. (Visits only by prior arrangement with CTS.) The Museum of Revolution is in the north wing of the Museum of National History, with its entrance in Changan Avenue.

The Monument to the People's Heroes (4) stands directly south of Tiananmen, approximately on the site of the old outer gate of the Imperial

THE FORBIDDEN CITY AND THE PALACE MUSEUM

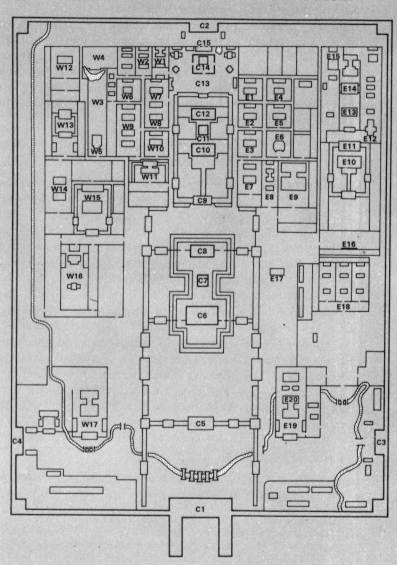

Central palaces (from south to north)
and main gates:

C1	Meridian Gate
C2	Gate of Inspired Military Genius
C3	East Flowery Gate
C4	West Flowery Gate
C5	Gate of Supreme Harmony
C6	Hall of Supreme Harmony
C7	Hall of Complete Harmony
C8	Hall of Preserving Harmony
C9	Gate of Heavenly Purity
C10	Palace of Heavenly Purity
C11	Hall of Heavenly and Earthly Intercourse
C12	Palace of Earthly Tranquillity
C13	Imperial Garden
C14	Hall of Imperial Tranquillity
C15	Gate of Perfect Rectitude

City, the Zhonghuamen, destroyed in 1952. The monument was the focus of attention during the Qingming Festival incident in 1976, when the wreaths brought by the people to honour the late Zhou Enlai (Chou En-lai) were removed by the police.

Chairman Mao's Memorial Hall, on the south side of the square, was started in November 1976, and completed in nine months. Its colossal style matches that of the Great Hall of the People and the History Museum, dwarfing the Qianmen gates, which have miraculously escaped the modern town-planner's zeal. The Memorial Hall can be visited by prior arrangement with CTS, or with your host organization.

The Qianmen inner and outer gates were completed in 1419, with a semi-circular enclosure (followed by the modern road) and small side gates to the east and west, the only ones in permanent use in imperial times. The towers on top of the gates were burned down in 1900 during the Boxer Rebellion and rebuilt shortly thereafter. The outer one, destroyed a second time in the 1930s, owes its modern style to the Germans.

The Forbidden City (1), a maze of palaces, each with its own walls, was built between 1417 and 1420 and covers 73 hectares. It was the seat of government as well as the residence of the emperor and his family. The grey crenellated wall surrounding it is pierced by four gates: Wumen (Meridian Gate) to the south, Shenwumen (Gate of Inspired Military Genius) to the north, Donghuamen (East Flowery Gate) to the east, and Xihuamen (West Flowery Gate) to the west. The basic design of the buildings inside this wall is believed to have been adapted from a tent; the structure is raised on a platform and the roof is supported by pillars, not by the walls. These golden roofs are probably the most gorgeous sight in the Forbidden City. You may wonder why their gently up-turned ends are decorated

---

Eastern palaces (from north to south):

E1 Palace of Pure Affection
E2 Palace of Heavenly Favours
E3 Palace of Great Benevolence
E4 Palace of Great Brilliance
E5 Palace of Eternal Harmony
*E6 Palace of Prolonged Happiness
E7 Palace of Purification
E8 Palace of Nurtured Happiness
E9 Hall of Worshipping the Ancestors
E10 Hall of Imperial Supremacy
E11 Palace of Peaceful Old Age
E12 Pavilion of Pleasant Sounds
E13 Hall of Cultivation of the Character
E14 Hall of Delight in Longevity
E15 Well of the Zhen Concubine
E16 Nine Dragon Screen
E17 Arrow Pavilion
E18 Imperial kitchens
E19 Hall of Literary Glory
E20 Pavilion of Literary Profundity

Western palaces (from north to south):

W1 Studio of Pure Fragrance
W2 Palace of Mighty Glory
†*W3 Hall of Righteousness and Equipoise
† W4 West Garden
† W5 Pavilion of Raining Flowers
W6 Palace of Prolonged Happiness
W7 Palace of Accumulated Elegance
W8 Palace of the Emperor's Assistant
W9 Palace of Eternal Spring
W10 Palace of Longevity
W11 Hall of the Culture of the Mind
† W12 Hall of Heroic Splendour
†W13 Palace of Longevity and Peace
† W14 Palace of Vigorous Old Age
† W15 Palace of Benevolent Tranquillity
† W16 Garden of Benevolent Tranquillity
W17 Hall of Military Prowess

*destroyed   † closed to the public

with a procession of ceramic figures. In 283 B.C. Prince Min of the state of Qi in Shandong province, who was a cruel tyrant, was captured by his people — with the help of a few well-disposed neighbouring princes — and punished with no less cruelty. He was tied to the end of a roof until he died. For his eternal punishment, he is represented sitting on a roof-end on the back of a hen, his retreat cut off by a fierce-looking *zhiwen* (a kind of dragon). Between Prince Min and the *zhiwen* is a row of as many as eleven ferocious animals (dragon, phoenix, lion, unicorn, winged horse) ensuring that he will stay there forever. The dragon, a motif repeated throughout the Forbidden City, is a symbol of the emperor, and the phoenix — or the peacock — a symbol of the empress.

The palaces and the Palace Museum are open from 9 a.m. to 5 p.m.; admission until 3 p.m. only. Closed Mondays.

The central palaces: To anyone entering the Forbidden City from the south — once an imperial privilege — the Wumen (Meridian Gate) (**C1**) is a powerful symbol of how forbidden the Palace once was. From the pavilions at each of the four corners of the U-shaped gate, drums and bells would be struck every time the emperor entered or departed. Officials attending imperial audiences — always before sunrise — had to use the side gates: the Xihuamen (West Flowery Gate) (**C4**) was reserved for military officials; civilian officials used the Donghuamen (East Flowery Gate) (**C3**). The courtyard behind the gate is crossed by the Golden Stream which originates at the Jade Fountain Spring near the Summer Palace. Here again the stream is spanned by five marble bridges beyond which the sumptuous Taihemen (Gate of Supreme Harmony) (**C5**) guards the entrance to the Three Great Halls, which are elevated on a marble terrace.

The first of these, the Taihedian (Hall of Supreme Harmony) (**C6**), presides over the vast and empty courtyard where thousands of kneeling officials would wait for the arrival of the emperor. The Taihedian, with its eleven-bays-wide facade and its double roof, is the largest building in the Forbidden City. On the terrace in front of it, a sundial on the right and a *jialing* (grain measure) sheltered by a miniature pavilion remind visitors that time and measures were standard throughout the empire. The Hall of Supreme Harmony is the formal throne hall used on the emperor's birthday and for the major festivals, and no woman, not even the Dowager Empress Ci Xi, ever set foot in it. Behind it, the smaller Zhonghedian (Hall of Complete Harmony) (**C7**) was used by the emperor while preparing for audiences. The third hall, the Baohedian (Hall of Preserving Harmony) (**C8**), was where he received tribute-bearing envoys from vassal countries and also scholars who had passed the official examinations. It now houses a display of archaeological finds. The stepping-stone at the back of the Baohedian, carved with clouds and dragons, is the largest monolithic carving in the palace (over 16 m long). It was first sculpted in the Ming dynasty and re-carved in 1761.

The next three halls, known as the Inner Court, were the residential halls of the Ming emperors. The first Qing emperor, Shun Zhi, reposed in the Qianqinggong (Palace of Heavenly Purity) (**C10**) until a propitious day for his burial was chosen and the compound was never again used as a residence. The Qianqinggong is an imposing nine-bays-wide hall reached by a marble 'causeway' adorned in autumn by two rows of pomegranate trees in tubs. Two famous banquets were given there, by Kang Xi in 1711 and by Qian Long in 1785, for men over sixty, on the occasion of their sixtieth birthdays. The next hall behind the Qianqinggong is the Jiaotaidian (Hall of Heavenly and Earthly Intercourse) (**C11**), a throne room for the empress and the hall where imperial weddings were held. This is also where the imperial seals were kept. The last of the three smaller halls, the Kunninggong (Palace of Earthly Tranquillity) (**C12**), was the private apartment of the empress during the Ming dynasty, but during the Qing dynasty became the bedroom of the emperor on his wedding night. The two bridal chambers in the east wing are decorated in red, the colour of happiness. The west wing was used for the practice of secret shaman rites on imperial birthdays and lunar New Year's Eve and also had an altar to the Kitchen God.

The Yuhuayuan (Imperial Garden) (**C13**) awaits you through the Kunning Gate (Gate of Earthly Tranquillity) at the back, very tame and artificial with its man-made rockeries, its borders of peonies, its twisted old cypress framed by pebble-mosaic paths, and its kiosks and pavilions. In the centre stands the Qinandian (Hall of Imperial Tranquillity) (**C14**), a temple dedicated to the God of Fire, surrounded by its own walls.

For many visitors, the tour of the Forbidden City will end there. They will leave the garden by the Shunzhenmen (Gate of Perfect Rectitude) (**C15**), walk across the 'perimeter of defence' with the barracks of the imperial guard in rows along the wall, and emerge through the Shenwumen (Gate of Inspired Military Genius) (**C2**), associated with unhappy memories. It was through this gate, in 1644, that the last Ming emperor, Chong Zhen, having killed many of his concubines and asked the empress to commit suicide, left the palace in the middle of the night and hanged himself from a tree on Coal Hill (**23**), rather than face the humiliation of seeing the palace invaded by the rebel Li Zicheng.

If you have time to spare, however, you will want to come back to the Forbidden City and visit the eastern and western palaces.

The eastern palaces: These palaces were for the most part residences and now contain the collections of the Palace Museum. The exhibition rooms are open on alternate days of the week and a special exhibition of old paintings is mounted every autumn, from 1 October.

Leaving the Imperial Garden by the south-eastern gate, you will come to a 'street' leading south, contained by red walls. The first gate on the left leads into the Zhongcuigong (Palace of Pure Affection) (**E1**) and to the adjacent Jingyanggong (Palace of Great Brilliance) (**E4**), once the apartments of female members of the imperial family, now housing a collection of fabrics. South of these, also entered from the street, are the Chengqiangong (Palace of Heavenly Favours) (**E2**) and the Yonghegong (Palace of Eternal Harmony) (**E5**), containing the display of ceramics of the Museum. The Chengqiangong, when it was deserted by the imperial family, became a winter sanctuary for goldfish and birds. The next palace on the east side of the street, the Jingrengong (Palace of Great Benevolence) (E3) was the residence of the strong-minded Zhen Fei, known as the 'Pearl' Concubine, the favourite of Emperor Guang Xu. The next palace to the east, the Yanxigong (Palace of Prolonged Happiness) (E6), has been destroyed. The Zhaigong (Palace of Purification) (E7), the last one of this group along the street, now contains an exhibition of bronzes. This is where the emperor fasted and meditated for three days before offering sacrifices for the New Year and other festivals. The neighbouring Yujinggong (Palace of Nurtured Happiness) (E8) was traditionally the residence of the heir apparent. East of it, the Fengxiandian (E9) was an ancestors' temple and now contains an exhibition of sculpture.

The two easternmost larger palaces are associated with Emperor Qian Long and the sinister Dowager Empress Ci Xi. To the south, a superb Nine Dragon Screen (E16) protects the gate of the first palace from evil spirits. Qian Long had this Ningshougong (Palace of Peaceful Old Age) (E11) built for his retirement and he lived there after 1795, when his son Jia Qing ascended the throne; it is a replica on a smaller scale of the Qianqinggong. The Museum's collection of paintings is exhibited in the Huangjidian (Hall of Imperial Supremacy) (E10), the former reception room of the palace and the Ningshoudian (Hall of Peaceful Old Age), and once used for the practice of shaman rites.

The palace to the north was the private residence of Qian Long, and later of the Dowager Empress Ci Xi. The imperial treasure is now housed in its two main halls, the Yangxindian (Hall of Cultivation of the Character) (E13) and the Leshoutang (Hall of Delight in Longevity) (E14). West of these, in a separate courtyard, is a private theatre, the Changyingge (Pavilion of Pleasant Sounds) (E12), and another building to the north from which the opera- and drama-loving empress used to watch performances. Behind the main residential quarters are more pavilions set in a garden, and on the left near the north gate of the compound the well (E15) where Zhen Fei, the favourite 'Pearl' Concubine, drowned mysteriously on the night of 14 August 1900. It seems she had had the temerity to suggest that Guang Xu, who after all was the emperor, should stay in Beijing and try to hold the fort as the foreign allies, having defeated the Boxers, advanced on the capital. But his mother, the Dowager Empress, was not about to surrender power to her son; having disposed of the unfortunate Zhen Fei, she buried her jewels and, dragging the emperor with her, fled through the north gate of the compound, the Shunzhenmen, dressed in blue denim like a peasant woman.

The southeastern area of the Forbidden City has few buildings. Next to the vast imperial kitchens (E18) is the Jianting (Arrow Pavilion) (E17) which houses a collection of stone drums. The large compound south of it is the Wenhuandian (Hall of Literary Glory) (E19), resting place for civilian officials attending an imperial audience, and the Wenyuange (Pavilion of Literary Profundity) (E20), which was the main library, its roofs covered in blue-green tiles.

The western palaces: These follow a plan similar to the eastern ones. Entry is from the south-west corner of the imperial garden, near the Yangxingzhai (Studio of Character Training), which was at one time the residence of Sir Reginald Johnston, the private tutor of Xuan Tong, the last emperor, better known as Mr Pu Yi. The three small compounds to the north are the Shufangzhai (Studio of Pure Fragrance) (**W1**), a theatre with a stage, the Zhonghuagong (Palace of Mighty Glory) (**W2**), and a third palace which was destroyed by fire in 1923. Still further west, there is the West Garden (**W4**) — overlooked on the east side by the blue-tiled Jianfugong (Palace of Established Happiness), a mourning chapel — and the site of the Zhongzhengdian (Hall of Righteousness and Equipoise) (**W3**), burned mysteriously in the fire of 1923, together with the dynastic treasures stored in it. The hall was not rebuilt and a tennis court was laid out on the site. Only the Yuhuage (Pavilion of Raining Flowers) (**W5**) remains, a lama temple with an unusual roof decorated with dragons, and north of it, the Baohuadian (Hall of Precious Splendour), formerly a Taoist temple, then a Buddhist temple. Unfortunately, this northwestern area is at present (1978) closed to the public.

The next series of palaces, the residences of imperial concubines and empresses, have been left furnished as they were. These are the Xianfugong (Palace of Prolonged Happiness) (**W6**) and east of it, the Chuxiugong (Palace of Accumulated Elegance) (**W7**), where the consort of Emperor Xuan Tong lived until 1912. The Yikungong (Palace of the Emperor's Assistant, i.e., the consort) (**W8**) was the residence of several empresses, and the Dowager Empress Ci Xi's residence when she first entered the palace as Emperor Xian Feng's concubine. The larger palace to the west is the Changchungong (Palace of Eternal Spring) (**W9**) where the Dowager Empress Ci Xi lived during Emperor Tong Zhi's reign. The gallery round the hall is decorated with murals relating to the Ming novel, *The Dream of the Red Chamber,* with *trompe l'œil* perspective effects. Among the furnishings, note the layers of quilted silk bed covers reminding one of the fairy tale of the Princess and the Pea, the richly embroidered bed curtains and hangings; the *kang*, a heated platform used as a day bed, with its hard elbow-cushions, the writing table and writing implements. In winter, the halls were hung with quilted linings which could be placed over the doorways, making the rooms draught-proof. Note also the cloisonné charcoal-burners which, with the *kang*, were the only forms of heating.

The smaller Yongshougong (Palace of Longevity) (**W10**) to the east was also a residence for imperial concubines, and, to the south, another fairly large palace, the Yangxindian (Hall of the Culture of the Mind) (**W11**) was the residence of several emperors, including Guang Xu, the unfortunate monarch who spent the last eight years of his life as a prisoner of the fearful Ci Xi, and died in this palace. His successor, Xuan Tong (Pu Yi), also lived here after his abdication in 1924. This hall is one of the few that still have carpets covering the polished flagstones. It contains curtained bookshelves and three rare pieces of calligraphy collected by Emperor Qian Long.

In the extreme north-west corner of the Forbidden City, there is a lama temple, the Yinghuadian (Hall of Heroic Splendour) (**W12**) and directly south of it the Shouangong (Palace of Longevity and Peace) (**W13**), also a temple. Both are closed to the public, as are the next three palaces to the south: the Shoukanggong (Palace of Vigorous Old Age) (**W14**), a temple; the Cininggong (Palace of Benevolent Tranquillity) (**W15**), one of the oldest buildings in the whole complex; and, on a smaller scale, the Cining-huayuan (Garden of Benevolent Tranquillity) (**W16**), better known as the Garden of the Fallen Favourites. Lastly, the Wuyingdian (Hall of Military

Prowess) (**W17**), near the Xihuamen (West Flowery Gate) of the Imperial Palace, traditionally a waiting hall for military officials, was used by the peasant leader Li Zicheng when he occupied Beijing in 1644. He obviously knew the imperial protocol.

Temples in the Imperial City. The Imperial City abounds in old temples, most of which are closed to the public, but they can easily be spotted from the street and you may have a chance to sneak in if you find the gate open.

First, on the west side of Tiananmen, there is the Zhongshan Park (**2**), named after Sun Yatsen, the Republican hero (pronounced 'Sun Zhongshan' in northern dialect). The Altar of Land and Grain, built by the emperor Yong Le, stands in the park, inside a wall. The next compound west of the park is the Zhongnanhai (Middle and South Lake) (**25**), a former imperial 'resort'; it was one of Chairman Mao's official residences, and is now the residence and offices of Politburo members. The southern gate, originally a pavilion built by Qian Long for his Fragrant Concubine, is nearly unapproachable: the guards take their duty seriously.

Going north on Beichangjie which runs between the Forbidden City and the Zhongnanhai, there are three temples: on the west side, the Temple of the God of Thunder, then the Temple of Prosperity, and on the east side, near the top of the street, the Fuyusi (Temple of Blessed Protection), where Kang Xi was sent as a child to escape an epidemic of smallpox in the Forbidden City.

The east side of the Imperial City almost mirrors the west side. East of Tiananmen, the 'Working People's Cultural Park' is a prosaic new name for the grounds of the Taimiao, the Ancestral Temple of the Ming and Qing (**3**), where the tablets of the deceased emperors and their consorts used to be honoured by their descendants. It is a superb enclosure with three main halls, built in 1462, and set in a courtyard graced with marble terraces and balustrades. Zhou Enlai's, and later in the same year Zhu De's, ashes reposed there during the period of official mourning. In the south-east corner of the Imperial City, separated from the Peking Hotel by Huangchenggen, the street built on the site of the west wall of the Imperial City, is a pavilion with yellow glazed tiles, the Tangzi or Ancestral Temple of the Manchu emperors, a private temple as opposed to the Taimiao, a dynastic temple. It was rebuilt on this site in 1900.

In the next block, on the east side of Nanchizi, there is the Mahakalamiao, also known as the Mongol Temple, dedicated to Shiva, the Hindu god, in one of his lamaist forms as 'Demon Protector'. This temple, formerly a palace, is where the emperor Zheng Tong lived after 1451 when he was released from Mongolia and plotted the fall of his brother Jing Tai who had ascended the throne in his absence. The palace was converted into a temple by Kang Xi in 1691. Further north, on the east side of Beichizi, is the Yunshenmiao (Temple of the God of the Clouds), and in the next block, also on the east side, the Fengshenmiao (Temple of the God of Winds), both in a sorry state.

Coal Hill. It seems that the name 'Coal' Hill (**23**) is a misnomer for 'Beautiful' Hill, both pronounced *mei* (though in different tones) in Chinese. It was renamed Jingshan, or Prospect Hill, by the Manchus. Situated directly north of the Forbidden City, it affords a magnificent view of the golden roofs, when the air is free of pollution. The hill, crowned with five pavilions, used to be planted with fruit trees and was a favourite pleasure garden for the imperial family. It has all but lost its charm now that millions of feet trample its grounds, ignoring the paths, and the Christmas trees planted all over it contribute little to its beauty. The tree from which Chong Zhen, the last Ming emperor, is supposed to have hanged himself can be seen on the east slope; though another tradition says that he strangled himself in the Wanchunting (Pavilion of a Thousand Springs) at the top. Early morning or late afternoon are the best time to climb Coal Hill and survey the Forbidden City and the town without being blinded by the sun.

Beihai Park. Beihai (North Lake) Park (**22**) is due west of Coal Hill, north-west of the Shenwu Gate of the Forbidden City. During the Liao dynasty, at the beginning of the tenth century, the emperor used to have his residence on the site of the park, but the lake was dug two centuries later, under the Jin. Kublai Khan had his palace in the Round Town, on the southern shore of the lake, and built Hortensia Island with the earth excavated from the lake. Emperor Yong Le, the indefatigable fifteenth-century builder of Beijing, had the three lakes (North, Middle and South — the latter two now being the Zongnanhai) and their shores redesigned into magnificent pleasure gardens.

Although the Round Town, Tuancheng, immediately west of the south gate (**G1**) of the park, is closely associated with Kublai Khan, little remains of his time. The circular wall dates from the fifteenth century and the two main buildings inside were rebuilt in the eighteenth century. The Chengguangdian (Hall of Inherited Brilliance) (**R1**), built in the shape of a Maltese cross, used to contain the statue of a white Buddha. The small blue-tiled pavilion (**R2**) to the south, built by Qian Long, shelters a large 'Black Jade' wine bowl given to Kublai Khan in 1265.

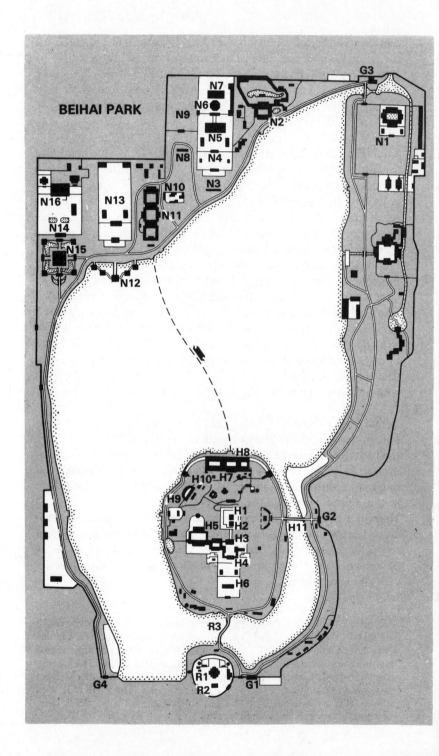

BEIHAI PARK

Hortensia Island, at the south end of the lake, is crowned by the White Dagoba (**H1**), nicknamed the Peppermint Bottle, which was built in 1652 in honour of the fifth Dalai Lama when he visited Beijing. On the south side of the terrace of the White Dagoba is the Shanyinsi (Temple for Cultivating the Good Deeds) (**H2**), a small shrine made of glazed tiles and bricks, once the abode of a fierce-looking lamaistic god. On the next level down the south slope are the Puandian (Hall of Universal Tranquillity) (**H3**) and the Zhengjuedian (Hall of Spiritual Perception) (**H4**), north and south of the same terrace respectively. To the west of this terrace the two-storied Qingxiaolou (Tower of Auspicious Skies) (**H5**) was built at the spot where Qian Long used to watch skating parties on the lake. The Yonganσι (Temple of Everlasting Peace) (**H6**) stands at the bottom of the southern slope of Hortensia Island, behind a *pailou* (triumphal arch).

The largest building on the northern slope is the Yilantang (Hall of the Rippling Waves) (**H7**), a palace with several buildings, half-way along the covered way, which are the grand setting of the Fangshan Restaurant (see RESTAURANTS). A visit to Beihai should be combined with a sampling of the Empress cuisine there. Get, if you can, a table in the Bizhaolou (Tower which Reflects the Azure of the Sky), which is built over the covered way. Continuing westward along the covered way to the end, one comes to the Yuegulou (Tower for Inspecting the Ancient Calligraphy) (**H9**) with over four hundred stone tablets set in the walls, going back to the second century A.D. Behind the Hall of the Rippling Waves is a marble column carved with spiralling dragons and clouds supporting a small figure of a man holding a plate to the sky. It is called the Chenglupan (Plate for Receiving the Dew) (**H10**), erected in memory of Emperor Wu Di of the Han dynasty who used to have slaves standing with a dish to collect the dew which he would drink, believing it was an elixir of immortality. You can leave the island on the east side by the Zhishanqiao (Bridge for Ascending the Hill) (**H11**), and walk along the shore towards the north.

Just before reaching the north gate of Beihai Park, a high wall to the right now hides what is the Altar of Silkworms (**N1**). The path turns west

---

Beihai (North Lake) Park

Gates
G1 Front (south) Gate
G2 East Gate
G3 Back (north) Gate
G4 West Gate

Round Town
R1 Hall of Inherited Brilliance
R2 Pavilion of the Black Jade Bowl
R3 Bridge of Eternal Peace

Hortensia Island
H1 White Dagoba
H2 Temple for Cultivating the Good Deeds
H3 Hall of Universal Tranquillity
H4 Hall of Spiritual Perception
H5 Tower of Auspicious Skies
H6 Temple of Everlasting Peace
H7 Hall of the Rippling Waves
H8 Fangshan Restaurant
H9 Tower for Inspecting the Ancient Calligraphy

H10 Plate for Receiving the Dew
H11 Bridge for Ascending the Hill

East and north shore
N1 Altar of Silkworms
N2 Studio of Peaceful Mind
N3 Temple of the Small Western Heaven
N4 Hall of the Heavenly Kings
N5 Hall of Great Wisdom and True Compassion
N6 Ten Buddha Pagoda
N7 Great and Precious Hall with Glazed Tiles
N8 Nine Dragon Screen
N9 Former Temple of Thousand Buddhas
N10 Former site of Fangshan Restaurant
N11 Pine Hill Restaurant
N12 Five Dragons Pavilions
N13 Temple of Happy Meditation
N14 Temple of the Great Western Heaven
N15 Tower of Guanyin
N16 Tower of Ten Thousand Buddhas

over a bridge and the first walled compound on the north shore is the Qing-xinzhai (Studio of Peaceful Mind) (**N2**), now closed, a summer house and a garden where Empress Ci Xi used to enjoy resting. Further west, a triple archway of glazed tiles adorns the entrance to the Xiaoxidian (Small Western Heaven) (**N3**), founded in the Ming dynasty and rebuilt by Qian Long. The temple, as its name suggests, is dedicated to Amitabha Buddha who presides over the Western Heaven. At the back is a pavilion named the Ten Buddha Pagoda (**N6**), and the last building is the large Daliulibaodian (Great and Precious Hall with Glazed Tiles) (**N7**). Immediately to the west of the Small Western Heaven is the Nine Dragon Screen (**N8**), as beautiful as the one in the Forbidden City, which used to frighten the evil spirits away from a temple which is no longer there. The next compound to the west of the screen is the Pine Hall Library (**N11**), rebuilt by Qian Long. Further west, the Five Dragons Pavilions (**N12**), originally built in 1602, symbolize five brothers who lived in Shandong province in the second century B.C.; all became famous scholars and were known as the 'Five Dragons of Learning'. The temple north of the Five Dragons Pavilions is the Chanfusi (Temple of Happy Meditation) (**N13**), now a pioneer's club.

The last group of buildings along the north shore is the Daxidian (Great Western Heaven) (**N14**), with an unusual detached hall standing to the south, surrounded by a little moat: the Guanyinge (Tower of Guanyin) (**N15**). Inside the temple, the Wanfolou (Tower of the Ten Thousand Buddhas) (**N16**), a three-storeyed building, presides over the main court which is now used as an open-air cinema. Behind it and to the west is a small dagoba protected by a pavilion.

Boating and skating bring the Pekingese to the Beihai which reopened in 1978 after eight years of being Jiang Qing (Madame Mao's) favourite and exclusive riding ground — so the gossip goes.

The Drum Tower and its surroundings. The Drum Tower (**50**), north of Coal Hill, was built by Yong Le in 1420 with materials scavenged from the old drum tower of the Yuan capital. The drum used to be sounded before daybreak to call the officials to imperial audiences and at nightfall. The Bell Tower (**51**), a few hundred metres north of the Drum Tower, used to house a large bell which was struck in response to the drum. The present structure dates from 1745. West of the Drum Tower is the Shichahai, Lake of the Ten Monasteries (**21**), with temples on its shores. From Dianmen-wai Street, go north towards the Drum Tower and take the first *hutong* (alley) west after the old hump-back bridge. It will lead to the Houshenmiao, built in 1734 and dedicated to the God of War, the God of Wealth and the God of Fire. Continue along the shore past the Kaorouji restaurant, which specializes in barbecued lamb, leaving the bridge on your left until you reach the Guanghuasi, Temple of Religious Transformation, and in the next block, the palace of Prince Chun, father of the last Manchu emperor. Sadly, little of this palace can be seen behind its well-kept and guarded walls. Going north to the main street, West Drum Tower Street, the high yellow roofs of the Ancestral Hall of Prince Chun can be seen across the street. It is used as a residence for the Panchen Lama.

The Lama Temple and its surroundings. The Yonghegong (Palace of Peace and Harmony) or Lama Temple (**52**) is approached from the northern extension of Dongsi Beidajie. The last compound on the east side before reaching the moat, its approach is heralded by a set of three *pailou* (triumphal archways). Emperor Yong Zheng was born in the palace and his son Qian Long, following an ancient custom, turned it into a temple in 1745. The monks used to come from Tibet or Mongolia. The temple consists of three main halls and a three-storeyed building which can be seen from the street and shelters a giant statue of Maitreya Buddha. East of the Lama Temple, there is a large Buddhist temple hidden behind grey walls, which cannot be visited. It is the Bolinsi, Temple of the White Cypress Grove, built in the Yuan dynasty and which served as a retreat for monks studying the sutras.

Going back to the main street, on the west side, a small shaded street leads to the Temple of Confucius (Kong Miao) (**53**) the second largest such temple in the country (see pp. 114-15). A stele on the north side of the street warns passers-by that they have to dismount beyond this point. Two *pailou* span the street — a rare sight in modern Beijing. The main hall, Hall of Great Perfection, stands on a marble terrace in the middle of a courtyard with a gallery on either side. West of the temple is the Hall of Classics, formerly a school for the study of the classics. The main building is the Imperial Schoolroom, a circular pavilion set in a pool of water. It is now the Municipal Library.

The south-east quarter. The Observatory (**41**) stands on the site of the former east wall of the Inner City. When it was built in 1296, it marked the south-east corner of the Yuan dynasty wall. When Emperor Yong Le rebuilt the city, he extended it to the south, but the observatory remained where it had been. Emperor Jia Jing had it rebuilt in 1522.

Following a tradition which had started under the Yuan, the Ming appointed Moslem astronomers to calculate the calendar, but in 1610 the Jesuits, who had gained access to the capital, outwitted the Moslem astronomers in predicting an eclipse; eventually, in 1629, they were put in charge of the observatory. Father Verbiest designed a set of five astronomical instruments in 1674; a sixth is said to have been a present from Louis XIV of France. The instruments were removed to Potsdam as spoils after the Boxer Rebellion but the Germans returned them in 1919, and the ones in position on the observatory terrace today are presumed to be the originals.

In 1970, the east wall of the Inner City was torn down and work on the subway started shortly thereafter, undermining the tower-like structure which has in any case been closed to the public for at least twenty years on the grounds that it is unsafe.

The Old Legation Quarter (7), bounded on the north by East Changan Avenue, on the east by Zhongwenmennei Street (or Hatamen North), on the west by the Museum of National History and on the south by the new Sanmenjie (Three Gates Street), was built on the site of the old wall between the Inner and Outer cities. The former 'glacis' to the east has been turned into a park. The Old Legation Quarter (see Appendix for a plan) can be easily visited on foot from the Peking or Xinqiao Hotels.

The Dongdan covered market, at the corner of Dongdan and East Changan Avenue, is a colourful and crowded place where you will have a chance to see what the Chinese buy for their dinner, how long they have to wait at each counter to be served in the evening, which items are rationed, how the traditional scales are used, and will be amazed at the infinite variety of dried foodstuffs.

The western quarters.   Due west of Xisi corner on Fuzhengmennei Street, on the north side, is the large Guangjisi, Temple of Universal Rescue (64), now the headquarters of the Chinese Buddhist Society and the only officially active temple in the area. It can be visited by prior appointment. It was gutted by fire in 1832 and rebuilt entirely in bricks and concrete imitating the complicated structure of wood supporting the roofs.

Further west, but set one block north of the main street, is the Temple of the White Dagoba (Baidasi) (60), originally built in the Liao dynasty and much more elegant than the better-known 'Peppermint Bottle' in the Beihai. The front court of the temple is now occupied by a vegetable market and the walls have fallen down on the east side, making it possible for once to take a good look without asking anyone. North-west of the White Dagoba is the Lu Xun Museum (35), more often closed than open, in a house the writer (see p. 162) once lived in.

At the Arts and Crafts Factory at Xinjiekou, in the north-west quarter, you will admire the deftness of the artists who decorate glass snuff bottles on the inside, the skill and perseverance of jade carvers (it takes two to five years to carve a piece of jade), the patience of those who reproduce paintings by hand, and the technique of making cloisonné ware.

Christian churches. The Northern Cathedral (**19**) is west of the National Library, off a narrow alley; its twin spires can be seen from the main street. It was moved to its present site in 1888 by imperial order because it used to cast an unlucky shadow over the palaces of the Zhongnanhai. It withstood a long siege by the Boxers in 1900. The Western Cathedral (**20**) is on the south side of Xizhimen Street. Both it and the Northern Cathedral are now closed. The Southern Cathedral (**14**) now overlooks the new Sanmenjie, at the corner of Xuanwumen Street. It was built on the site of Father Matteo Ricci's residence, and rebuilt after 1900. Catholic services are still held there every Sunday, mostly for the foreign community. St Michael's Church, with its two fallen crosses, is situated in the former Legation Street, a few hundred yards west of the Xinqiao Hotel. It is used as a storeroom and no one knows the fate of its excellent organ. The Eastern Cathedral (**18**), off Wangfujing on the east side, south of the junction with Dengshikou, has been rebuilt three times since its foundation in 1666; it is now a school.

THE OUTER CITY AND THE SUBURBS

The Temple of Heaven. As you honk your way down Qianmen Dajie towards the Temple of Heaven (**12**), think that the emperor used to be carried over the road, cleared of stalls, traffic and people, in complete silence, accompanied by an interminable procession.

The enclosure of the Temple of Heaven is nearly 5 km long, and almost perfectly square except for the curved north wall which was to protect it from evil influence borne by the north wind. To the north of the enclosure stands the Qiniandian (**d**), with its glorious deep blue roof in the shape of a triple umbrella. Here the emperor used to pray, in the spring, for a good harvest. The hall is approached from a raised marble causeway (now covered with concrete slabs) which has a square terrace extending on the east side (**c**), used for erecting the emperor's yellow tent.

Passing through the double gate buildings, one enters a rectangular court-yard, with the Hall of Prayer for Good Harvest raised on a three-tiered marble terrace. The roof is topped with a gilded knob. Inside, four pillars (made of a single tree trunk), one for each point of the compass, support the vault of the roof, decorated with a central motif of a dragon within a circle of clouds. Twelve outer pillars, for the twelve months of the year and the twelve watches of the day (periods of two hours), support the outer wall. This masterpiece of architecture originally built in the fifteenth century, during the reign of Yong Le, was burned to the ground in 1889, for which thirty-two officials and guardians lost their heads. The tree trunks used to rebuild the hall came from Oregon in the United States.

Retracing our steps south on the causeway, we should see to the west the Palace of Abstinence (Zhaigong) (**e**), where the emperor fasted in

THE TEMPLE OF HEAVEN

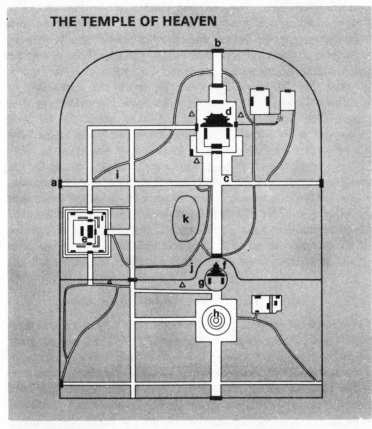

a West Heavenly Gate
b North Heavenly Gate .
c Terrace for imperial tent
d Hall of Prayer for Good Harvest
e Palace of Abstinence
f Imperial Vault of Heaven

g Echo Wall
h Altar of Heaven
i Children's playground
j Open-air café
k Mole hill

preparation for a different ceremony, the sacrifice offered to heaven at the summer and winter solstice. Alas, a sacrilegious gigantic mole hill has been deposited west of the causeway, obscuring the view, as a consequence of four years of digging air-raid shelters in the city. The Palace of Abstinence now contains an open-air theatre. The causeway ends at a wall enclosing the Huangqiongyu (Imperial Vault of Heaven), and the Altar of Heaven. The wall (g) is circular, with one gate to the south, and is known as the Echo Wall because two people facing it at opposite points can hear each other whisper. However, when dozens of people try the echo at the same time, it is a disappointing experience. The Huangqiongyu (f) is an octagonal building made entirely of wood with a roof of dark blue glazed tiles (or so they should be, but they were simply painted over in 1977). The temple used to contain the tablets of the Manchu imperial ancestors and the tablets to heaven which were used during the sacrifice.

The Altar of Heaven (Tiantan) (**h**) is also familiarly called the Round Mound because of its shape. (In fact it gives its name to the entire Tiantan compound, which we wrongly call 'Temple' of Heaven.) The altar is a triple terrace of white marble representing Heaven at the top level — following an ancient Chinese belief that the sky is circular — then Earth, and Man at the lowest level. A supremely sacred place, the Altar of Heaven was only opened to the public in 1912 and even in this age of tourism conveys an unmistakable feeling of approaching heaven.

Chaoyang Gate and its surroundings.   The gate is no more, but in this area, so easily accessible from the diplomatic compounds, there are a few buildings worth mentioning. East of the moat, on the south side, a glazed tile triple archway stands opposite a large temple on the north side, now turned partly into a military establishment and partly into a school. It is the Dongyuemiao (Temple of the Eastern Peak) (**59**), dedicated to Taishan (see pp. 108-13). The temple dates from the Yuan dynasty and contains a vast number of small shrines to all kinds of Taoist gods.

Inside the old city, crossing the temporary bridge over the moat near the Ritan Park, after a few turns one comes to a beautiful gate guarded by two lions, and the shiny dark blue (almost black) roofs of a large temple can be seen over the wall. It is the Zhihuasi (Temple of the Transformation of the Intellect) (**62**), built by the powerful eunuch Wang Zhen (1444) who manipulated Emperor Zheng Tong of the Ming dynasty. A good view of the very beautiful two-storeyed hall at the back can be had from outside the eastern and western walls.

The Tianningsi and south-western quarters.   The Tianningsi (Temple of Heavenly Repose) (**58**) and its Song dynasty pagoda is perhaps the worst case of neglect and abuse of a fine temple in Beijing. What may be the oldest temple in Beijing is situated outside the west moat, north of Guanganmen Street, and it is used as a factory and surrounded by junkyards, with makeshift workshops furiously spitting black smoke at it. To make things worse, a gigantic factory chimney was built to the north-west, dwarfing the miserable pagoda. Its graceful carvings are slowly disappearing from its sides.

North of it is the large and once opulent Boyunguan (Temple of the White Cloud) (**57**), last repaired by Qian Long, where a very popular temple fair used to be held for two weeks after the New Year. It is a Taoist temple, now turned into army barracks. Inside the former city walls, on Niujie, Ox Street, in the heart of the Moslem quarter of Beijing, is the beautiful old mosque, the Qing-zhensi (**17**), so like a temple from the outside except for its orienta-tion, to the west, facing Mecca. At the back of the buildings is a school for Moslem children.

The northern suburbs. Due north of the Zoo (**36**), and reached by turning east after the White Stone Bridge (Baishiqiao), after about 1 km on the bank of the canal, you come to the Wutasi (Five Stupas Temple) (**39**). Built in 1465, the main structure still standing is a square tower, decorated with rows of Buddhas with a platform at the top on which stand five stone stupas. North of it, and reached by an east turn off White Stone Bridge Road opposite the Institute of the Minorities, is a tall temple building, popularly known as the Big Buddha Temple (**61**) because it contains a large statue of Buddha. It can only be seen from the fields on the west side, being now incorporated into a housing compound.

Turning right on the North Circular Road, after about 2 km, you will see on the north side the circular grey roof of the Big Bell Temple (**55**), a tower built in 1733 for a large bell cast in 1406 and inscribed with the Diamond Sutra. A path leads from the main road to the east gate of the temple. Continuing east on the North Circular Road, after the Changpinglu crossroads, you will see on the south side the gold and white dagoba of the Yellow Temple (**54**), recently restored. A path leads through the fields to this lama temple, whose marble dagoba was built by Qian Long in 1781 in memory of the sixth Panchen lama who died of smallpox in Beijing.

ENVIRONS OF BEIJING

A number of day-trips and shorter excursions are possible from Beijing; you can visit some of the following sites by taxi if you do not have the use of a car.

Marco Polo Bridge. The bridge is about 15 km south-west of Beijing, on the way to the Western Qing Tombs and Zhoukoudian, site of the discovery of Peking Man. From Sanmenjie, leave the city by the Xibianmen (Western Side Gate) and turn left towards the south-west where the road forks. You drive for about 10 km until you reach a Y junction under a railway line. Take the right branch which will take you through the walled and picturesque village of Wanping.

The bridge spans the Yongding River and its parapet decorated with lions was described by Marco Polo, hence its name; the Chinese call it Lugouqiao, Black Moat Bridge. It was built in 1192 and several imperial steles have been erected at one end or the other. Popular tradition says there are so many lions carved on the stone parapets that they are impossible to count. When you examine them, you will see that apart from each large one, there are many little cubs crawling over their bodies and under them.

The bridge was where the Japanese war on China was restarted in 1938. Foreigners are not permitted to go beyond the far end of the bridge.

The Summer Palace. Several roads lead to the Summer Palace (**48**). You can start from the Sanlitun Foreigners' Compounds (**27**) and take the North Circular Road to the end and turn right. Follow the road to the T junction near Beijing University (Beida) (**45**), drive along the south and west wall of Beida until you reach another T junction just past a small marble bridge. A left turn will take you to the Summer Palace and on to the Western Hills; a right turn will lead to Qinghua University (**46**) and to the Yuanmingyuan (Garden of Perfect Brightness, i.e., the Old Summer Palace) (**47**). A prettier itinerary starts from downtown on West Changan Avenue, which you follow over the new West Moat Street, to one block past the Museum of the People's Revolutionary Army (**42**), where you turn north (right) on Wanshoulu (Longevity Road). Follow the Jingmi canal past the Balizhung Pagoda (Pagoda of the Eight Li Village) (**56**) on the left; the road zigzags for a while, crosses the canal and approaches the Summer Palace from the south. You can't go astray: foreigner's check-points indicate where *not* to turn.

The Summer Palace — in Chinese *Yihueyuan*, Garden of Harmony in Old Age — is very recent. The Anglo-French troops burned the old Yuanmingyuan in 1860 and at the same time, the former Qingyiyuan (Park of Pure Rippling Waves), built by Qian Long on the site of the present Summer Palace, was also largely destroyed. The Dowager Empress Ci Xi began rebuilding it in 1873, with funds appropriated for the modernization of the navy, and it became her principal residence in her old age. The buildings and gardens of the Summer Palace are on the whole very representative of the ornate late Qing style with its fear of empty space resulting in chinoiserie crowding the architecture. It is sadly better known abroad than the more austere and classical Ming style.

The main entrance is the Donggongmen (East Palace Gate) (**G1**) which opens into the large courtyard of the Renshoudian (Hall of Benevolence in

Old Age) (E1), the main throne hall. Bronze lions, unicorns, deer and phoenix adorn the courtyard. The path turns left (south) towards the lake shore and a small island with the Zhichunting (Pavilion of Knowing the Spring) (E2). A massive tower, the Wenzhangge (E3), dedicated to the God of Literature spans the shore path which continues south to the Iron Ox (E4). This was erected in 1755 by Qian Long to stabilize the waters of the lake, following an ancient practice of Yu the Great, the Jade Emperor who tamed the flood waters (*c.* 2205 B.C.). Soon the gorgeous Seventeen Arch Bridge (E5) appears. Its more poetic name is the Xiuyiqiao, Bridge of Embossed Ripples, and it leads to the Longwangmiao (Temple of the Dragon King) (E6), a Taoist temple built on a small island, and dedicated to the dragon who controls the waters of the lake.

Retracing our steps over the bridge and then north, we come to the Yulantang (Hall of the Jade Waves) (E7), which had a clear view of the lake until the Dowager Empress had a wall built on its left side. This is where the unfortunate emperor Guang Xu used to be imprisoned when the Dowager Empress was in residence at the Summer Palace. To the northeast of this palace, but more easily reached from north of the Renshoudian, is a theatre which consists of a free-standing stage with an upper floor and the Yiledian, (Hall of Pleasant Smiles) (E8), from which the empress and her suite used to watch plays. (The Forbidden City and the Summer Palace have two theatres each, all built on a similar plan.)

Returning to the shore through a garden, we come to the palace where the old empress Ci Xi used to live, the Leshoutang (Hall of Happy Old Age) (N1), which is still furnished and reminds one of the western palaces of the Forbidden City. The small compound to the west was used by court ladies. The Covered Way (N2) starts there, and people say that when a young man and a young woman start walking together at this end, they will be engaged by the time they reach the Marble Boat at the other end. The beams supporting the roof of the 700 m long promenade are decorated with scenes from legend and famous lake views, which Chinese visitors love to discuss and interpret. Most of these pictures were white-washed over during the Cultural Revolution because people were supposed to forget the legends, and those too much damaged to be restored have now been replaced by stiff landscapes in academic style.

Half-way along the Covered Way we come to a large open space with a wooden *pailou* (triumphal arch) and on the north side the Wanshoushan, Hill of Longevity. On the lower level is the Paiyundian (Hall which Towers into the Clouds) (W1), the main hall of a palace over which towers in turn the Foxiangge (Pavilion of Buddha's Fragrant Incense) (W2), a four-storeyed tower which dominates the lake and has a view of the hills to the west. The small hill to the west with two pagodas cut out against the sky is the Jade Fountain Hill, the source of the water which feeds the Kunming Lake and is channelled to Beijing and the Forbidden City. It is a jealously guarded summer residence for Politburo members. From the tower, you can also see the much nearer Bronze Pavilion (Baoyunge, Pavilion of the Precious Clouds) (W3), on the western slope of the Hill of Longevity. It was built in 1755 from castings made by Jesuits. On the east side there is a Tibetan prayer wheel. A steep path and steps lead further up outside the enclosure to a temple made entirely of glazed tiles, the Zhihuihai (Temple of the Sea of Wisdom) (W4), which stands at the peak of the hill. The half-ruined palaces and temples on the north slope (W6, 7, 8) have great charm

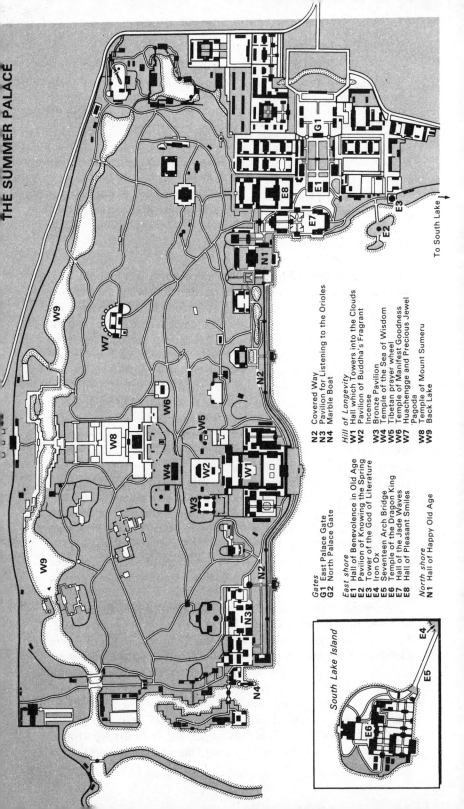

THE SUMMER PALACE

Gates
G1 East Palace Gate
G2 North Palace Gate

East shore
E1 Hall of Benevolence in Old Age
E2 Pavilion of Knowing the Spring
E3 Tower of the God of Literature
E4 Iron Ox
E5 Seventeen Arch Bridge
E6 Temple of the Dragon King
E7 Hall of the Jade Waves
E8 Hall of Pleasant Smiles

North shore
N1 Hall of Happy Old Age
N2 Covered Way
N3 Pavilion for Listening to the Orioles
N4 Marble Boat

Hill of Longevity
W1 Hall which Towers into the Clouds
W2 Pavilion of Knowing Buddha's Fragrant Incense
W3 Bronze Pavilion
W4 Temple of the Sea of Wisdom
W5 Tibetan prayer wheel
W6 Temple of Manifest Goodness
W7 Huachengge and Precious Jewel Pagoda
W8 Temple of Mount Sumeru
W9 Back Lake

South Lake Island

To South Lake

and are worth exploring if you have the time.

Climbing down Longevity Hill again, you will find yourself back on the terrace outside the Paiyundian and soon on the western half of the Covered Way. The Tingliguan (Pavilion for Listening to the Orioles) (**N3**), an old theatre now used as a restaurant (see RESTAURANTS), is on the left, perched on a high terrace. The Covered Way ends in sight of the Marble Boat, an extravagant achievement of bad taste. If you have the energy, you can start walking around the lake from there and enjoy looking at the palaces and temples from a distance and in relative solitude.

The Summer Palace is a favourite park with the Pekingese who go boating and swimming in summer; in winter, the frozen lake adds a dimension to the often crowded park and provides an incomparable setting for skating.

The Western Hills. From the Summer Palace, you take the road which leads in a northwest direction after following the Summer Palace's east wall. When you come to the Jade Fountain compound with its two pagodas, you will see on the north side of the road the stele tower, red with yellow roof, of Ming emperor Jing Tai. Keep going north-west past the junction with the south road of the Jade Fountain Compound, now closed to foreigners, until you come to a crossroads. The road going south leads to the Badachu (Eight Great Places), a valley in the Western Hills with eight old temples, now also closed to foreigners; the road going north will take you to the Wofosi (Temple of the Sleeping Buddha). It is one of the oldest temples in the Western Hills, founded in the Tang dynasty, and is approached by a stone path lined with venerable cypresses. One enters through a triple archway. The gate building, hall of Maitreya Buddha and Hall of the Three Buddhas are now empty. They were desecrated during the Cultural Revolution and the three Buddhas replaced by a giant white plaster statue of Mao Zedong. Mao is no longer there but a large bronze statue of Buddha, fully dressed but with bare feet, was spared and can once again be seen. Devotees used to make offerings of shoes to this image, which was cast in 1331.

Returning to the main road, you turn right (north) towards the Hills and through a big village. Just at the end of the main square, the road forks right (north) towards the Biyunsi (Temple of Azure Clouds), whose marble stupas can be seen from a long distance. Built in 1366, the temple was restored by Yu Jing, a favourite eunuch of the Ming emperor Cheng De, and enlarged with corruption money by another eunuch, Wei Zhongxian. Qian Long had the Diamond Throne built in 1792, a white 'marble' terrace with one large pagoda in the centre, and six stupas with fine carvings around it. Sun Yatsen's body reposed here until his mausoleum was built in

Nanjing. Only two of the halls still have Buddhist statues: the Hall of the Coming Buddha with a statue of Maitreya — the Four Heavenly Kings have gone — and, in an outbuilding on the left, the images of Five Hundred Lohans. The shape of the Diamond Throne was directly inspired by Indian temples.

Returning to the village square, you turn right up the hill to the Hunting Park, which also has an entrance near the Biyunsi. It was a game park in the Yuan dynasty and contains a few interesting buildings: a glazed tile pagoda, the Pavilion of Introspection, enclosed to the south by a semi-circular wall, and the remains of the Zhaomiao, a temple in Tibetan style in front of which stands a beautiful archway. There is a good restaurant, the Xiangshan Restaurant, set in the grounds of a former palace west of the main gate.

The Ming Tombs. The valley of the Ming Tombs is about 50 km north of Beijing. From the North Circular Road, take the Changping Road, the third major right turn from Sanlitun. If you are starting from downtown, leave the town by Deshengmen (the Gate of Righteous Victory) and keep going north. The turning for the Ming Tombs is 4 km past Changping village.

Thirteen of the sixteen Ming emperors (the Chinese call the site Shisanling, the Thirteen Tombs) repose in this valley protected by a crescent of mountains to the north. The first emperor, Hong Wu, is buried in Nanjing; the second, his grandson, was ousted by his uncle Yong Le and became a monk. Jing Tai, the seventh emperor, who ascended the throne after his brother Zheng Tong was taken prisoner by the Mongols, was buried in a simple tomb on the north side of the road to the Western Hills, opposite the Jade Fountain Pagoda compound. The others are here.

When Yong Le designed his tomb, he followed the Tang and Song tradition of laying a 'Spirit Way', with a guard of honour constituted by stone animals and dignitaries, only, unlike the Tang and Song imperial tombs which each had a guard of honour, the thirteen tombs are approached from a single 'Spirit Way'. It begins with a superb marble *pailou* (triumphal arch) (**a**) with five archways, now to the right of the modern road. The arch was once painted, but four centuries of weathering have almost entirely erased the colours. The road continues through the Great Red Gate (**b**) which was the real entrance to the valley of the Ming Tombs, once protected by a wall beyond which no common mortal was allowed, and which was only opened for an imperial procession on foot, with the dead emperor being carried to his tomb, or for the present emperor, also being carried, coming to pay his respects to his predecessors. Now the valley is planted with persimmon and apple trees and several villages have sprouted inside the sacred enclosure, still incredibly unaffected by the twentieth century. The best time — though the atmosphere is magical all the year round — for a visit to the Ming Tombs is in the autumn, when the leaves of the persimmon trees have fallen revealing the orange fruit still hanging from the black branches against the crisp blue sky.

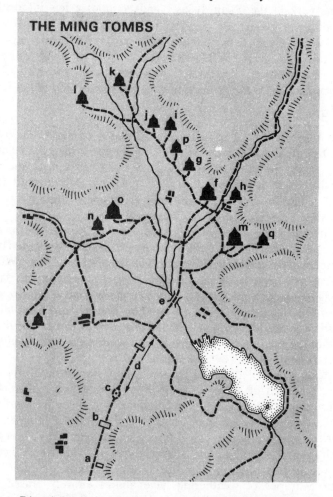

THE MING TOMBS

a	Triumphal arch	j	Maoling (tomb of Cheng Hua)
b	Great Red Gate	k	Tailing (tomb of Hong Zhi)
c	Stele Pavilion with Cloud Pillars	l	Kangling (tomb of Cheng De)
d	Imperial Guard of Honour	m	Yongling (tomb of Jia Jing)
e	Bridge	n	Zhaoling (tomb of Long Qing)
f	Changling (tomb of Yong Le)	o	Dingling (tomb of Wan Li)
g	Xianling (tomb of Hong Xi)	p	Qingling (tomb of Tai Chang)
h	Jingling (tomb of Xuan De)	q	Deling (tomb of Tian Qi)
i	Yuling (tomb of Zheng Tong)	r	Siling (tomb of Chong Zhen)

We come to the Stele Pavilion with four Cloud Pillars (c), literally Columns Bearing the Sky, engraved with cloud patterns and found only in imperial architecture. The stele, or tablet, (*bei*) is carried on the back of a tortoise which symbolizes the universe: its shell represents the sky and its belly the earth. The Imperial Guard of Honour (d) starts here with pairs of standing (male) and crouching (female) animals: lions, unicorns, camels, *qilin* (mythical creatures), horses, elephants; civilian officials, military officials and scholars. All the carvings are monolithic, even the enormous elephants. Lastly comes the triple *pailou,* called Lingxingmen (Gate of the Lintel of the Stars), which is also the name given to the gate of a Confucius temple. The road then goes over a modern hump-back bridge (e) adorned with the marble balustrade stripped from the old one below. You can already spot some of the tombs scattered in the foothills, each with a red rectangular outer wall and a stele tower standing in front of the tumulus enclosed in a crenellated circular wall. The burial chambers are under the tumulus. Each tomb is designed on the same basic plan (see p. 72) although they vary greatly in size.

Changling (f) is the tomb of Yong Le, the third Ming emperor (1403-25) and probably the last great monarch of the dynasty. It is the largest, most magnificent and best preserved. The lofty sacrificial hall is built with forty pillars each made of a single trunk of aromatic *nanmu* supporting a coffered ceiling decorated with dragons. The second courtyard contains an altar finely carved out of a single block of stone with stone incense-burners — most other tombs were assaulted during the Cultural Revolution and the incense-burners smashed. The stele tower stands on a square base pierced by a tunnel which leads to the door of the tomb. You can climb the steps to the tower and walk around the tumulus.

Xianling (g), tomb of Hong Xi (1425-26), is very dilapidated and the stele tower has almost disappeared under the trees. Hong Xi reigned only for ten months. Jingling (h) is the tomb of Xuan De (1426-36), a moderate emperor.

Yuling (i) is the tomb of Zheng Tong (1436-65), who reigned a second time, after a year in captivity to the Mongols, under the name of Tian Shun (1457-65). Zheng Tong was a typical product of the 'Inner Court', educated and pampered by eunuchs, who after his capture by the Mongols in 1450, promptly installed his brother Jing Tai on the throne. Zheng's return in 1451 caused little embarrassment except to his brother who eventually had to step down (1457) and conveniently died within a year.

Maoling (j) is the tomb of Cheng Hua (1465-88), well-meaning but whose authority was outweighed by that of the eunuchs. Tailing (k), tomb of Hong Zhi (1488-1506), is unusual, with its forecourt and main court separated by a double wall and a stream. Kangling (l) is the tomb of Cheng De, a gifted but dissolute emperor (1506-22).

Yongling (m) is Emperor Jia Jing's tomb (1522-67), remembered for his persecution of Buddhism and his commitment to Taoism. Yongling is the third largest tomb, still beautifully preserved with exquisite carvings on the

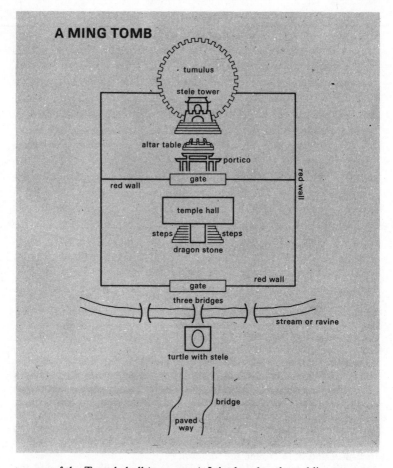

A MING TOMB

- tumulus
- stele tower
- altar table
- portico
- gate
- red wall
- red wall
- temple hall
- steps
- steps
- dragon stone
- gate
- red wall
- three bridges
- stream or ravine
- turtle with stele
- bridge
- paved way

terrace of the Temple hall (now gone). It is closed to the public at present. and rumoured to be in the process of being excavated.

Zhaoling (**n**), in a superb position overlooking a mostly dry torrent bed, is the tomb of Long Qing (1567-73), whose reign was very short.

Dingling (**o**) is the second largest tomb, where the long-reigning Emperor Wan Li (1573-1620) is buried. His tomb was excavated in 1956-8 and the 'underground palace' where the emperor and his two wives repose can be visited. Most of its contents have been removed and replaced by copies. Wan Li reigned first with the help of a competent minister, Zhang Juzheng; after Zhang's death in 1582, Wan Li, uninterested in government but much attached to imperial pomp, dipped happily into the coffers. Qingling (**p**) is the tomb of Tai Chang, son of Wan Li, who ascended the throne and died within two months (1621).

Deling (**q**), tomb of Tian Qi (1621-28), classically designed and decayed to a degree which enhances its romanticism, is my favourite. Sadly, the emperor who lies buried here may be the greatest single culprit for the fall of the Ming dynasty. Spending quiet days with a saw and a chisel in his workshop, he left power in the hands of the infamous eunuch Wei

Zhongxian, who diverted money from the imperial coffers into embellishing the Temple of Azure Clouds in the Western Hills, where he hoped to secure a heaven for his retirement.

Siling (r) is the tomb of the unlucky last Ming emperor, Chong Zhen (1628-44), who committed suicide on Coal Hill. It was built by order of Shun Zhi, the first Qing emperor, in 1659; during the interval of fifteen years, Chong Zhen lay temporarily in an imperial concubine's tomb, inside a 'borrowed' outer coffin. The tomb is accessible only on foot through a hamlet.

The Great Wall. You must make the 80 km trip (by car or by train) to the Great Wall, even if it means that you won't have time to see the Summer Palace. Still better, go there at sunset or at dawn, and look north over the hills whence the hordes of 'barbarians' came to attack the Nankou Pass. This formidable defence line, which the Chinese call the Wall of Ten Thousand Li (about 5,000 km), was linked up and extended under the Qin emperor Huang Di (221-208 B.C.) with the labour of 700,000 prisoners, soldiers, and men rounded up in the villages. The legend was that it could not be completed until 10,000 men had been buried underneath. The wall was repaired, abandoned and even moved several times through the centuries. The Yuan neglected it, having come from the other side, and it was rebuilt extensively for the last time under the Ming, who kept the 'barbarians' at war with each other while they were strong, and eventually lost the empire to the Manchus. It has been restored in three places: at Shanhai Pass in Hebei province, Nankou Pass near Beijing and Jiayu Pass in Gansu province.

As you approach the wall, you will see segments of ruined fortifications clinging to the hillside. They are ruins of the Great Wall at the Juyong Pass which were left to decay after the Mongol conquest. The fortifications round the garrison town — now a hamlet — can still easily be traced and in the middle of it stands a beautiful gate built in 1345. It is not part of the fortifications and no one really knows whether it was put there to celebrate the conquest or is simply a Buddhist monument. It is built of blocks of marble and sculpted on the inside of the archway with four giant statues of Heavenly Kings and inscriptions in six different languages: Chinese, Mongol, Uighur, Tibetan, Sanskrit and Tangut, which have puzzled philologists for a long time.

A visit to the Great Wall takes half a day and is easily combined with a detour to the Ming Tombs.

2 Hebei Province and Tianjin (Tientsin)

Although both Beijing and Tianjin, the other large city of the area, are separate municipalities, they lie within Hebei province, which extends to the north, west and south of Beijing, and is bordered on the east by the Bohai Gulf. The seaside resort of Beidaihe is much frequented by foreign residents in Beijing, and other places of interest in the province are easily accessible from the capital.

BEIDAIHE (Peitahe) (44)*　北戴河

Beidaihe (North Dai River) is a seaside resort on the Gulf of Bohai, about six hours by fast train from Beijing. There are several through trains to and from Beidaihe, both day and overnight. The resort itself is about 15 km south-east of the little town of Beidaihe and visitors are met at the station and driven to their hotels.

Beidaihe was developed at the beginning of this century when Europeans living in the concessions in Tianjin and in the legations in Beijing took up the new fad of bathing in the sea. The entire staffs of embassies moved to Beidaihe for three months during the steaming hot summer. Beidaihe itself is very humid during the summer but sea breezes make it bearable. The greater part of the villas and hotel bungalows there were built by foreign missionaries, businessmen and diplomats, each nationality building houses in a different area, but a number of 'westernized' Chinese families also had summer villas there. Foreign residents in Beijing still spend the summer in Beidaihe. The Beijing International Club runs a hotel complex of bungalows and new buildings in what was formerly a White Russian settlement. But the resort is increasingly used by Chinese holidaymakers as well, who have their own beaches, and is being opened to foreign tourist groups.

A branch of Kiesling and Bader of Tianjin operates a restaurant and a bread and cake shop during the season. In addition there are two other restaurants in the village which are worth a visit: the Gongnongbing restaurant, near Lu Xun public park, and a seafood restaurant on the west side of Main Street, over the top of the hill.

At whatever time of the season you go there, you should bring some woollens, a plastic raincoat and some mosquito repellant.

*Bold-face numbers following certain place-names refer to locations numbered but not named on the Tourist Sketch Map at p. 4.

From Beidaihe you can make a half-day excursion to SHAN-HAIGUAN (The Pass between the Mountains and the Sea), the easternmost section of the Great Wall. The massive fortified gate there, the First Gate Under Heaven, was first built in the Tang dynasty (618-907) and rebuilt in 1639 when the pressure from the Manchus to the north increased. In 1638, the Manchus raided forty cities including Tianjin and Jinan (Shandong). During these raids, the Great Wall was the scene of bloody battles, but ironically the final breakthrough took place without a struggle.

In 1644, the commander of the Shanhai Pass was General Wu Sangui, a native of the former province of Liaodong — on the north side of the pass. He was very much in love with a certain Chen Yuanyuan (Round-faced Beauty) whom he had left in Beijing in the care of his father. When he heard that Li Zicheng, the peasant rebel, had captured his beloved, he made a pact with the Manchu commander stationed on the other side of the Shanhai Pass to surrender himself and his troops, on condition that the Manchus would help him drive Li Zicheng out of Beijing. Li Zicheng, learning this, immediately sent Chen Yuanyuan back to Wu Sangui, but it was too late. (A less romantic account has it that Wu Sangui, summoned to the capital by emperor Chong Zhen, arrived to find the emperor dead and the rebels entrenched inside the Forbidden City. Caught between Li Zicheng's armies to the south and the Manchu troups massed north of the wall, Wu Sangui chose to surrender to the northern forces.) In any event, the Manchus did 'liberate' Beijing from Li Zicheng and his rebels, but overstayed their welcome for another three centuries.

The Shanhai Pass is defended by a square fortress which used to have four gates, one at each point of the compass. The east gate is the finest and best preserved. A small temple outside the gate is dedicated to Meng Qiangnu, a woman who lived during the Qin dynasty. Her husband had been sent to help build the wall and never returned. She went to the wall to look for him, but in vain, and her tears made the wall crumble down.

The Qing Tombs. Unlike the Ming emperors, who had their tombs built in a single area after they moved their capital to Beijing, the Qing are buried in two different sites. Emperor Shun Zhi's tomb was built about 110 km east of Beijing, near the Great Wall, in Zunhua county. Emperor Yong Zheng was advised by his geromancers that the eastern site would not be propitious, and they selected another site for his tomb, about 75 km south-west of Beijing, at the foot of the Taihang Mountains, in Xingcheng county. Later Qing emperors chose the eastern or western site, according to their geromancers' recommendations.

Dongling, the Eastern Tombs, are magnificently situated at the foot of the Yan Mountains, in an area covering 2,500 sq. km and bounded on the north by the Great Wall. A Spirit Way, lined on either side by eight pairs of monolithic carvings of animals and dignitaries, leads to a cluster of five emperors' tombs, each one flanked by the tomb of an empress. In addition to the tombs of these five emperors (Shun Zhi, Kang Xi, Qian Long, Xian Feng and Tong Zhi) and eight imperial consorts (including Dowager Empress Ci Xi), there are six other tombs of imperial princes and princesses, and even the tombs of Kang Xi's wet-nurse and governess.

Yuling, the tomb of Emperor Qian Long (1736-96), is sometimes open to the public. It lies to the west of the Spirit Way and is built on a plan similar to the Ming tombs. The main temple hall is a lofty structure built on a marble terrace and supported by pillars made of the fragrant hard wood *nanmu*. There are four underground burial chambers lined with stone walls decorated with low-relief Buddhist art motifs and figures.

Xiling, the Western Tombs, are also surrounded by a wall but are more scattered than the Eastern Tombs. One Spirit Way leads to Emperor Yong Zheng's tomb and another to that of Jia Qing. Dao Guang's tomb lies west of both these tombs and cannot be reached from either Spirit Way. Nor can Guang Xu's tomb, which is to the north-east and inside a separate walled enclosure, near the railway built by the Manchus to facilitate their visits to the Western Tombs. The imperial consorts are buried in separate tombs beside their emperors.

TIANJIN (Tientsin) 天津

Tianjin (The Heavenly Ford) is situated in a flat and marshy area near the Bohai Gulf, about 120 km south-east of Beijing. Although it is possible to fly there, most travellers go by train or by road from Beijing. The Hai River and its tributary wind their way slowly through the plain, depositing vast amounts of silt which have made it necessary to move the harbour to Xingang, 40 km to the east. Floods were frequent until the completion of flood-control projects. The city suffered major destruction during the July 1976 earthquake and was not reopened to tourism until 1978. Tianjin, with a population of over 6 million, is one of the municipalities directly under the central government. It can be visited in one day.

History. Tianjin has been populated since the Warring States period (476-221 B.C.), but it became an important trading centre only after the capital was moved to Beijing under the Yuan. The Grand Canal which passes through Tianjin was the main means of transportation to Beijing of the grain produced in Henan. Tianjin was also a major centre for trans-shipment between the southern coastal provinces and the capital. In the Ming dynasty, the strategic importance of Tianjin increased and fortifications were built round the town and at Dagu, at the mouth of the estuary. The arrival of the Europeans in 1858, when Tianjin became a Treaty Port, was to change the physical aspect of the city and further increase its importance as a trading centre. In addition, it rapidly became one of the nation's largest industrial centres (textiles, metallurgy, chemicals). After the Boxer Rebellion, the walls of the Chinese old town were demolished because the rebels attacking the foreign concessions had sheltered there.

Places of interest. Although known as 'the Shanghai of the North' Tianjin is lacking in glamour, and is not really a city which attracts tourists. It is the city in China where foreigners are most stared at and the municipal government has so far been powerless to change this. Though it has a few parks, its architecture is an incredible mixture of European styles which blend neither with the local style nor with each other. The European or Japanese visitor touring the former concessions will see a caricature of his national architecture in a strange setting. The housing situation which was already very grim has been worsened by the 1976 earthquake during which many of the badly maintained European buildings collapsed; one hotel used for tourists was destroyed in the quake. Most foreigners are now accommodated in the *Haihe Hotel* (also called No. 1 Hotel, formerly the Victoria Hotel), 198 Jiefanglu, tel. 34 996, old-fashioned but fairly comfortable. The *Tianjin Grand Hotel* (formerly Astor House), 219 Jiefanglu, tel. 31 114, is less 'luxurious' than the Haihe and only used for foreign guests when accommodation is short. Both hotels are within walking distance of the Friendship Store, also in Jiefanglu.

Apart from tourists, many foreign residents in Beijing pay regular visits to Tianjin's commission shops, most of which are situated on Heping and Dongma Roads. The Yilinge Antique Store at 175 Liaoning Road attracts many buyers because of the quality and price of its antiques, generally better than in Beijing.

Another reason for visiting Tianjin is purely gastronomical. It is famous for its seafood (crabs) and its dumplings, popularly called *'goubuli'* (dogs won't touch them). Several restaurants serve them, including the Baozi Restaurant at 97 Shandong Road. If you have a problem in ordering *'goubuli'*, ask for Tianjin Baozi, which is now the noncommittal official name for them. The seafood at the Dengyinglou, 94 Binjiangdao, tel. 23 757, is highly recommended.

The former Austrian Restaurant, Kiesling and Bader, now called the Tianjin Restaurant, at the intersection of Suzhou and Shanghai

Streets, still serves crab *au gratin, Wiener Schnitzel* and *café Liègeois* in the best tradition. It has a bread and pastry shop on the ground floor. Hygiene, unfortunately, is no longer part of the tradition.

Visitors to Tianjin are often taken to visit the No. 1 Carpet Factory, which employs 1,400 people. The factory specializes in Tianjin cut-pile carpets, an early twentieth-century addition to the range of Chinese carpets in which an embossed effect is achieved by shaving the pile round the decorative motifs in different colours.

YANGLIUQING, a village 15 km west of Tianjin, has been famous since the seventeenth century for its woodblock prints of New Year Pictures. (Two other centres share its fame: Weifang in Shandong and Taohuawu in Jiangsu.) These New Year pictures are pasted up on doors or inside houses for the Chinese New Year and usually stay until the next year, when they are not torn apart by the wind and rain. They are usually representations of fat children playing or eating, or, more rarely nowadays, figures of popular gods. They are painted in a profusion of pinks and reds and carry couplets wishing luck and prosperity.

Tianjin is also famous for its kites; the famous craftsman, Wei Yuantai, nicknamed 'Fengzheng Wei', Kite Wei came from there.

CHENGDE (Jehol) (**43**)　承德

Chengde (Inherited Virtue) is better known as Jehol, a name which comes from the Rehe, or Warm, River, a tributary of the Luan River, in northern Hebei province, which never freezes. The trip to Chengde, 250 km from Beijing, until recently took about six hours by train, the last part of the route up a zigzag rail 'staircase'. A fast day train has now been added, bringing the city within four and a half hours of Beijing. Visitors should spend a minimum of one day in Chengde, arriving and leaving by the night train. There is so much to see, however, and the scenery is so attractive, that it would warrant a two- or three-day visit.

Chengde has two hotels, the *Palace Guesthouse*, near the Qing summer palace, which is not at present (1979) receiving foreign guests, and the *Chengde Hotel*, situated in town, to the south of the palace. The latter offers simple accommodation and very bad food: it is wise to arrive with a small provision of fruit and snacks.

The Qing emperors used to spend up to half the year in their summer palace at Jehol, **Bishushanzhuang** (Mountain Village for Escaping the Heat). Begun in 1706 under Kang Xi and completed in 1790 under Qian Long, the palace is surrounded by a 20 km long red wall which snakes up and down the hills. Outside the wall, to the east and the north of the summer palace, are a number of temples — there were originally eleven, though war and neglect eventually brought the number down to eight (now only seven) — built between 1713 and 1780. Whereas the style of the palace buildings is Chinese, similar to that of the Imperial Palace in Beijing, several of the temples outside are in Tibetan style. Emperor Kang Xi, who started the building of these temples, was well aware of the importance of supporting the Dalai Lama's claim to political as well

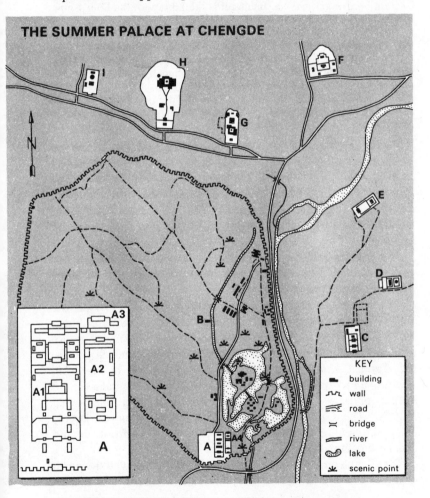

THE SUMMER PALACE AT CHENGDE

KEY
- building
- wall
- road
- bridge
- river
- lake
- scenic point

A Bishushanzhuang: the Four Palaces
  A1 Front Palace
  A2 Hazel Grouse Studio
  A3 Palace of the Wind in the Pines like
     Ten Thousand Streams
  A4 East Palace
B Wenjingge (Library)

C Temple of Universal Love
D Temple of Universal Joy
E Temple of Distant Tranquillity
F Temple of Universal Peace
G Temple to Mount Sumeru
H Potala
I Temple of the Image of Wenshu

as spiritual power, as a means of keeping the Mongol forces in Tibet in check; and Emperor Qian Long built most of the later temples in Tibetan and Mongol style to please and flatter the envoys who came to pay tribute in Chengde.

The Bishushanzhuang (**A**) comprises four palaces:

The Zhenggong (Front Palace) (**A1**), to the west, is the largest and contains the main throne hall, the Hall of Tranquil Respect for Sincerity (Danbojingcheng), also called the Nanmu Hall, because it is built with the fragrant hard wood, *nanmu*. Behind it is the Library of the Four Knowledges and the private apartments.

The Songhaozhai (Hazel Grouse Studio) (**A2**), east of the Zhenggong, also quite large, used to be the residence of Qian Long's mother.

The Wanhesongfeng (Wind in the Pines like Ten Thousand Streams) (**A3**), immediately north of the Songhaozhai, a much smaller palace, was used as a school by the young Emperor Qian Long.

The fourth palace, to the east of the Songhaozhai, is simply called the Donggong (East Palace) (**A4**). It is where the emperor used to receive vassal kings.

To the north-east of the palaces is the lake area with kiosks and pavilions studding its shores. A hot spring rises on the north-east shore. It was in a pavilion on the north shore of the lake that Qian Long received Lord Macartney, the first-ever envoy to China from the King of England, in September 1793. On a small island is the House of Mist and Rain, a two-storey building used by the emperor as a study.

The palaces and the lake cover only one-fifth of the grounds within the wall. The rest is hills covered with trees and has a few buildings, including three temples.

The Wenjingge (**B**) to the north-east was built in 1774 to house the 79,000-volume *Sikuquanshu*, Complete Library of the Four Treasuries (classics, history, philosophy and literature), a major anthology ordered by Qian Long, and the 10,000 volume encyclopaedia, the *Gujin Tushujicheng*. Seven copies were made of the *Sikuquanshu* and the one kept at Jehol was sent to the capital after the burning of the Old Summer Palace, Yuanmingyuan, outside Beijing in 1860. The *Gujin Tushujicheng* was left in Jehol and largely destroyed and dispersed during the years of warlordism and Japanese occupation.

The Eight Temples Outside, in the hills to the east and the north of the palace, are described from south-east to north-west:

The Purensi (Temple of Universal Love) (**C**) is the oldest. It was built in 1713 to commemorate the visit of Mongol princes to Chengde for the celebration of Kang Xi's sixtieth birthday.

The Pulesi (Temple of Universal Joy) (**D**) was built in 1766 specially for a visit to Chengde of envoys from the Kazakh and Eleuth minorities. It has an unusual circular hall with a double umbrella-shaped roof covered with yellow tiles, standing on two-storey terraces with stupas on the lower level.

The Anyuanmiao (Temple of Distant Tranquillity) (**E**), built in 1764, sadly is in bad condition. It was copied from a temple in the Ili valley, in western Mongolia, which the Qing armies had occupied in 1755-7. The three-storey tower in the temple enclosure is covered in deep blue glazed tiles bordered with yellow. It contains a gilded statue of the Bodhisattva, Ksitigarbha, guardian of the world and ruler of the netherworld. Known in Chinese as Di Zang, he is also the protector of little children.

The Puningsi (Temple of Universal Peace) (**F**), built in 1755 after the 'pacification' of western Mongolia, is a large temple in Tibetan style. Inside, a stele commemorating the 'pacification' is inscribed in four languages: Manchu, Chinese, Mongol and Tibetan. The Great Mahayana Hall, a five-storey square tower roofed with gilded bronze tiles, untarnished after two hundred years, rises on the Red Terrace, which is really a fortress in the style of Tibetan and Mongol temples which often had resident garrisons to protect their considerable treasures. The Mahayana Hall, itself raised on a White Terrace, contains a gigantic statue of Guanyin with a thousand eyes and arms. The temple has also a Hall of Brightness of the Rising Sun, with a magnificent dome-shaped coffered ceiling decorated with a pattern of dragons in the centre; a Hall of the Brightness of the Moon; and a glazed pagoda at the top.

The Xumifushoumiao (**G**), built in 1780, is dedicated to the mythical Mount Sumeru, the central mountain peak of the Buddhist universe, abode of Indra (in Chinese, Yindolo), the warrior deity of India who figures in lamaic Buddhism as an attendant to Sakyamuni Buddha. The temple was built in honour of the sixth Panchen Lama, who visited Chengde in 1781 and later died of smallpox in Beijing. A residence was built for him to the west of the Red Terrace, which is three storeys high and pierced with many windows, a true stronghold. A glazed pagoda stands on the highest point of the grounds, to the north, and a triple glazed archway commands the entrance to the Red Terrace. This temple and the next one to the west, the Putuozhongshengmiao, combine harmoniously Tibetan and Chinese styles.

The Putuozhongshengmiao (**H**), largest of the seven surviving temples, was built between 1757 and 1771 and is a close reproduction of the Potala, the palace of the Dalai Lama, built a century earlier in Lhasa. Behind the temple, a White Terrace is crowned by five stupas, a symbolic image of Mount Sumeru, and further on, a triple archway of glazed tiles stands across the path to the impressive Red Terrace, itself a copy on a smaller scale of the one at the Potala in Lhasa, down to its asymmetry which is so alien to Chinese architecture.

The last temple to the north is the Shuxiangsi (Temple of the Image of Wenshu [Manjusri]) (**I**), built in 1774 as a replica of the Tongming Temple in Wutaishan, Shanxi. Its lamas were all Manchus and spent eighteen years translating the sutras into Manchu.

The eighth temple, now destroyed, was the Pushansi (Temple of Universal Virtue), presumably a casualty of the Japanese occupation or of the civil war.

3 The Northeast

The three provinces Liaoning, Jilin (Kirin) and Heilongjiang lie to the northeast of the Great Wall, though what was once the province of Liaodong, including the Liaodong peninsula, was part of the Chinese empire under the Yuan and the Ming. Under the Ming it was administered as part of Shandong province because communications were easier between the two peninsulas than through the Shanhai Pass in the Great Wall. Liaodong, the richest province of the Manchu homeland, was closed to Chinese immigration from 1668, to preserve its Manchu character and also to leave the control of the lucrative ginseng trade in Manchu hands. Ginseng, a root supposed to have invigorating and aphrodisiac properties, being a monopoly, was a great source of income for the Qing emperors in the eighteenth century.

One-third of the industry of the People's Republic is concentrated in the Northeast, where the population is relatively small (70 million). The winters are bitterly cold, and visitors usually come between April and October.

SHENYANG (Mukden) 沈阳

Shenyang (North of the Shen River), the capital of Liaoning province, is situated at the centre of the bleak plain of the Liao River, on the north bank of one of its tributaries, the Han River; some 850 km from Beijing, it can be reached by train in twelve hours and by plane in one and a half hours.

Visitors usually stay at the *Liaoning Hotel* (**a**), near Beiling Park in the northern part of the city, or at the *Liaoning Guesthouse* (**b**) near the centre, at the intersection of Nanjing and Zhongshan Roads. The latter has art-nouveau stained-glass windows and a cavernous billiard room. There are two reasonable restaurants in the city, the *Nanfang* and the *Beifang*, both near the main railway station, on opposite sides of Shengli Street which runs past the station. Shenyang is no gastronome's paradise, so do not expect too much.

The main shopping streets are Taiyuan Street, a block east of the railway station, where there is an antique shop; and Zhong Street, in the eastern part of the city, which is lined with incongruous houses with archways and wrought-iron balconies.

History. From the tenth century A.D., under the Liao dynasty, Shenyang was a major centre for trade between the nomadic peoples and the north of China, and became part of the Chinese empire during the Yuan dynasty. Its importance was suddenly enhanced at the beginning of the seventeenth century when Nurhachi, the founder of the Manchu state, having accepted the title of 'Dragon General' from the Ming emperor, stopped paying tribute to the Ming, and in 1616 himself took the title of emperor, of the Qing dynasty. In 1625, he moved his capital to Shenyang (Mukden), where he employed Chinese architects and sculptors to build him a palace to compare with the Ming palace in Beijing. He died in 1626 and is buried in the Dongling, to the east of Shenyang. His successor, Abahai (also spelt Abukai), led the conquest of China but died before Beijing fell (1643) and is buried in the Beiling, to the north of Shenyang. After the Manchu conquest, completed during the reign of the third Qing emperor, Shenyang remained a secondary capital, but by the end of the nineteenth century the emperors seldom resided in the Northeast.

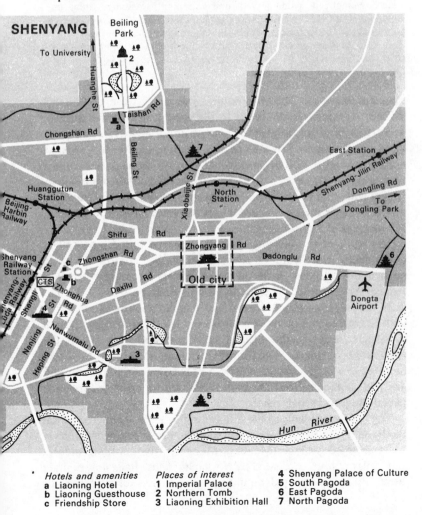

Hotels and amenities
a Liaoning Hotel
b Liaoning Guesthouse
c Friendship Store

Places of interest
1 Imperial Palace
2 Northern Tomb
3 Liaoning Exhibition Hall

4 Shenyang Palace of Culture
5 South Pagoda
6 East Pagoda
7 North Pagoda

The Liaodong peninsula was ceded to Japan in 1895, after the first Sino-Japanese war, and by 1897 Russia had obtained the right to extend the Trans-Siberian Railway through Manchuria. Japan too began to develop industries in Liaodong, and a scramble for the control of Manchuria's rich coal and iron ore deposits began. In 1900, the Chinese sided with the Boxers in expelling the Russians from Manchuria, but they managed to re-occupy their former positions in Mukden and along the railway. Shenyang became an important rail centre and grew into a modern city. The Sino-Japanese war ended in 1905 with Liaodong in principle under Chinese administration, but Japan obtained the lease of the Liaodong peninsula and the lease on the Russian railway.

By the early 1930s, mounting nationalism in China threatened Japan's hold on Manchuria and the 'Mukden incident' (an attack on the railway in 1932) was the pretext for an invasion which led to the creation of the puppet state of Manchukuo (1933-45). The Japanese created an industrial base in Manchuria which served their sweeping invasion of China until their defeat in 1945. The victory of the Communists in 1949 paved the way for a return of the Russians, in their new incarnation as Soviet experts. With their help, Mukden rebuilt its war-damaged industry, which has continued to expand ever since. By the 1970s its population, about 100,000 in 1910, had grown to close to 3 million.

Places of interest.   The university is to the north-west, not far from Beiling (Northern Tomb) Park. To the south is the Korean quarter, which has shops catering for the Korean minority, including a book-store where you can buy a set of Mao Zedong's works in Korean, a department store selling ginseng and gaudy Korean dresses, and a restaurant which serves cold dog meat and cold noodles generously spiced with chili powder. In the south-west is the former Japanese quarter where the houses are semi-detached, with little gardens, reminiscent of English suburbia.

The walls of the old city have disappeared but can be traced easily from the layout of the streets. At its centre two main north-south and two main east-west streets frame the Imperial Palace (1) (entrance in Dadong Road). Built between 1625 and 1637, the palace covers an area of 50,000 square metres, as compared with 720,000 square metres for the Forbidden City in Beijing. It is on a homely scale — the official halls are well apart from the residential courtyards. The throne room is an octagonal one-storey building in a large courtyard. The roof is covered with yellow and green tiles and in front are two pillars decorated with ferocious gilded dragons in high relief.

The four small halls to the left and right of the main court were the Banners Halls, one for each of the banners — originally military units grouped by race (Manchu, Mongol, Tibetan, etc.) under a particular colour — created by Nurhachi. These halls now contain arms, uniforms and palanquins. A gate to the left (west) leads to the living quarters, which contain a three-storeyed Harem Tower and the Wenshu Gallery, repository of one of the seven copies of the *Sikuquanshu* (anthology) of Qian Long (see p. 80). Of the smaller halls, some have been left furnished and others, emptied to help refurnish the Forbidden City, now contain exhibitions of ceramics, cloisonné ware, jewellery, imperial costumes and paintings.

The Beiling, or Northern Tomb (**2**), is a large and majestic compound where Abahai (Abukai), the second Qing emperor, honoured with the posthumous title of Tai Zong (Great Ancestor), lies buried. Tai Zong, who engineered the conquest of China, died before his armies entered Beijing. The scale and layout of his tomb make it quite unlike the Ming Tombs outside Beijing. The entrance is through a triple red archway which leads to a large park planted with evergreens, containing a stele pavilion. An elegant three-storeyed tower built on top of a massive crenellated wall commands access to the second courtyard, which contains the Ancestor's temple. At the far end of the second court is the mound with the stele tower in front of it.

The Dongling (Eastern Tomb), in the eastern suburbs of Shenyang, is the tomb of Nurhachi, father of Abahai and founder of the Qing dynasty, who died in 1626. He was given the posthumous title of Tai Zu, the Great Progenitor, given only to the first emperor of a dynasty. The Hun River flows to the south of the tomb, which is built on a plan similar to the Beiling but on a smaller scale.

You can also visit the Liaoning Exhibition Hall (**3**), a Soviet-style building in the south-west quarter, and a number of factories including machine-tool, electrical, textile, metallurgical and chemical.

LUDA (Dalien, Dairen) (**48**) 大辽

Lüda (Great Junction) is a port on the bay of Dalien, at the tip of the Liaodong peninsula. Together with Lüshun (Port Arthur) it was leased in 1905 to the Japanese, who enlarged and modernized the harbour, which is free of ice the year round.

Lüda has many industries, from a shell-picture factory to a locomotive plant, as well as a Naval Academy. The town is surrounded on three sides by hills and is built of small, attractive houses with wooden balconies in Russian style. It is a seaside resort, with three main beaches on the other side of the hill south of the town: Dongshan beach, Tiger Bay beach — with rock formations looking like crouching tigers — and Xinghai beach.

Foreigners stay in the *Dalien Guesthouse*, built in 1907 in grand Victorian style. It is rather gloomy and in need of modernization, but the restaurant serves excellent seafood.

ANSHAN (**49**), 70 km south of Shenyang, and FUSHUN (**50**), 60 km east of Shenyang, are both major industrial towns, and the centres for steel and coal respectively. Go there if you must!

CHANGCHUN 长春

Changchun (Eternal Spring), the capital of Jilin (Kirin) province, with a population of about 2 million, is situated about 280 km northeast of Shenyang. A settlement grew up on the banks of the Yitong River when the Russians constructed the Trans-Siberian railway at the turn of the century. Changchun was the capital of Manchukuo between 1933 and 1945, and was built on a grand scale by the Japanese, with wide avenues and tall buildings; most of the former administrative buildings are now used by the university. It is the largest centre for the automobile industry and produced the Jiefang (Liberation) trucks in the early 1950s, the first motor vehicles made in China.

There is a ski resort in the south of Jilin province, in the Longgang mountains at Tonghua, 250 km south-east of Changchun, and 220 km due east of Shenyang.

JILIN (**51**) 吉林

Jilin (Happy Forest), 80 km east of Changchun on the banks of the Songhua (Sungari) River, is surrounded by hills covered with forest. Its traditional resources are ginseng root, deer antlers (both used in traditional medicine and as aphrodisiacs) and sable furs. It is a centre for power and chemical industries.

HARBIN 哈尔滨

Harbin is the capital of Heilongjiang province, the northernmost province of China, which takes its name from the Amur, or Black Dragon, River which marks the border with the Soviet Union. It is a major centre of the Northeast's railway network and grew up with it. The city has wide, tree-lined streets bordered by buildings painted (when they are) in pastel colours. The residential areas have houses with small gardens planted with flowers and vegetables, and a pleasant promenade runs along the Sunghua River which borders the town to the north. Europeans are often surprised to see this entirely occidental city with a population now entirely Chinese.

DAQING (Taching) (52)　大庆

Daqing (Great Reward) oil field is about two and a half hours by train from Harbin. The train stops at Anda and the rest of the journey must be made by road. There is no such thing as a 'downtown' in Daqing, but visitors can be accommodated overnight in a rudimentary guesthouse situated in one of the many hamlets scattered over the oil field. If the guesthouse seems spartan, it is luxurious by comparison with the mud houses and temporary dwellings in which the population live. In this northernmost province, where the climate is quasi-Siberian, there are few amenities for the workers, and often not even running water.

What attracts the population, or — since many of those who work there were not given a choice — what sustains them is that they will in their time there acquire valuable technological training and experience and the right kind of political background. Daqing is a model industrial community; when there are calls for self-reliance in industry one hears the slogan, 'In industry, learn from Daqing'. Exploratory drilling began in 1959, and production rose at the rate of 20 per cent a year until 1974. In 1975 Daqing was supplying 80 per cent of the Republic's oil; thereafter, however, production began to taper off. Daqing's oil reserves are diminishing rapidly now and this may explain why so little has been done to improve living conditions for the workers.

4 Shanxi and Shaanxi

Shanxi and Shaanxi provinces, in central China, are bordered on the north by Inner Mongolia, and separated by the Yellow River. The region is one of loess plateaus, almost completely bare of trees, with a few important rivers, the Yellow River and its tributaries the Fen and the Wei. It is in this area that Chinese civilization developed, the loess being a light and easy soil to till. The main staple crops are wheat and millet. Deforestation through the centuries has caused a drop in humidity, however, and extensive erosion of the soil by wind and water, so that agriculture is dependent on irrigation; precipitation occurs mainly in the summer season. The winters are extremely dry and windy, with temperatures below zero C. for four months of the year. The area is fairly rich in coal and iron ore which have enabled industry to develop.

DATONG (Tatung) 大同

Datong (Great Togetherness) is situated on a 3,900 ft.-high plateau in the north of Shanxi province, lying between two stretches of the Great Wall. The winters are cold and windy (min. temp. −30°C.) and the summers hot (max. temp. +29°C.). Most of the rain falls in August and September (only 400 mm).

However, the summer is still the best season for visiting Datong, which is eight hours by train from Beijing. The sites of historical interest there can be visited in one day, so that you can arrive and leave by the night train. If you do stop there, the hotel for foreigners, the Datong Guesthouse (a), is located at the southern end of the town's fortifications. It was built in the 1950s for Soviet experts and is rudimentary; the food is rather bad.

Its proximity to Inner Mongolia gave Datong a strategic importance. It was the capital of the Wei empire until A.D. 494, and later became the northern capital of the Liao empire (A.D. 960). In the Ming dynasty, it was a garrison town, and the fortifications built round it at the time are for the most part still standing but are fast disappearing through the combined efforts of the local population and natural erosion.

Places of interest.   Three temples in the town are open to visitors: the Upper Huayan, the Lower Huayan and the Shanhua monastery. A fourth, dedicated to Confucius, lies in the south-east quarter of the town (**6**) and cannot be visited.

The Upper Huayan temple (**1**) was founded in the Liao dynasty, in the tenth century A.D. Climbing a steep flight of stairs, one comes to the terrace of the Daxiongbaodian (Precious Hall of the Great Hero). Rebuilt in 1140, it faces east, which is unusual. Behind its severe exterior is a richly decorated hall containing 52 statues of the Ming period, the walls covered with murals of the Ming and Qing dynasties. Five large Buddhas, of wood or of clay, stand in the centre, representing the five directions: centre, north, south, east and west, with a row of ten saints on either side, leaning forward at a

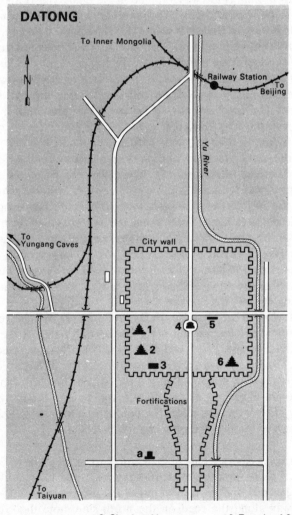

a Hotel	**3** Shanhua Monastery	*•***6** Temple of Confucius
1 Upper Huayan temple	**4** Drum Tower	
2 Lower Huayan temple	**5** Nine Dragon Screen	*not open to the public

perilous angle. A wooden model of a corner tower of one of the city walls, destroyed in the Qing dynasty, is displayed on the left in front of the altars. Coming out of the temple, one has a magnificent view of the town, with its fortifications, the other temples and, in the centre, the Drum Tower.

Between the Upper Huayan and the Lower Huayan, one passes a platform where once stood a temple building destroyed by the Jin. At the back of this platform is the large City Bell, which once hung in the Bell Tower (destroyed in the 1950s).

One enters the Lower Huayan temple (**2**) through a little side gate in the north wall. It too was founded in the Liao dynasty and partly rebuilt in the Ming and Qing. The main hall, built in 1048, contains a valuable library of Buddhist sutras (13,000 volumes) and a number of magnificent statues of the Liao period. The books are stored in locked cupboards on three sides of the hall, designed to look like rows of little two-storey houses with a gallery running half-way up. A large bell and a large drum still stand inside the hall by the entrance. The forebuildings, of no special architectural interest, now house the City Museum, containing a collection of objects found in tombs near by, some dating from the fifth century A.D., and on the south side, an exhibition of vegetable and animal fossils.

The Shanhua Monastery (**3**), also called the Nansi, or South, Monastery, was founded in the eighth century but completely rebuilt in the twelfth. Only four halls now survive: the Tianwangmiao, (Temple of the Celestial Guardians), the Sanshengdian (Hall of the Three Saints), a two-storey pavilion rebuilt in 1953, and the Daxiong-baodian (Precious Hall of the Great Hero), the largest of all, which contains some fine pieces of sculpture of the Liao dynasty and later periods. Note the statue of Guanyin (Kuanyin) with six arms and the rich Ming dynasty frescoes on the walls.

In Datong you can also visit the Drum Tower (**4**), built in the Ming dynasty and standing on the main north-south street of the inner town (under repair, 1978), and near it the Nine Dragon Screen (**5**), or wall. The latter, covered with glazed tiles of five different colours representing nine dragons fighting for balls of fire (the sun) on a background of sea waves and clouds, was built in the early Ming dynasty. The town also offers the unique opportunity of visiting a steam-engine factory, the only one left in China.

The Yungang caves.   One of the main reasons for going to Datong is to visit these famous caves, 16 km west of the town, with their giant figures of Buddha carved out of the hill.

Half-way along the road on the north side, note the Guanyin Temple, with its Three Dragon Screen, in the same style and of the same period as the one in the town. Founded in the eleventh century and rebuilt in the twelfth, the temple is in a very bad state of repair and guarded by armed sentries; visitors are not allowed, but it is worth stopping to have a look at the outside. Note also the pointed earth-coloured beacons on the tops of the hills along the way.

The Yungang caves cover a stretch of about 1 km, with 53 caves, some of them no more than niches carved high in the sandstone cliff, 21 of which can be visited. They were built for the most part between A.D. 460 and 494, and five of them (Nos. 16 to 20), built by a monk called Tan Yao on Wei emperor Wen Cheng's order, are among the earliest examples of Buddhist stone sculpture in China, their style deriving from the Graeco-Buddhist sculpture evolved in Gandhara, North India, from the first century A.D.

The Old Temple of the Stone Buddhas (Shifogusi), built in 1652, through which one enters the site, is the only surviving temple among the caves, but traces of others can be seen on the face of the cliff. (Note the open-air stage built opposite the entrance to the temple on the south side of the road.)

Eastern caves: **Nos. 1** and **2**, built on a similar plan with a carved pagoda-pillar in the centre and Buddhas in niches on the walls, are very eroded. Note the inscription above the entrance to No. 2: Yun Shen Chu (Place where the Clouds are Thick). **No. 3**, the largest of the caves although the entrance is small, contains one Buddha and two Bodhisattvas in the western part, dating probably from the seventh or eighth century; the eastern part of the cave is unfinished. **No. 4** is small with a square pillar at the centre; the statues have almost disappeared. A ravine separates the four eastern caves from the central caves.

Central caves: **No. 5** is well preserved and protected by a four-storey structure. A statue of Buddha 17 m. high stands in the middle. Like much Chinese stone sculpture it is plastered over, to protect it from erosion, and gilded; the eyeballs are made of glazed ceramic. Note the flying *apsarah* (angels) in high relief on either side of the entrance and visible from the second floor — perfect examples, with their full faces and serene smiles, of the mature Northern Wei style.

The centre of **No. 6** is occupied by a square two-storey pagoda-pillar, with one main statue of Buddha on each face and surmounted by four nine-storey pagodas borne by elephants. The sculpture on the central pillar and on the walls and ceiling is sumptuous and of exceptional quality; bas-reliefs on the east and south walls depict the life story of Buddha.

A wooden structure still protects the entrance to **No. 7**. Note the Bodhisattva, Manjusri (Wenshu), on a lion throne in the back cave and the six praying Bodhisattvas above the doorway. The outside wooden structure outside **No. 8**, its counterpart, has disappeared and the statues inside are badly worn. Note the Vishnu with five heads and six arms riding on a peacock on the left and the Shiva with three heads and eight arms riding on a bull on the right, illustrating a blend of Indian, Chinese and even Greek motifs. At the entrance to **No. 9** are octagonal pillars borne by elephants. The lintel above the doorway has a magnificent decoration of garlands of lotus flowers hanging from a roof, and rich carvings decorate the walls. No.

10, the other one of this pair, has the same octagonal pillars at the entrance, the same rich decoration inside.

In No. 11, carved in A.D. 483 (see the inscription on the right-hand wall near the entrance), most of the statues are eroded and covered with plaster. The walls are decorated with an intricate pattern of niches with ornate Buddhas and pagodas. No. 12 is decorated with little Buddhas and Bodhisattvas carved in niches; note the musicians playing different kinds of instruments on the north wall. The large statue inside is of a later period. A large statue of Maitreya Buddha sitting cross-legged occupies the centre of No. 13, with a little four-armed Vajra supporting his right arm.

Western caves: The front of No. 14 has fallen off and the sculpture inside is very eroded. The walls of No. 15 are decorated with little Buddhas in niches arranged in rows.

In No. 16, the first of the five earliest caves carved under the supervision of the monk Tan Yao, a massive statue of Buddha stands with its head reaching the ceiling. In No. 17, carved in A.D. 480, an impressive giant statue of Buddha sits cross-legged in the centre, with a seated Buddha on the left and on the right, representing the past and the future. A large Buddha stands in the centre of No. 18, his robe richly decorated with bas-reliefs of a thousand Buddhas, his left arm folded on his chest. The severity and massiveness of the main Buddha contrasts with the pairs of Bodhisattvas on either side, which are of a finer and gentler design. No. 19, which comprises one central cave and two smaller side caves, contains a giant figure of Buddha with a column supporting his right arm. The giant statue of a seated Buddha in No. 20 is visible from far off. The outside wall of the cave has fallen off and the statue, typical of the severe early Northern Wei style, is left exposed.

Separated from No. 20 by a series of little caves and niches carved at different levels in the cliff, No. 21 has sculpture dating from the late Wei dynasty. A five-storey pagoda stands in the middle.

Many of the carvings in the Yungang caves are damaged, or missing; some examples of the sculpture, removed and sold to somewhat unscrupulous art lovers at the beginning of the century, have found their way into museums in Europe and North America.

TAIYUAN 太原

Taiyuan (Great Plain), the provincial capital, lies in a depression of the Shanxi province plateau, watered by a Yellow River tributary, the Fen. The climate is more continental than in the North China plain and agriculture suffers from drought. The Taiyuan basin is rich in iron ore and coal deposits and has been developed into an important industrial region. The population is now nearly 2 million.

Taiyuan is thirteen hours by overnight train from and to Beijing and can be visited in two days. The three hotels for foreigners are situated in the main east-west street, Yingzi Dajie. Accommodation at the *Bingzhou Hotel*, built in the 1950s, is primitive and the food is very bad. The *Yingzi Guesthouse*, also called the Eight Corner Guesthouse, opposite the Yingzi Park, has a good view of the town from the rooftop; built in the 1970s, it is fairly comfortable. A new hotel for foreign visitors is being built in the western suburbs on the banks of the Fen River. The Friendship Store is in Wuyi Road, just north of the main square. *Fen jiu*, a strong local wine, is produced in vineyards north of the city.

History. The area has been populated for a very long time and numerous remains of neolithic settlements have been found. Taiyuan has either been a bastion defending the north of the empire against invasion, or, when the central power was weak, has been left to enjoy a great measure of autonomy. The city has a strong tradition of rebellion against the empire, and was completely razed to the ground in A.D. 979. Called Jin Yang at the time, it then lay south of present-day Taiyuan, near the Jinci temple. It was rebuilt on its present site and renamed Bing Zhou. The modern name of Taiyuan (Great Plain) was first used in the second century B.C. The town prospered through commerce, under the north barbarian dynasties as under the Chinese dynasties. The city walls were fortified under the Ming and kept in good repair until 1949, after which their systematic destruction began.

Places of interest. The No. 2 Shanxi Provincial Museum, open 8-12 a.m., 2-6 p.m., is situated off the main Wuyi square (to the north-west), in an old Taoist temple, the Chunyanggong, extensively restored in 1734. It is a very rich and eclectic provincial museum, displaying ceramics, bronzes, a large collection of stone sculpture (note the Western Han Tiger), a collection of Northern Wei Buddhist sculpture, some very good examples of Tang Buddhist sculpture, including a now headless and armless Bodhisattva showing clear Greek influence in the draperies of his robe, and an imposing statue of Laotze.

The courtyards also contain good samples of cast iron sculpture, typical of the local craftsmanship which has a tradition going back to the Song dynasty. The No. 2 museum also has a good collection of painting and calligraphy, including works by a local artist, Fushan (early Ming dynasty), master of calligraphy, painter and doctor, who invented a soup — called *Tou Nao* for his old mother — which is now famous in the city and eaten at the Spring Festival. The museum also has a display of lacquer ware and embroidery.

The Chongshansi (Temple where Goodness is Worshipped) is also known by the name of a temple that once stood on the same site, the White Horse Temple. The present hall, a classic example of Ming dynasty architecture, with a double roof, is all that remains of the temple, which was destroyed by fire in 1864. Two bronze lions guard the entrance. This temple is still active and possesses a remarkable collection of Buddhist sutras (5,480 volumes) including Yuan dynasty books, woodblock printed sutras from the Song dynasty, fifteenth-century sutras hand-painted in gold leaf, and an exceptionally rare and beautiful illustrated book of the life of Buddha, painted in the ninth year of the reign of Cheng Hua (1483). The hall contains three large statues of Bodhisattvas: in the centre, Wenshu painted in gold leaf and flanked by Guanyin and Puxian. The two bronze lions and the bell outside were cast respectively in 1391 and 1449.

The No. 1 Shanxi Provincial Museum is directly to the south, in a temple which was once part of the Chongshansi and was turned into a Confucian temple after the fire of 1864. It has a collection of Jin dynasty sutras printed on scrolls.

The house of Yan Xishan, in Shengli Jie, now the headquarters of the Shanxi Provincial Revolutionary Committee, was rebuilt at the beginning of this century by the famous general-dictator who supported the republicans against the Manchus and ruled the province until 1949.

The Two Pagodas, in the southern suburbs in the grounds of the Temple of Everlasting Happiness (Yongzuosi), were built during the reign of the Ming emperor Wan Li. They appear on the city flag. One cannot visit the pagodas but can get a view of them from the roof of the Yingzi Guesthouse.

Environs of Taiyuan. The Jinci, situated on the west bank of the river Fen about 25 km south of Taiyuan, at the foot of the Xuangweng Mountains, is the most famous group of temples in the area, dating from the Northern Wei dynasty (386-543). It is a family temple, built in memory of Prince Shu Yu of Tang, second son of King Wu of the Western Zhou dynasty. A modern gate built in traditional style commands the entrance, while the old gate is on the left. Note the three locust trees, said to be 1,300 years old, and the two Ming cast-iron lions.

The first building, slightly to the right of the main axis, is the Water Mirror Platform, built in the fourteenth century. It is a stage and is still used several times a year for opera performances. One then comes to the Iron Men Terrace, with four statues of warriors cast in the eleventh century, but the south-western figure is the only one of the originals left.

The Hall of the Sacred Mother, built in 1102 by Emperor Ren Zong of the Song dynasty in honour of Prince Shu Yu's mother, is the oldest wooden structure in Taiyuan. The main pillars supporting the roof are decorated with curling dragons in high relief, and larger-than-life-size statues of Celestial Guardians stand either side of the entrance into the hall. The statue of the Sacred Mother herself is in the middle of the hall behind a glazed tile altar, with life-size terracotta statues of twenty-two of her companions lining each side of the hall. These include ladies-in-waiting, servants, an opera actress disguised as an old man (on the right), and a much-esteemed cook (on the left), all of them remarkable for their realism and individuality. Frescoes depicting the life of the Sacred Mother are painted above the windows on the outside. To the right of the Hall, the

Descendants' Temple (Miaoyitang) is now empty, but has a fine nine-panel fresco, representing children at play, on the wall above the windows.

Still further to the right, up a flight of steps, is the Temple of Prince Shu Yu of Tang, originally built in the Northern Wei dynasty, and rebuilt in the Ming and Qing dynasties. To the right of this temple is the pavilion of the Tang Tablets, which commemorates the visit of Emperor Tai Zong, second emperor of the then newly founded Tang dynasty, to honour this prince, Shu Yu, of the much respected Zhou dynasty. The inscriptions are said to be in Tai Zong's own handwriting.

Immediately to the left of the Temple to the Sacred Mother is the Taitai Temple, dedicated to a legendary figure said to have tamed the waters of the Fen River. It is now empty. Still further to the left is the Water Mother Temple (Shuimulou), closed, but with the statue of Shui Mu, spirit of the source of the river Jin, visible behind the door. A pavilion is built over the spring which comes out of a deep well and is called the Spring Eternally Young (Nanlaoquan). The water is very limpid and flows at a constant rate and temperature; below, it collects in a small pool with a marble boat which is a favourite background for visitors having their picture taken.

The Jinci contains two small museums: one dedicated to the local painter, Fushan, and another containing various objects found in the neighbourhood. Another spring, the Yuzhao, is traversed by a cross-shaped bridge, rebuilt during the Song dynasty and a unique specimen.

Further along on the Jinci road is the Xuanzhongsi (Temple of the Dark Centre), founded in A.D. 472. It is best visited with the Jinci, in one day-long expedition; the temple can provide restrooms, and one can take a picnic lunch provided by the hotel in Taiyuan.

The Xuanzhongsi, also known as the Yongmingcansi, is in Jiaocheng country, birthplace of Chairman Hua, about 60 km south of Taiyuan. The last 4 km of the road take one up a mountain track, barely accessible by car, which winds past the monks' cemetery with its 'forest' of stupas. The last few yards of the climb have to be made on foot. Only a white dagoba is visible from the road; the temple itself is completely hidden until one reaches the gates. It is still active and was left undisturbed during the Cultural Revolution. Most of the temple was destroyed by fire about a hundred years ago.

The first hall of the entrance contains a Ming statue of Maitreya Buddha and four celestial guardians. Drum and bell towers stand on top of the temple walls, on either side of the entrance. The next hall, a small pavilion, shelters statues of the god of war and Weituo, guardians of the Buddhist religion. Then come two pavilions with steles. The next hall, which is the largest, contains a statue of Amitabha Buddha standing, dating from the Ming dynasty and surrounded by scrolls representing sixteen worshippers. The next hall, the only building still standing from the Ming dynasty, contains seven Buddhas of gilded wood sitting on lotus thrones. The roof of this, the main prayer hall, is adorned with lively little figures on either side of three small stupas: a dragon at the corner, a rider on horseback, a bridge, another rider. The roof is partly glazed and can be best seen from the hall of the Thousand Buddhas at the top. On either side of the Seven Buddha Hall are symmetrical buildings containing steles and bas-relief carvings, some of which date back to the fourth century.

The uppermost temple hall is the Thousand Buddha Hall, which contains small Tibetan bronze statues of Buddhas and Bodhisattvas gathered from a number of temples in the province, and also some more common Chinese images in lacquered wood. The secondary shrines at the sides, including one dedicated to Guanyin which still contains some statues, only receive visits from birds nowadays.

It was in the Xuanzhongsi that in the fifth century was founded the sect of the Pure Land (Jingtu), whose main deity was Amitabha Buddha. The sect traced its origins to a monk of south China named Hui Yuan (334-416) who preached that the simple act of faith of calling the Buddha's name would ensure salvation. Jingtu made converts in Japan in the eighth century, and a small shrine in a courtyard to the west of the main buildings is dedicated to prominent Chinese and Japanese monks, members of the sect

To the south-west of the small town of PINGYAO, some 110 km south of Taiyuan and accessible from there by road or rail, is the Shuanglinsi (Temple of the Two Forests) which was founded in the Northern Wei period, but largely rebuilt in the nineteenth century. It contains an extraordinary collection of statues of the Song, Ming and Qing dynasties, altogether about 1,500, spanning a period of some 800 years. The Hall of the Heavenly Kings contains four giant statues of the guardians of the Buddhist religion, of the early Ming dynasty, which are rendered in a particularly forceful and individual-istic style. The second courtyard features two large lateral halls, the Hall of the Thousand Buddhas on the right and the Hall of the Pusa (Bodhisattvas) on the left, both containing a large number of statues, mostly of the Ming dynasty, of great realism. The Hall of the Great Hero in the middle of the second courtyard is a seven-bay-wide building with Ming dynasty figures of Buddha in the centre and a dozen life-size statues of Lohans (disciples), of the Song dynasty, in painted clay over wood. All these figures are set against a back-ground of stucco frescoes representing mountains, rivers and palaces in a very good state of preservation; the effect is un-expectedly homogeneous because the main characteristic of the statues is their vitality.

Although Wutaishan, about 200 km northeast of Taiyuan, is not at present open to the public, it cannot be left out. It is one of the four sacred mountains of Buddhism, dedicated to the Bodhisattva Manjusri (Wenshu). Its temples enjoyed a great popularity during the Tang dynasty and numerous pilgrims' gifts made them amongst the most prosperous temples in the country.

DAZHAI (Tachai) (45)　大寨

Dazhai (Great Outpost) is a production brigade centred round a village in the Taihang Mountains in Shanxi province, about 120 km west of Taiyuan. One goes by train to the town of Yangquan and drives 60 km south to Dazhai. The railway timetable makes an overnight stay compulsory. Accommodation for foreign visitors in Dazhai Guesthouse is very simple, in rooms partly dug out of the rock like most dwellings in this area of north China. A bowl of millet gruel always appears at the end of the meal, for *couleur locale*.

If you did not know it already, you will soon be aware that Dazhai is the 'model' production brigade. The slogan *Nongye xue dazhai* ('In agriculture, learn from Dazhai') turns up all over the country on walls, rocks, roofs, and traced in stone on the ground. It has become the practice to reward model workers with a pilgrimage to the model commune, and in all seasons you will see groups winding their way up and down the terraces in long lines following red flag bearers.

The brigade is located in dry and stony hills cut by streams which turn into torrents when the rain falls in the summer. The first agricultural co-operative, comprising fifty families, was set up there in 1953 and doubled the agricultural production in four years. In 1958, following disastrous floods which destroyed most of the terraced fields and housing, the retaining walls of the terraces were built in curved lines with deeper foundations and using big boulders hacked out of the mountains. Instead of rebuilding individual houses for the commune members, collective housing was designed in the valley, consisting of rows of rooms faced by rows of kitchens on the same level, the rooms being allocated to each family according to its size. Since 1976, the Dazhai commune members have begun re-levelling the terraces to make larger fields allowing the use of farm machinery.

Dazhai has the highest yield in the area and chemical fertilizers are increasingly used as well as traditional night soil and composting. The Dazhai conferences of 1975 and 1976 outlined a programme to set up 'Dazhai-type counties' in two-thirds of the country. Chen Yonggui, the peasant-leader of Dazhai, was made a member of the Politburo in 1973. He is usually represented — in particular in Huxian-type paintings (see below, p. 103) — wearing a turban made of a white towel, in the peasant fashion.

YAN'AN (Yenan)　延安

Yan'an (The Long-time Peace) is in central Shaanxi province, 320 km east of Taiyuan. The town is surrounded by an amphitheatre of hills and situated on the banks of the Yan River from which it takes its name. It is only accessible by plane from Xi'an (see below) or Taiyuan and flights are often cancelled or delayed if the visibility is poor. Flight schedules make a minimum stay of two days necessary and although the area has a few temples and rock carvings, they are not included in the tourist itinerary which consists exclusively of revolutionary sites. Yan'an Hotel is simple and the food frugal.

In October 1934 the Central Red Army and a body of civilians, both men and women (about 100,000), forced out of their base at Ruijin in Jiangxi by the Nationalist blockade, set off on the Long March. The exodus lasted one year, and after crossing eighteen mountain ranges and fourteen rivers, they arrived in the small town of Wuqi, north-east of Yan'an, in October 1935. The Communists set up their capital in Yan'an in 1937, having preserved the party organization intact, and gathered some 50,000 troops under a unified command. The loess hills of northern Shaanxi afforded some protection against bombing and the Communists, like the local population, lived in cave-dwellings. The blockade was total, though, and the army had to produce its own food to survive.

Yan'an's revolutionary sites include the former residence of Chairman Mao at the foot of Fenghuang Hill, which is very near the hotel; another one in the Qiangliang Hills at Wangjiaping, near the Revolutionary Museum; one to the north at Yangjialing, near the University, and a more distant one to the north-east at the Zaoyuan (Date* Orchard). In the ten years of the Yan'an government, Chairman Mao and his colleagues of the Central Committee moved several times to escape the Nationalist bombings; they were eventually forced out of Yan'an in 1947.

At Wangjiaping, you can see the Assembly Hall in which the 1945 Party Congress was held. It is a reconstruction of the original one, destroyed in 1947 by the Nationalists, and it looks amazingly like a church. You will also be shown the plot of land cultivated by Mao Zedong who was following his own directive of self-reliance and growing tobacco and red peppers to feed his chain-smoking habit and season his food in the Hunanese fashion.

The Baota (Precious Pagoda), which is the symbol of the town, can be seen from everywhere. It is the only building remaining of a temple founded during the Song dynasty in the tenth century. It was severely damaged in 1947 but has since been restored.

The Museum of Revolution is large but, mercifully, has a sitting room half-way through. When I visited it in 1976, it was almost

---

Zao, commonly translated as 'date', is the jujube.

totally empty of heroic figures except for Mao Zedong, Zhu De and Zhou Enlai. All the former companions, by then disgraced, were either absent or presented as traitors.

NANNIWAN is a production brigade 50 km southwest of Yan'an where the first construction and production brigade of the army was set up, under the leadership of Wang Zhen, later Vice-Chairman and member of the Politburo. Responding to Mao's call for self-sufficiency, the army settled on poor and empty land and began cultivating it, building housing and setting up workshops. Nanniwan is now a 'Cadre School' for party and other cadres of the Xi'an region. They usually spend a period of six months doing manual labour to keep themselves in touch with peasant life.

XI'AN (Sian) 西安

Xi'an (Western Peace), the capital of Shaanxi province, was intermittently the capital of the empire for over a thousand years. It has a wealth of archaeological remains unequalled elsewhere in China, including imperial tombs of eleven dynasties, from the Zhou in the twelfth century B.C. to the Tang in the eighth century A.D. The city is worth a two- to three-day visit.

Situated a few kilometres south of the Wei River, a major tributary of the Yellow River, in the fertile loess plain of Guangzhong which is bordered to the north by the loess plateaus of Huangtu and the Qin hills to the south, greater Xi'an has a population of 2.5 million. It is a major industrial centre (textiles, mechanical engineering, light industry). The climate is of the North China continental type, with dry cold winters and a humid summer season.

Xi'an is about twenty hours by train from Beijing. Foreign tourists stay in the *Renmin Tasha* (People's Hotel) (**a**), a vast and unhospitable hotel, originally built for the Soviet experts, in Dongxin Street. The food is very plain, starchy and greasy. A new hotel is being built (1979) with state funds and should be completed shortly.

Some simple, attractive brown-glaze or blue and white pottery can be bought at ironmongers' and pottery shops in the city. A whole street is given over to the making and selling of baskets and wicker furniture. There is also an antique shop.

History. The Wei valley is one of the cradles of Chinese civilization. It has been settled since the palaeolithic era, and important remains of a settlement in the neolithic era have been found in the village of Banpo, in the western suburbs.

During the Zhou dynasty, the capital moved several times in the vicinity of Xi an until 770 B.C., when it fell into the hands of western barbarians. The first emperor Qin (259-210 B.C.) established his capital in modern Xianyang, on the north bank of the Wei, and his tomb is at the foot of

Mount Lishan, 30 km east of the city. The first emperor of the Han dynasty destroyed many of the palaces built by Qin Shihuangdi and established his capital also on the north bank, just north of present-day Xi'an, and named it Changan (Everlasting Peace). It was the starting point of the Silk Route, going west towards Persia.

After an interregnum of three hundred years, the Sui reunified the empire and chose a site south of the Wei, almost exactly that of modern Xi'an, for their capital in A.D. 582. Under the Tang the city knew its most prosperous times, becoming a truly cosmopolitan place where a large population of merchants and envoys from western Asia and even Europe were allowed to practise their trade and religions. For the most part

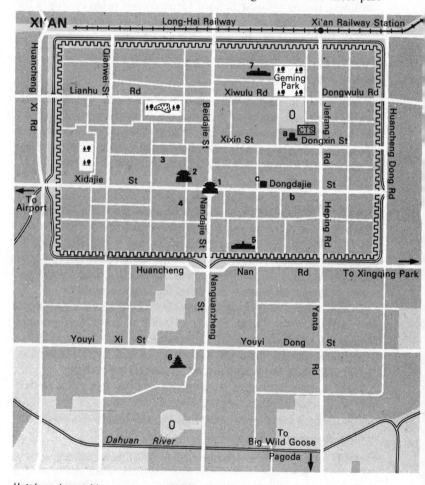

Hotels and amenities
a People's Hotel
b Xi'an Restaurant
c Department Store

Places of interest
1 Bell Tower
2 Drum Tower
3 Mosque
4 Bamboo Fence Market
5 Shaanxi Provincial Museum
6 Small Wild Goose Pagoda
7 Memorial Museum of the Eighth
  Route Army Xi'an Office

destroyed after the fall of the Tang, Xi'an was never again to be a capital of the empire. Under the Ming, it was rebuilt on a smaller scale, with walls and a palace for a son of emperor Hong Wu (fourteenth century). It was a garrison town during the Qing dynasty but fell to the republicans without a fight in 1911, after which the Manchus were massacred.

Xi'an is a dusty but attractive city where most people still live in traditional houses in courtyards. The Ming dynasty walls and some of the gates have been preserved and one hopes will not be pulled down. The people are proud of living in a former imperial capital city.

Places of interest. Both the Bell (1) and Drum (2) Towers have been restored recently, but only the Bell Tower can be visited. It was rebuilt at its present location in the sixteenth century, but the original bell inside has disappeared. (The upper storeys of a bell tower are usually built round the bell, which can only be replaced by a smaller one — as small as the largest gate in the tower.) From the third floor one has an excellent close-up view of the Chinese roof-truss system, fundamentally different and more elaborate than in the West. Each main transverse beam supports a pair of queen-posts, which in turn support a shorter transverse beam, rising step by step to carry a curved roof, while the 'bracket-arm' system is used to support the overhanging, turned-up eaves. The Drum Tower, also rebuilt in the Ming dynasty, stands on the site of the tower built there in the Tang dynasty, when the main north-south axis of the town was one block west of where it is now.

Xi'an used to have over a hundred temples, mosques and even Nestorian churches. The present-day mosque, Qingzhensi (3), behind the Drum Tower in Huajuegang Jie, was first built in the Tang dynasty and heavily restored in the fourteenth century. The prayer hall, still in use, has a fine coffered ceiling.

The Shaanxi Provincial Museum (5), in the grounds of a former temple of Confucius, has a collection of historical relics, including Persian, Arabic and Byzantine coins; beautiful glazed pottery horses and figurines found in Tang tombs; some exquisite murals from the tomb of Princess Yongtai, daughter-in-law of Empress Wu Zetian; Zhou dynasty bronzes; and ceramics.

The Gallery of Stone Carvings, the richest in the country, with more than 70 pieces from the Han dynasty, second century B.C., to the Tang, early tenth century A.D. , contains the high-relief carvings of the Six Horses of Tang emperor Tai Zong, two of which are now in the United States, and monolithic sculptures of large animals.

The famous 'Forest of Steles' (*beilin*), a most unusual sort of library, was started in 1090, during the Song dynasty, from a collection of 114 steles engraved with the 12 classics in 837. Eventually brought to Xi'an, the collection now has over 1,000 steles. One of them commemorates the founding of a Nestorian Christian church in Xi'an in 781. Others are engraved with inscriptions by famous calligraphers and record the evolution of the art of calligraphy.

The Small Wild Goose Pagoda (Xiaoyanta) (**6**) used to stand on the north-south axis of the Tang city, right at the centre, but is now just outside the south wall of Xi'an. It was erected in A.D. 707 on the grounds of the Daqianfu Temple, built by the ferocious but devout Empress Wu Zetian a few years earlier. It is 45 m high and now 15 storeys high, the two top storeys having collapsed after an earthquake in 1555. The lintels above the north and south entrances are finely carved with ivy patterns and Buddha figures.

A major landmark of Xi'an, about 4 km south of the city, is the Big Wild Goose Pagoda (Dayanta), built in A.D. 652 to house the Buddhist sutras brought back from India by the monk Xuan Zang, whose epic journey to the West was described in the popular sixteenth-century novel *Xiyou Ji* (translated as *Monkey*). The square brick pagoda, 64 m high, has 7 storeys, with spiral staircases inside leading to the top.

A stele set inside the west archway at the base depicts Buddha preaching against a background of Chinese-style buildings of the Tang period. Two other steles inside the archways, have inscriptions by famous and not-so-famous calligraphers: the custom used to be for successful candidates in the imperial examinations to engrave their names on the steles. They are now protected from further defacement.

The Xingqing Park, east of the city walls, is on the site of the palace of the Tang emperor Xuan Zong (713-75) who moved there with the court in 728. His love for the beautiful Yang Guifei caused the ruin of this great monarch, remembered above all for his patronage of the arts. In 755, An Lushan, a general rumoured to be Yang Guifei's lover, seized the capital and the emperor fled to Sichuan and abdicated. The Park still contains a few buildings in Tang architectural style: the Chenxiang (Garuwood) Pavilion and the Hua'exianghui (Flower-Shedding Brilliance) Gallery. The base of the former throne hall, the Qinzhengwuben (Diligent in Government Affairs and Proper Calling) can still be seen.

Environs of Xi'an. The region around Xi'an and especially the hills on the north bank of the Wei River are of great interest to archaeologists with their dozens of imperial tombs and the remains of several imperial capitals and palaces. A number of sites have not yet been excavated and are not open to visitors.

The neolithic Banpo village, 10 km east of Xi'an, first excavated in 1954, gives a remarkably complete picture of the life of men 6,000 years ago. They cultivated the land, made pottery, stored food in pits, raised cattle, fished and hunted. The geometric and figurative designs on the pottery are particularly beautiful. The Banpo museum has a hall showing reconstructions of the life of the Banpo people, and another displaying some of the objects unearthed. In addition, a 3,000 sq. m area of the site has been covered over and is open to visitors.

HUXIAN, about 35 km southwest of Xi'an, has become famous in the last decade as a centre for peasant painting. These paintings, which belong to a 'naïve' school, are really poster art, done in bright colours and depicting people at work and the countryside. Both characters and landscapes are idealized and the subject matter has a political content. Many of the Huxian paintings have been reproduced in the form of greeting cards which can be bought at the Rongbaozhai in Liulichang, in Beijing.

Several emperors built palaces at the Lishan (Mountain of the Black Horse) Hot Springs, some 35 km east of Xi'an, to enjoy the hills and the springs rising at their foot. The 'Precious Concubine' Yang Guifei of Tang dynasty emperor Xuan Zong used to bathe there and one of the pools bears her name. In 1936 the resort was the scene of the so-called 'Xi'an Incident', when Chiang Kaishek, who was staying there, was betrayed by one of his generals, Zhang Xueliang. He was arrested after trying to escape in the Lishan. Zhou Enlai negotiated his release in exchange for a pledge to join the Communists against the common enemy, Japan.

Not far from the Huaqing Hot Springs, and far more interesting, is the Tumulus of Emperor Qin Shihuang, who died in 211 B.C. after having united the Chinese empire for the first time in its history. The tumulus, visible from Xi'an, is 40 m high, surrounded by a square inner wall and an oval outer wall. The tomb itself has not yet been excavated, but excavations undertaken near the tumulus in 1974 have revealed a pit containing 558 life-size terracotta figures of warriors, some in war chariots drawn by teams of four horses. All these pieces are rendered with extraordinary realism and carry real arms. They are displayed in a museum built on the site, 500 m north of the tumulus.

The Qian Tomb, about 80 km northwest of Xi'an, on Mount Liangshan, is that of the third Tang dynasty emperor, Gao Zong, and Empress Wu Zetian, remembered for her ruthless ambition and her devotion to the Buddhist faith, who ruled as regent after Gao Zong's death and even crowned herself 'Emperor' in 690, a unique instance in Chinese history. The Qian tomb has not been excavated but the 'Guard of Honour' of stone carvings leading to the tumulus is well worth a visit.

Amongst the minor tombs in the vicinity, that of Princess Yong Tai, a daughter-in-law of Empress Wu, has been excavated and has particularly fine and well-preserved murals depicting scenes of everyday life at the Tang court.

Zhaoling, the tomb of the ruthless but able Li Shimin, the second Tang emperor, who took the dynastic title of Tai Zong, Great Ancestor, is on the mountainside — a departure from the established custom of building mounds in the plain — about 60 km northwest of Xi'an. The burial chambers have been turned into a museum. The walls are decorated with exquisite murals — alas, unprotected from the public. Several stone tablets found in the tomb tell the story of the last years of the Sui and the reconquest of the empire by Li Shimin and his father, Li Yuan. A beautiful collection of pottery figurines, all with individual features, accompanied the emperor in his tomb. Among them are a number of foreign persons bearing tribute, with beards and moustaches painted hair by hair.

5 Shandong

The eastern extremity of Shandong (Shantung) province forms a peninsula with a rocky coastline and several natural harbours. The western part belongs to the North China plain and mountains rise in the heart of the province. The west is mainly agricultural and in the east, apart from fishing and related industries, the exploitation of coal and iron ore, which was begun in the nineteenth century, has been a major factor in the industrialization of the province. The Yellow River runs through the north of the province, but has changed its course several times, sometimes flowing into the Yellow Sea, south of the peninsula. The climate of Shandong reproduces its geographical diversity: continental in the west, although more humid than in Beijing, and maritime in the peninsula.

JINAN (Tsinan) 济南

The Yellow River, known as 'the sorrow of China', flows a few miles to the north of Jinan (Safe Crossing South), capital of Shandong province, and the Taishan mountain ranges lie to the south. The muddy river, carrying its slow traffic of junks with patched sails, affords a glimpse of eternal China. The area is often threatened by floods, for the level of the river is above that of the plain, and has to be contained by dykes.

Traditionally a centre for the silk industry, Jinan is an important junction on the Beijing-Shanghai and Qingdao railway lines, and its industries have diversified considerably since 1949. It has a population of about 1.7 million.

Jinan is just over nine hours by train from Beijing. Two days is ample time to visit the 'City of Springs', so called because of the more than a hundred natural springs that bubble up in the city proper, and whose waters flow into the Daming Lake. A good time for a visit is after the summer rains when the water level is high.

One hotel for foreigners, the *Jinan Hotel* (tel. 35351) is in Jing'er Road, west of the old city; set in a pleasant garden, it has spacious rooms, but the restaurant is no gastronome's paradise. The luxury *Nanjiao Hotel*, in a beautiful area to the south of the city, has now also been opened for foreign tourists. Reserved until 1979 for high-ranking Chinese officials, the Nanjiao is Jinan's best hotel, with 700 rooms, an indoor swimming pool, air-conditioning and a good restaurant.

The Huiquan restaurant near the Baotu Spring has a selection of local dishes, and another, on the shore of the Daming Lake, serves fish from the lake, but both suffer from a lack of basic hygiene.

History. The region of Jinan has been settled since the neolithic era and important archaeological remains belonging to the **Longshan Black Pottery** culture have been found. The city's first walls were built in the sixth century B.C., and its name was Le until the Han dynasty (206 B.C. — A.D. 220), when it was renamed Jinan. A provincial capital since the Song (960-1280) dynasty, it has always been prosperous. The coming of the railway and the leasing of trading concessions to foreigners — first to the Germans, later to the British — at the end of the nineteenth and beginning of the twentieth centuries contributed greatly to the development of the place. In the 1940s, the KMT armies were deeply entrenched in Shandong province and in Jinan in particular, and put up a fierce resistance against the advancing Red Army. Jinan was won over in 1948 and suffered greatly during the fighting.

Places of interest. The Baotuquan (Jet Spring) **(1)**, at the southwest corner of the old inner city, is now a pleasant park with many pavilions and bridges. In one of the ponds dwells a strange 'hermit

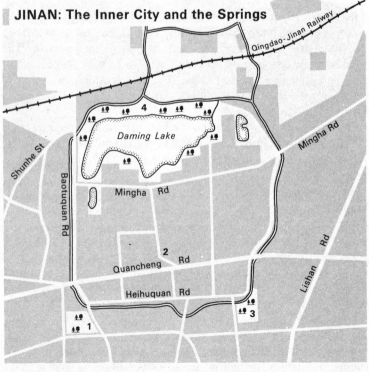

JINAN: The Inner City and the Springs

1 Baotuquan Park **2** Zhenzuquan **3** Heihuquan Park **4** Daminghu Park

seal' who occasionally comes out of hiding and emits harsh noises. The park has a former temple now used as an exhibition hall for local handicrafts, and a little museum, the Li Qingzhao Jinianguan, dedicated to a poetess of the eleventh and twelfth centuries, in a charming house near the hermit seal pond where the poetess, Li Qingzhao, is said to have stayed before fleeing to the south when the 'barbarian' Jin invaded Shandong.

Other springs in Jinan include the Zhenzhuquan, or Pearl Spring (2), in the centre of the inner city, where the water comes through the porous stone at the bottom of the pond, sending up myriads of bubbles, and the Heihuquan, or Black Tiger Spring (3), at the south-east corner of what was once the wall of the inner city, where the water flows from three tigers' heads of black stone.

The outer city wall of Jinan has been obliterated, and the inner city wall is only traceable by its moat. The banks of this moat have been planted with trees and shrubs and the local people come with their stools and fishing rods to spend a few peaceful hours. It is worth taking a walk down any little alley in this area which has kept a medieval flavour.

The Daming Lake, in the north of the old inner city, is a favourite recreation area (4). Boats can be hired, and several old buildings and pavilions are scattered on the shores, some of them used as tea-houses or restaurants. The Beiji Miao, Temple of the North Pole, a former Taoist temple built at the top of three flights of steps, is particularly striking. The present buildings date from the Ming dynasty and they now house a small ceramic museum, in which some fine examples of Longshan Black Pottery are exhibited.

The park of the Golden Ox (Jiuniu) to the north of the city, at the foot of the Wuying Mountains, has a quite charming temple but it is empty of all carvings. To the south, the Qianfoshan, Mountain of the Thousand Buddhas, once had some fine rock carvings dating from the Northern Wei to the Sui dynasty. Alas, the Red Guards were let loose on the Thousand Buddhas during the Cultural Revolution, and only the temple buildings — now a small museum — and two elegant archways survived.

The Shandong Provincial Museum, in West Wenhua Road just inside the old outer city, has a particularly rich collection of the Longshan Black Pottery which originated in Shandong near the small town of Boxing, north-east of Jinan, around 2500 to 1500 B.C. Characterized by its jet-black colour and a near-perfect shape, the pottery's delicacy (it is sometimes no more than 1 mm thick) and its satin gloss comes from firing at a very high temperature.

Environs of Jinan. About 38 km south of Jinan, in the direction of

Mount Tai, is the village of Liubu, with the remains of the Shentong monastery, founded in the sixth century A.D. The monastery itself, at the top of the cliff, is not open to the public; most of the buildings are fairly recent. Along a path leading down from it are many statues of Buddha, in niches at several levels. The earliest carvings of this Thousand Buddha Cliff (Qianfoya) date from the seventh century (Tang dynasty), some of them life-size and others rows of tiny seated Buddhas in niches. On a lower level, near the rocky bed of a torrent, stand the ruins of the old monastery and the Longhuta (Pagoda of the Dragon and the Tiger), a brick pagoda built in the Tang dynasty. At the foot of these ruins lie the stupas, over forty of them in varying states of repair, erected in memory of the monks who died in the temple. The earliest and most interesting of the temple remains is the Simenta, the Four Gate Pagoda, a stout stone structure with a square base pierced with four archways, with no ornament other than a pointed stupa at the top of the four-sloped roof. Inside the pagoda are four seated Buddhas flanked by a pair of standing Bodhisattvas. The pagoda and carvings date from A.D. 544 and give an impression of simple and forceful beauty.

A few miles south of Liubu are the remains of a temple dedicated to Guanyin with a Nine Point Pagoda.

TAI'AN (39) 泰安 and MOUNT TAI (Taishan) 泰山

Taishan (Exalted Mount), about 85 km south of Jinan, is the highest peak (1545 m) in the mountains of central Shandong. An expedition to this most sacred of the five sacred mountains of Taoism can be completed in a week-end from Beijing, sleeping two nights on the train, one night at the top of Taishan. The rail journey is via Jinan, but there are some through trains to Tai'an, the town at the foot of the southern slope of Taishan.

Tai'an's main function is and has always been to accommodate visitors to the mountain, although the area is also known for its orchards. For those who want to stay the night in the town and not on the mountain, there is a hotel for foreigners (b) near the Taishan Great Bridge. In addition, there is a Reception Centre (a) just outside the north-east corner of the wall of the Daimiao (Temple of Mount Taishan) (1), one of the few ancient buildings in Tai'an to survive the Japanese occupation.

The Daimiao was already in existence at the beginning of the Han dynasty and was restored and remodelled during each successive dynasty. In 1928 it was stripped of its altars and statues and turned into offices and shops, and no major restoration was undertaken until after 1949.

Outside the south entrance stands the Triumphal Portal of the Eastern Peak (Dongyuefang) — the Eastern Peak being another name for Taishan — erected in 1672. In the forecourt, on the west side, a particularly large stele (over 7 m high) was erected in A.D. 1009 during the reign of the Song dynasty emperor Zhen Zong, who bestowed upon Taishan the title of 'Good and Holy King Equal to Heaven', and was the last emperor to make sacrifice to the mountain. In the first courtyard to the east are five cypresses said to have been planted by Han Wu Di, the founder of the Han dynasty. North of this courtyard is a hall built in 1770 for the Qing emperor Qian Long who used to stay there.

The main temple hall is an imposing building with nine bays and a two-tier roof covered with yellow tiles. It has been empty since 1928 but the Qing dynasty frescoes on the walls have recently been restored. They represent an imperial pilgrimage to Taishan, with its colourful procession stretching from the west wall to the east wall — an exercise so costly that it was not repeated after 1008. Many tablets are set in the walls of the courtyard.

Ascending Mount Tai.   The ascent can be made in three to four hours at a brisk pace, but most people will spend the day climbing, having lunch and a rest at the half-way point, the Zhongtianmen (Gate Half-way up to Heaven). It is possible to spend the night at the Zhongtianmen Resthouse (**d**). Other resting places are dotted along the paths, but they get fewer as one nears the top. The visitor who has overestimated his or her strength and is not afraid of losing face can be carried in a chair, on the way up or down. CTS recommends that visitors take as little as possible with them on the climb, and leave their luggage at the hotel in Tai'an. Drinks and snacks can be bought along the way, getting more expensive the higher one gets, because everything has to be carried up on a man's back. The air can be very cold at the top and warm padded coats are supplied at the summit. A cable car and a new hotel at the top are under construction.

The emperor, who was the intermediary between Heaven and Earth — he was the Son of Heaven and the Father of the Chinese people — used to make sacrifice to the God of Mount Tai to ensure the prosperity and stability of the empire. The ordinary people also had favours to ask of the God of Taishan, and a visit to the place is enough to make a pilgrim of the twentieth century understand the fascination it may have had for generations of Chinese. 'A people who can so consecrate a place of natural beauty is a people with a fine feeling for the essential values of life': I can only hope, like G.H. Lowes Dickinson at the beginning of this century, that the coming of mass tourism and a cable car will not destroy the magic of Taishan.

Two paths lead to the top: the main path, which was used by the emperor, and the western path. The beginning of the main path is marked by a

monumental stone portal, the Daizongfang, or Portal of the Great Ancestor (2) (yet another name for Taishan). It was built during the reign of the
Ming emperor Long Qing (1570), rebuilt in 1730 and in the 1930s was
adorned with Sun Yatsen's calligraphy. Near the beginning of the path, off
on a side path to the right, is the Pool of the Queen Mother (3), called the
Jewel Pool during the Tang dynasty, where a spring rises inside the Temple
of the Queen Mother. Back on the main path, the First Heavenly Portal,
Yitianmen (5), awaits visitors at the bottom of the first series of steps. Just
behind it, another stone archway commemorates the Place where Confucius Rested Before the Ascent. It is overgrown with an old wistaria vine, but
the inscription has recently been restored. The next stone archway, also
built in the seventeenth century, bears the characters *Tianjie*, or Stairs to
the Sky.

Just before the Red Gate Palace (6), named after some red stones standing beside the path, the buildings of the former Lower Temple of the
Princess of the Azure Clouds (Bixiayuanjun), of the Ming dynasty, have
been turned into a teahouse (5). The Tower of the Ten Thousand Immortals, built right over the path, dates from the Ming dynasty; an inscription
commemorates a visit of the Qing emperor Qian Long. A Memorial to the
Heroes of the Revolution (7) has replaced another memorial, the Sun Wen
Obelisk, erected in honour of the founder of the republic, Sun Yatsen.

Still further up the steps, on the right is the Temple of the Goddess of the
Big Dipper, Doumugong (8), now used as a resting place where food, drinks
and books can be bought. It was once called the Monastery of the Dragon
Spring; on the other side of the path, two so-called 'Dragon Trees' grow
intertwined.

Shortly after the Doumugong, one should leave the main path and go to
the right, across the stream, to pay a visit to the Valley of the Stone Sutra,
where the stream flows over some large smooth rocks engraved in
the sixth century A.D. with giant characters of the Diamond sutra. The
main path eventually leads across to the other side of the torrent, where
one enters an area shaded by cypresses which is called the Cypress Arbour.
At the end of this section is the Heavenly Kettle Pavilion (Hutiange) (9), a
place marked by an archway, where the mountains form the shape of a
kettle. On the left through the archway, a tea and noodle shop has been set
up in a side building of the former Middle Temple of the Taishan Goddess
(Taishan Zhongbu Yuanjun Miao). After the temple, the path becomes
very steep and an archway signals that this is the Point Where the Horses
are Turned Back. Here the emperor had to dismount and get into a sedan
chair.

A long stretch of steep steps has to be climbed before arriving at the
Zhongtianmen, the Gate Half-way up to Heaven (11), and it is time to take
a rest. The Zhongtianmen Resthouse, a modern building, is a little way to
the left, at the top of the western path. Meals and, if necessary, rooms are
available to foreign visitors. Remember that this is the half-way point and
that the second half is harder!

The path continues to climb, this time gently, and is named the Happy
Three Li (1 *li* = ½ km). Numerous inscriptions have been carved on the
rock face by grateful pilgrims, including modern ones. It is only a few hundred metres until one reaches the Step into the Clouds Bridge (12), once
built of wood, but now made of stone; and one is confronted with a very
steep staircase which leads to the Five Pines Pavilion (13) and the ruins of
the Memorial Arch to the Knighted Pines. In 218 B.C., the Qin emperor

TAI'AN AND MOUNT TAI

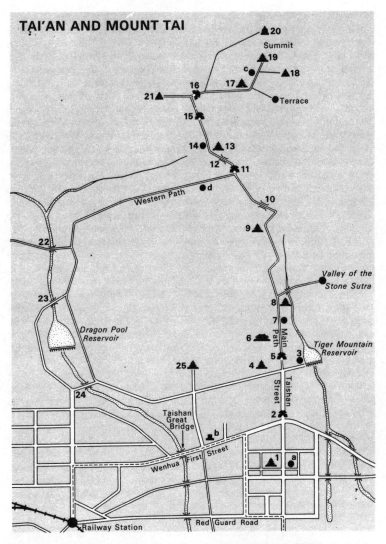

Hotels and amenities

a Tourist Information Centre
b Hotel
c Goddess's Resting Palace
d Zhongtianmen Resthouse

Places of interest

1 Daimiao
2 Portal of the Great Ancestor
3 Pool of the Queen Mother
4 Guandimiao
5 First Heavenly Portal
6 Red Gate Palace
7 Memorial to the Heroes of the Revolution
8 Temple of the Goddess of the Big Dipper
9 Heavenly Kettle Pavilion

10 Step into Heaven Bridge
11 Gate Half-way up to Heaven
12 Step into the Clouds Bridge
13 Five Pines Pavilion
14 Grotto Facing the Sun
15 Archway of Ascending Immortals
16 South Gate of Heaven
17 Temple of the Princess of Azure Clouds
18 Summit for Contemplating the Sun
19 Peak of the Pillar of Heaven
20 Tomb of the Princess
21 Summit for Contemplating the Moon
22 Changshou Bridge
23 Jiandai Bridge
24 Dazhong Bridge
25 Illuminate the Universe Temple

Shihuang was climbing Taishan when a violent storm broke out. He took shelter under some pine trees (no one knows how many and they have since disappeared), and expressed his gratitude by giving them the title of Officials of the Fifth Rank (hence the misnomer, Five Pines Pavilion).

The path continues along the Wanzhangbei, the Ten Thousand Feet Stele, carved with an inscription in very large characters in the hand of the emperor Qian Long. On the back wall of the small Grotto Facing the Sun, Chaoyang Dong (14), which is a sort of alcove hollowed out of the rock, is a particularly graceful portrait of the Taishan Goddess, engraved on a brass plaque set in smooth stone, like Western medieval brass. The rest of the path climbs through the Pine Tree Mountain and when you get to the Archway of Ascending Immortals (15), you wonder whether you have not become one already. The path is punishingly steep, but when you walk under the South Gate of Heaven, or the Third Gate to Heaven (16), you are almost at the top. A sharp turn to the right and the main temple of the Princess of Azure Clouds appears at the top of the long flight of stairs. To the left, some ruins indicate where the Temple of Confucius once stood.

The Temple of the Princess of Azure Clouds (Bixiaci) (17) is an imposing group of buildings with red walls and golden roofs, founded in the Song dynasty and known at that time as the Temple of Luminous Perfection. The temple was the goal of the climb and pilgrims used to offer sacrifice to the Taishan Goddess when they reached the top. The temple has two main courtyards, the roofs being covered in bronze tiles to resist the frequent gales at the top. Apart from the Mountain Gate to the north, there are three other gates which bear the poetic names of North, South and East Spirit Gates. A passage through the Hall of the Lingguan, or Spiritual Leader, north of the first courtyard, leads to the main court. Inside are two large bronze steles, the one on the left erected in 1615 on the orders of Ming emperor Wan Li, and the one on the right in 1625, on the orders of Tian Qi, in the hope of enlisting the help of the Taishan Goddess in repelling the Manchu armies threatening the empire, which was to fall anyway in 1644. A large incense burner stands near the Pavilion of Longevity (Wansuilou), which is the shrine to the Princess of the Azure Clouds. The statue of the Goddess, which used to be richly dressed, is still inside but somewhat damaged. Inside the main hall behind the pavilion, the inscriptions have gone but the cast-iron statues of various deities have been preserved, although dented by the assaults of Red Guards. Above the temple, to the left, is the famous Taishan inscription of the Tang dynasty, the Tang Moya (Yai) Keshi: nearly a thousand characters carved on the rock face. A Temple of the Eastern Peak used to stand in front of the inscription, but only a stele remains, to the right of where the gate once was.

A few more steps and you have arrived at the guesthouse, set up in an old temple, the Goddess's Resting Palace (Yuanjun Houqingong) (c). Accommodation is very simple: there is no running water, but thick quilts and padded coats are provided. An electric bell rings to rouse visitors who wish to see the sun rise. Its rise is sometimes obscured by the mist, but on a clear day one can see the rays of the sun lighting peak after peak, until it reaches Taishan peak, the highest. The sunrise is best seen from the Riguanfeng, Summit for Contemplating the Sun (18), where the rocks are level and form a sort of terrace.

A temple is built on the highest point, the Tianzhufeng or Peak of the Pillar of Heaven (19), dedicated to Yuhuang, the Jade Emperor, the supreme deity in the Taoist pantheon. The temple is now a souvenir shop, but the statues of the god and two acolytes remain. Outside the main gate of the temple stands a stele known as the Wuzibei, the Stele Without Characters, which, scholars agree, dates from at least the Han dynasty. Inside the Temple of the Jade Emperor, a balustrade encloses the rock which is the highest point in Taishan.

Before you begin the descent, pay a visit to the Tomb of the Princess, the Houshiwu **(20)**, over the top of the mountain. It is a delightful ruin overgrown with trees. And before you leave Taishan, remember that Emperor Qian Long ascended it eleven times. The descent is as hard as the ascent, but you may choose to go down the western path which branches to the right at the Gate Half-way up to Heaven.

Situated at the bottom of the western path, on a slope in the midst of a bamboo grove, is another temple, the Puzhaosi (Illuminate the Universe Temple) **(25)**, founded during the period of the Six Dynasties (222-589) and rebuilt during the Tang. Inside the main courtyard, under some pine trees said to have been planted during the Six Dynasties, is a Pavilion for Filtering the Moonlight (Shaiyueting), so named because the trees project their shade over it.

QUFU (38) 曲阜

Qufu (Crooked Mound), the birthplace of Confucius, reopened to the public on 1 April 1979 after fourteen years, is 140 km south of Jinan. From Jinan one travels by train to Yanzhou and then by road (about 12 km) to Qufu. Overnight accommodation is provided in a wing of Confucius's house which has been turned into a guesthouse.

History. Qufu was the capital of the vassal state of Lu during the Zhou dynasty (1122-221 B.C.). Confucius lived at the end of the period of Chinese history known as 'Spring and Autumn' (770-476), at a time when the suzerainty of the Zhou king was being challenged by the vassal states and when life was being deeply transformed by new discoveries. The use of iron revolutionized agriculture and warfare, trade increased, and the use of metal coins spread; travel by horseback accelerated communications within China and between China and the West. The technical revolution was matched in the field of ideas and a 'hundred schools of thought' flourished.

Confucius was born in Qufu in 551 B.C. into a family of impoverished local officials. The name Confucius is the Latinized form of Kong Fu Zi, i.e. Master Kong, Kong being his family name. He spent almost thirty years of his life peddling his ideas about social order at the courts of the vassal states, searching for an enlightened prince and making disciples. Towards the end of his life, he returned to his native state which he had left in semi-disgrace for having remonstrated with its ruler, Duke Ai of Lu, and confined himself to teaching. He died in 479 B.C. Confucius himself, if in fact he ever existed, wrote nothing, but shortly after his death his teachings were recorded by some of his disciples in a short book, the *Analects,* which successive generations of Confucianists have commented upon and interpreted. Duke Ai of Lu turned his house into a temple which received the favour of many an emperor thereafter and grew to cover an area of 22 *ha* (*c.* 54 acres).

The teachings of Confucius were a prime target of the Cultural Revolution, and Qufu was seriously damaged, but has been restored with care. The present layout of the town dates from the Ming dynasty.

Places of interest. The Temple of Confucius (Kong Miao) is entered by the main gate, the Lingxingmen, named after a star in the Great Bear constellation, south of the temple compound on the north-south axis of the town. The forecourt is planted with old cypress trees, some of which are said to date from the Han dynasty. A triple marble bridge spans a small stream. The central path leads through three gatehouses containing displays of ancient pottery and stone carvings. In a courtyard near the third gatehouse, many steles are gathered, some dating from the Han dynasty, which record the many restorations of the temple since its foundation.

The first and oldest temple hall is the Guiwenge, the Great Pavilion of the Constellation of Scholars, a wooden structure dating from the Jin dynasty (1190) with a lower roof, a wooden gallery running along the four sides, and a double roof above. The proportions and simplicity of the building are acknowledged in an inscription at the base of the building by the Ming dynasty calligrapher, Li Dongyang.

Behind the Guiwenge, thirteen imperial steles are arranged in two rows, under individual pavilions, on either side of an east-west street which leads right (east) to the residence of Confucius' descendants. The three main sanctuaries of the temple lie north of this street.

In the centre is the Great Temple, largest and most important of the sanctuaries. Access is through the Dachengmen, Gate of Great Perfection. Sheltered by a small pavilion just on the left, inside the courtyard, is the Confucius Tree, said to have been planted by the Master himself; several trees are supposed to have sprouted from the same roots. The first building on the main path is a pavilion with a rare form of roof, supported on four sides by triangular pediments. It is called the Altar of the Apricot Tree because Confucius is said to have taught under an apricot tree at this spot.

The main sanctuary dedicated to Confucius stands on a double white marble terrace, and is 31.89 m high and nine bays wide. The present building dates from 1724. The facade is supported by twelve large pillars each made from a single trunk of that very durable and heavy tree, the *nanmu,* still growing today in Sichuan province. Coiled dragons in low relief are carved on the pillars. A majestic double roof covers the building, where ceremonies were performed — as well as in every temple of Confucius in the country — by the local officials, and by the emperor himself, at the beginning of February, May, August and November. Alas, the very old statues of Confucius, the Four Companions and the Twelve Disciples are no longer there, but there is an extraordinary collection of musical instruments, some of which are very old and others are used only in Confucian temples.

A smaller hall north of the Great Temple of Confucius is dedicated to his wife. A gallery around the four sides of the courtyard used to contain shrines dedicated to meritorious civil servants. The last hall is the Shengjidian, the Memorial to the Sage, containing a series of stone engravings describing the life of the sage. On the west side, a separate temple complex contains two main halls: the Hall of Silk and Metal (string and percussion instruments) used to house the musical instruments when they were not in use; the second hall is dedicated to Confucius' father and has two marble columns carved with dragons. A smaller shrine at the back is dedicated to Confucius' mother. On the east side, in the third sanctuary, is a little building on the right called Confucius' Dwelling, supposed to be the site of his house. The next hall is known as the Shilitang, Hall of Poetry and Rites, because it was built on the spot where Confucius' father once asked him whether he had studied Poetry and the Rites. Confucius' well is behind the Hall of Poetry and Rites, and so is the Lu wall where, during the anti-Confucian persecutions of Qin Shihuangdi (221-206 B.C.), the ninth descendant of Confucius hid the Confucian books; they were rediscovered during the Han dynasty. The next hall to the north is dedicated to Confucius' Ancestors, and still further north, the last hall is a family temple containing the tablets of his descendants.

Next to the Temple of Confucius, at the east gate, is the Residence of the Descendants of Confucius. The sage himself lived in near poverty, but his descendants were honoured from the Han to the Qing dynasties. The present family compound, dating from the Jia Jing era of the Ming dynasty (1522-67), has 463 halls, rooms and buildings and in the 1940s was still lived in by the seventy-sixth descendant of Confucius.

The public area, or Yamen, occupies a large space on the main north-south axis and is flanked by the east (now largely ruined) and west wings, reserved for study and rest for the officials of the Yamen. From the Yuan dynasty, the descendants of Confucius were given official functions as magistrates and had a large staff to help them administer the vast estate, collect taxes and conduct the ritual ceremonies at the temple. The family enjoyed a surprising degree of autonomy, being answerable only to the emperor and enjoying his protection. In their living quarters, separated from the Yamen by a wall and the Neizhaimen, or Gate of the Inner Residence, is a Tower of Refuge, built for the family to escape attacks by bandits or armed revolts. A garden, with ponds and artificial hills laid out in the Ming dynasty, lies north of the living quarters.

Because of the imperial protection of the family and its estate, the Kong family archives have been preserved almost intact since the Han dynasty, and so has a vast collection of ceremonial robes, ceramics, furniture, and household items, so that a visit to the Residence affords a unique display of a mandarin's household in a very good state of preservation.

A road bordered with Yuan dynasty cypress trees leads north to the Tomb of Confucius, situated in the Confucian Woods, the largest man-made forest in China. Here, surrounded by a wall, nearly all the descendants of the philosopher are buried. The Master's tomb itself is a mound, about 5 m high and surrounded by a wall. An avenue of animals leads to a little temple hall in front of the tumulus.

About 4 km east of Qufu is the Tomb of Shao Hao, one of the five mythical emperors who ruled China during the Xia dynasty (2205-1766 B.C.). It is the only pyramidal tomb in China, made of large blocks of stone, and topped with a small temple hall.

QINGDAO (Tsingtao) 青岛

Qingdao (Green Island), about twelve hours by train from Beijing, is a pleasant seaside resort as well as a busy harbour on the south coast of the Shandong peninsula. Until 1898, when it was ceded by the Chinese to the Germans for ninety-nine years. Qingdao was no more than a fishing village on the bay of Jiaozhou. By the time the railway line — with cast-iron sleepers — was extended from Jinan to Qingdao in 1905, it had become a modern town and harbour. The Germans built a brewery which has continued to develop to this day. *Qingdao pijiu,* Qingdao beer, still has the reputation of being the best in China and is usually available in the major cities. Some of it is even exported.

After the First World War, the German-held territories were ceded to Japan, which caused much resentment among Chinese patriots, who considered that their interests had been coldly ignored in the Treaty of Versailles. The territories were only returned to the Chinese in 1923.

A visit to Qingdao can be completed in one day, but you may wish to stay longer and enjoy the beach. At present, the *Jianqiao Hotel,* 31 Taiping Road, receives foreigners. Situated north of the Qianhai pier, it is inconvenient for visitors who have to go to the beach, some distance to the east, by bus or by taxi, accompanied by a guide. Within a few years, accommodation more suited to the holidaymaker will be built. There is a regular passenger service by steamer from Qingdao to Shanghai.

The residential area with its large European-style villas stretches along the south coast of the promontory, dominated by Zhanshan (Limpid Mountain), on top of which is a temple, the Zhanshansi. In the west bay of the south coast, a jetty leads to an octagonal tower with a double roof called the Qianhai Zhanqiao, the Jetty Facing the Sea. The east bay, where the main beach is — very crowded in the summer — is dominated by a fortress and has an aquarium with hundreds of species of plants and fish.

A few miles along the coast to the east is the famous Laoshan (Mount Lao), with its mineral springs whose water is bottled and sold in large cities in the country and also exported.

Another seaside place on the Shandong peninsula that may be visited is YANTAI (Chefoo) (**41**), on the north coast, on the Bohai Gulf. A natural harbour, Yantai grew from a fishing village to a busy trading port at the end of the nineteenth century, but never had any foreign concessions. It now has about 150,000 inhabitants who also live from the growing of fruit in the surrounding countryside.

6 Henan

Henan province is situated in north central China, in the drainage basin of the middle Yellow River. The landscape is that of a loess plain, loess plateaus and gentle hills. There is no natural ground cover, but slender new trees grow round the villages and along the irrigation canals and roads. The climate is a mild variety of the North China type, with dry winters and hot and humid summers. As with most places in China, spring and autumn are the best times to visit the province.

Henan is crossed by two major railway lines, north-south and east-west, which meet at Zhengzhou, the capital of the province. Until the building of the railways at the turn of the century, the province had been almost exclusively devoted to agriculture; today a whole range of industries has been established in the larger cities of Zhengzhou, Luoyang and Anyang.

ANYANG 安阳

Anyang (Peaceful Sun) is situated in the very north of the province, east of the Taihang Mountains, in the drainage basin of the Wei River, a major tributary of the Yellow River. It has a population of about 430,000.

Anyang is about eight hours from Beijing by train on the main Beijing-Guangzhou railway line. The older Anyang Guesthouse in Jiefang Road, in the centre of town, is no longer used for tourists from Western countries, and the newly built *Taihang Guesthouse* in the eastern suburbs, in Dengta Road, although completed in 1978 to fairly modern standards, is not very professionally run. For this reason, and because at present only two places there of historical interest are open to the public, one day, or even half a day, is enough to spend on a visit to Anyang. However, a further day can be spent in visiting the irrigation projects in Linxian, mentioned below.

History. Anyang was the last capital of the Shang dynasty, from about 1300 to 1066 B.C. It was then called Yin and the late Shang dynasty is also sometimes referred to as the 'Yin dynasty'. When the Zhou overran the Shang in 1066 B.C., Yin was destroyed, its population dispersed and the ruins eventually ploughed over. The city was rebuilt east of its former site and renamed Anyang at the end of the Warring States period in 257 B.C. It remained a provincial trading centre until 1949, then gradually became industrialized. Modern Anyang has burst out of the walls of the old city, which have gradually been destroyed and can only be traced where the moat has not been filled in. However, the old city has changed little since liberation, most of the new buildings having been constructed outside the old walls.

Places of interest. The Wenfeng (Cultural Peak) Pagoda, built in A.D. 952 during the Five Dynasties period, is in the old city, in the grounds of the large Tianning Temple, which has been converted into a school. The pagoda is octagonal, narrower at the base than at the top. It is built of stone and wood on a lotus-shaped base, its five storeys surmounted by a bottle-shaped stupa standing 38 m high. One can climb to the top and hear the chime of the bronze bells hanging from the corners of the glazed-tile roofs. The passage to the uppermost storey is very narrow and portly visitors will find it difficult to squeeze through. If you have made it to the top platform, which is quite spacious, you will be rewarded by a panoramic view of the old city and its narrow lanes and houses built round courtyards.

The Yin Ruins — the remains of the old Shang capital from the thirteenth century B.C. — were discovered earlier in the present century, in an area to the west of the city, quite by accident. An official of the Qing dynasty, Wan Yirong, fell ill in 1899 and was prescribed some traditional medicine made of ground oracle, or 'dragon', bones.* Having an interest in archaeology, he asked to see the bones themselves and noticed that the ancient writing on them was similar to that found on Shang bronzes. He learned that the bones came from Henan province, where peasants were digging them out of their fields in an area near Anyang. Scholars became interested, but it was not until 1928 that serious excavations were undertaken, proving that this was indeed the site of the ancient Shang capital, then called Yin. In the meantime, a good many bronzes, pots and oracle bones had found their way into museums abroad; but in 1949 an end was put to this haemorrhage of treasures, and an archaeological station was set up. Unfortunately ordinary visitors are barred from the excavation sites, but a small museum has been opened in the archaeological station where some of the findings are on show.

The Shang capital covered an area of about 6 km from east to west, and 4 km from north to south. Ruins of the imperial palace (5) were found in a loop of the Huan (Anyang) River, acting as a protecting moat on three sides. On the north bank, the site of the imperial tombs (7) was found and

---

*Oracle bones, inscribed with an archaic form of picture-writing, were used for divination. When thrown into a fire, cracks would appear on the bones which provided an answer to the question engraved on them: the fate of a battle, a good or bad fortune, the weather, etc. Only about half of the 3,000 characters inscribed on such bones can now be deciphered.

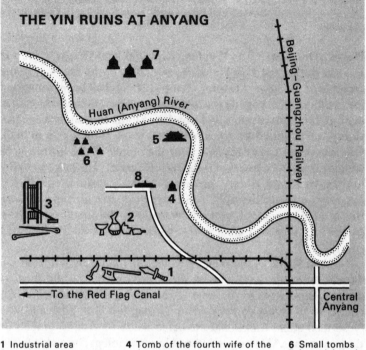

THE YIN RUINS AT ANYANG

Huan (Anyang) River

Beijing – Guangzhou Railway

To the Red Flag Canal

Central
Anyang

1 Industrial area	4 Tomb of the fourth wife of the	6 Small tombs
2 Living area	fourth emperor	7 Imperial tombs
3 Handicrafts and shops	5 Palace foundations	8 Museum

their excavation revealed that the Shang rulers were buried with a large number of slaves (a thousand or more), horses, dogs and other animals, usually buried alive. With the bodies in most tombs were found a fish, or a leg of ham or lamb beside the head, presumably as food for the after-life.

Of the twelve imperial tombs presumed to be in the area, eight were found before 1949 and two after that year; not all ten may have been the tombs of Shang emperors. In 1976, the tomb of the Fourth Wife of the Fourth Emperor (Sihaomu) was found in an area (4) south of the palace (to the east of the museum). The handicrafts area (2) was to the west of the site, and an industrial area (1), where bronze-casting remains were found, was to the south of the living area. In addition to the imperial tombs, more than a thousand small tombs (6) were discovered on the south bank of the river.

Among the most interesting pieces exhibited in the museum is a reproduction of a stone musical instrument with exquisite linear carvings, and bronzes at different stages in the casting process, from the clay moulds to the finished vessel. One of the thousand or more objects found in the Sihaomu tomb is a large *ding* cauldron, rectangular with four legs and two ears. Another cauldron, round and without any ornaments, was used as a coffin for the head slave.

LINXIAN (**37**) is about 40 km west of Anyang, in the Taihang Mountains, an area with thin soil and little water. In 1960 a large irrigation project began: the construction of the Red Flag Canal which would bring water from the Zhang River in Shanxi province through the mountains into Linxian. The project was completed in 1969. It includes 1500 km of canals, 134 tunnels and 150 aqueducts, and irrigates 600,000 *mu* (1 acre = 6.07 *mu*) of land. The drive to Linxian is through the mountains of western Henan, which are scenically attractive.

ZHENGZHOU (Chengchow) 郑州

Zhengzhou (Zheng Country), capital of Henan province, lies south of the Yellow River, in the plain. A major junction on the north-south Beijing-Guangzhou and the east-west Long-Hai (Xi'an-Shanghai) railway lines, the city is entirely industrial, with a population of 1.7 million, and has little to offer to tourists.

History. The city was founded in the Shang dynasty (sixteenth to eleventh centuries B.C.). Remains of a Shang dynasty capital, predating the Yin ruins in Anyang, were discovered in 1955. The name Zhengzhou first appeared in the sixth century A.D. Little of note took place in Zhengzhou between the Shang dynasty and the construction of the railway at the beginning of the present century. In February 1923, the railwaymen called a strike which was crushed mercilessly by the warlord Wu Peifu. In 1954 Zhengzhou won from Kaifeng the title of capital of the province.

There is little to see in Zhengzhou, and three hours is enough time to spend in the city, if CTS can arrange your journey onwards within the same day. If you do stay overnight, the *Zhongzhou* (Middle Province) *Hotel*, in Jinshui Road on the way to the airport, is one of the grandest Soviet-style hotels I have ever stayed in, but also one of the scruffiest; both Chinese and foreign guests use it. Zhengzhou does boast a 'scenic' restaurant, the *Jinshui*, over the Golden (Jinshui) River in the People's Park near the centre of the city. The speciality of the house is fresh fish from the river.

The Provincial Museum, also by the river, off Jinshui Road, is in a building completed in 1954, the elegance of whose exterior contrasts sharply with the rough finish of the interior. It exhibits reproductions (the originals of major pieces are in Beijing) of archaeological finds from the Xia to the Ming dynasty unearthed in Henan province. The museum also has a large section devoted to revolutionary history and a smaller section at the back with an exhibition of paintings.

A map in the museum shows the location of the old Shang capital, bordered on the north by the Jinshui River, on the east by Chengdong Road, on the south by the Xiong'er (Bear's Ear) River and on the west by Shuncheng Street. As in the Yin ruins at Anyang, the palaces were in the north-east, the shops in the west and south, and the burial grounds outside the town to the west, south and east. Bronzes and other finds at Zhengzhou tend to prove that the ruins there are of the earliest of the Shang capitals now being excavated in Henan province.

The earliest porcelain vessel as yet unearthed in China was also discovered at Zhengzhou. It is a wine vessel with a light green glaze over buff-coloured clay, dating from the Shang dynasty. There are several interesting musical instruments: a stone instrument with fine engravings found at Anyang, a set of bronze bells and a wood *si* (a string musical instrument, flat and played on a table) of the Spring and Autumn period (770-476 B.C.).

On the second floor of the museum is an exquisite oil lamp of the Warring States period (476-221 B.C.) in the shape of a man holding a shallow bowl. There is also an imperial insignia of the Qin dynasty in the shape of a tiger cut in half lengthwise: one half was kept by the emperor, the other by one of his generals, who could move his troops only if the emperor sent him the second half of the tiger with his orders. Funerary pottery of the Han dynasty, found in 1959 in the suburbs of Zhengzhou and very beautiful and well-preserved, represents buildings, watch towers and farm houses, one of which has a guard dog by the gate, pigs in the pigsty and chickens on the roof. Another beautiful and elaborate example of funerary pottery is a large model of a Ming dynasty palace made between 1513 and 1577, its many buildings free-standing and arranged around multiple courtyards.

From Zhengzhou, you can visit HUIXIAN (**36**), about 80 km north of the capital on the Anyang-Zhengzhou railway line. Besides water conservation projects and a fertilizer plant, you can ask to see the hot springs at Baiquan (Hundred Springs), just north of the town. The springs rise at the foot of the Taihang Mountains and gather in four artificial lakes, which are surrounded by monuments of historical interest.

KAIFENG 开峰

Kaifeng (The Open Peak), the former capital of Henan province, is a fine old city of about 500,000 inhabitants, situated a few miles south of the Yellow River, about 80 km east of Zhengzhou, in the North China plain — flat, monotonous and endless. The climate is that of North China, dry and cold in winter and hot and humid in summer.

The city is under constant threat from floods and has been destroyed several times by the waters of the Yellow River. The ground level rose after each flood and the most ancient monuments of the town sit a few feet deep in silt. The massive medieval walls of Kaifeng are almost intact, because in places they are almost entirely in the ground and would be impossible to demolish. Along the east wall, a small railway transports gravel from the city to the banks of the Yellow River. Coolies pull the gravel in their collapsible tri-cycle-carts from the main railway station to the little train, then pedal back to the station. The chain of coolies is continuous throughout the day and one thinks of the Yellow River swallowing tons of gravel every day, fed by generations of thin and sweating coolies.

Kaifeng has very little industry, but is famous for its handicrafts. One and a half to two days are enough to spend in the city, which is only an hour and a half by train from Zhengzhou; there are few through trains, however, and a visit to Kaifeng often involves spending time in the Zhengzhou station waiting room, which is far more comfortable than the Zhongzhou Hotel there.

If you do stay in Kaifeng, the *Kaifeng Hotel*, which accommodates both Chinese and foreigners, is fairly comfortable. It is in a complex of several buildings in the old town, in Ziyou Road, near the Xiangguo Temple. There is a Frendship Store in a narrow lane immediately to the east of the temple, with an entrance also in the outer courtyard of the temple itself. There you can buy the Bian embroidery which is the most famous local handicraft, made with hair-like stitches of silk thread; it takes a year or more to do a piece 20 cm square, and is priced accordingly.

History. Kaifeng first became a capital during the Three Kingdoms era which followed the fall of the Han dynasty (A.D. 220-265). During the Tang dynasty it was no more than a provincial centre, but after the break-up of the Tang empire into a northern and a southern kingdom Kaifeng became the northern capital during the period of the Five Dynasties. When the Song reunited the empire in A.D. 960, they rebuilt Kaifeng on an imperial scale as their capital. The city used to be surrounded by three concentric walls marking the limits of the three concentric cities: the Imperial City, the Inner City and the Outer City, as in Beijing. Kaifeng had 1½ million inhabitants during the Northern Song dynasty and became known as Bianjing or Bianliang; the small river which runs through the town, the Wenshui, was then known as the Bianshui.

Kaifeng's days of glory came to an abrupt end in 1126, when the 'barbarian' people of the Jin empire in Beijing invaded and looted the capital, taking with them the emperor, who died in exile and in the cold and barren Northeast. The dynasty continued as the Southern Song and the capital eventually moved to Hangzhou in Zhejiang province.

In 2500 years of recorded history, the Yellow River changed its course 26 times and broke its dikes some 900 times in Henan province alone. Kaifeng suffered a catastrophic flood in 1642 which destroyed most of the town, and two years later the dikes were broken by the supporters of the failing Ming dynasty, to stop the advance of the Manchus. Most of the ancient buildings still standing were rebuilt during the Kang Xi and Qian Long eras in the Qing dynasty. In 1852, the Yellow River once again broke through its dykes and changed to a northern course. Another disastrous flood was provoked deliberately in 1938, when the KMT armies tried to stop the advance of the Japanese; the river ran uncontrolled for nine years.

Until the beginning of this century, Kaifeng had a small community of Jews who came probably in the thirteenth century, intermarried with the local population and after a few generations became assimilated. The synagogue was destroyed by floods in 1842 and not rebuilt.

Kaifeng, which was slow to industrialize, ceased to be the provincial capital in 1954.

Places of interest. A visit to the Bian embroidery factory will make you understand why the work, unbelievably fine and slow, is so expensive to buy. The factory, situated in the Two Dragons Street where two Song dynasty emperors were born and grew up, exhibits a reproduction in Bian embroidery of the precious scroll painting, *Spring Festival in Kaifeng*. The original of the painting, which depicts the capital in the Song dynasty, is in the Palace Museum in Beijing.

A drive through town to some of the other sights will show you the busy narrow streets and open-fronted shops with a 'cock loft' above where the shopkeeper lives.

The Xiangguo Temple, in the south-east corner of the former Song imperial city, is a 1400-year-old centre of Buddhism. It was founded in 535, during the Southern and Northern dynasties and was then called the Jianguosi. It was destroyed by fire and rebuilt in 712 during the Tang dynasty by Emperor Li Dan, who renamed it Xiangguosi because he had held the official title of Xiang Wang before ascending the throne. When Kaifeng became the imperial capital, the temple was extensively rebuilt and enlarged and was the largest Buddhist monastery in the country. It used to own 540 *mu* (about 100 acres) of land and about 3,000 resident monks lived in its 64 courtyards. It was destroyed by floods at the end of the Song dynasty, rebuilt during the Yuan and again during the Qing, in 1766. At that time however it had become much smaller and had only about 300 monks. In 1927, the warlord Feng Yuxiang turned the monks out, melted the copper statues to make bullets, and the temple became a bazaar.

The temple is missing its first courtyard, the bell and drum towers and the First Hall. The Second Hall contains an exhibition on the history of the temple and a few objects which escaped the vengeful hand of Feng Yuxiang, including a set of four copper statues of Lohans of the sixth century and part of a set of porcelain bowls inscribed with the words *Zhong Zhou Xiang Guo Si* (the Xiang Guo Temple of the Middle Province).

The Third Hall or Daxiongbaodian (Precious Hall of the Great Hero) now houses the town museum where the exhibits are unusually well selected and displayed. They include some Ming and Qing ceramics and lacquerware, Qing dynasty clothes and uniforms, including a saddle of emperor Qian Long and a military uniform for the emperor weighing 20 kg. There is also some cloisonné ware, ivory and hardwood carvings, samples of old Bian embroidery, material woven by minorities, inkstones, brushes, ink slabs and jade carvings.

The Fourth Hall is octagonal and has a gallery running round it with an exhibition of archaeological finds from the area. Inside the hall is a very large statue of Guanyin, carved between 1736 and 1794, made of gilded ginkgo wood; too large to be removed and useless for making bullets, it is now the only piece of sculpture in the temple still in its original place. A popular legend is attached to this 'thousand-eyed and thousand-handed' deity, which in fact has 1048 arms with an eye in each palm. In the Zhou dynasty lived an old man with three daughters. When he fell ill he was told that the only medicine which would cure him would have to be made with one arm and one eye of one of his daughters. Both the elder daughters refused, but the youngest consented. The gods, moved by her sacrifice, sent her 'perfect' hands and 'perfect' (*quan*) eyes, but the message became confused on the way and she was given a thousand (*qian*) arms and a thousand eyes instead.

The Iron Pagoda is situated in the north-east corner of the walls of the town, at a place where the walls were originally 6 to 8 m high, but are now almost totally embedded in silt. Numerous graves can be seen north of the north wall.

The Iron Pagoda, Tie Ta, built of bricks and faced with brown-glazed bricks and tiles, takes its popular name from its brown colour. Rebuilt like a wooden structure in 1049, during the Song dynasty, on the site of an earlier pagoda made of wood, it is thirteen storeys high, but the base and first (ground) storey have disappeared in the silt of the great flood of 1842.

The monastery of which it was part was originally founded during the Northern Qi dynasty in A.D. 559. Originally called the Feng-chansi, it changed names many times through the successive dynasties, each change being accompanied by repair or rebuilding. The great flood of 1842 destroyed the temple buildings, and the Iron Pagoda suffered further during the occupation of Kaifeng by the warlord Feng Yuxiang and during the Japanese advance in 1938. No repairs were undertaken until 1957, when the pagoda was almost entirely rebuilt, and tiles and bricks remade after the original moulds which had been preserved.

To the south of the pagoda a pavilion shelters a large Song dynasty statue of a standing Buddha covered with gold leaf. It is 5.14 m high and is known as the Jieyingfo, the Welcoming Buddha. East of the temple several recent buildings house a small museum dedicated to the history of the temple. A local artist sells her paintings from a small house at the back of the museum.

The Pota, or Pagoda of the Po family, in the south-east quarter of Kaifeng, is all that remains of the Tianqingsi, or monastery of Celestial Purity, built under the Song dynasty and destroyed in 1841. The Song dynasty pagoda was originally nine storeys high but the top three storeys collapsed during the Yuan dynasty. Three miniature stories were built at the top. The pagoda is made of bricks, hexagonal in shape, and decorated with row upon row of small Buddhas. At present it can only be viewed from the Music Terrace near by. The grounds were taken over by a factory during the Cultural Revolution and workmen's housing has been built in its courtyard. The city of Kaifeng is in the process of claiming back the land and the pagoda which is in great need of repair.

The Old Music Terrace (Guchuitai), in Bianjing Park, is also known as the Terrace of Yu the Great (Yuwang Tai). This mythical ruler is said to have built a clay lock in the Bian River under the city gate which used to stand at this point; immersed at a secret place, the lock cannot be destroyed because it will rise with the water. The Music Terrace is believed to have been built by the musician Shi Kuang during the Spring and Autumn period (770-476 B.C.), but the present buildings date from the Qing dynasty.

The first hall has ten panels of calligraphy by the Qing dynasty reformist Kang Youwei embedded in its walls. It leads to a main courtyard, disfigured by an ugly modern gateway, which has a central hall and two wings. A gateway to the east leads to another courtyard with a small hall called the Sanxiansi (Temple to the Three Famous Persons). Six tablets tell the history of the terrace as told by the officials who carried out the renovations. A covered gallery runs round the terrace with many more calligraphies engraved on stones set in the wall. North of the terrace, down a few steps, there is the Zhongting (Middle Pavilion), with a stele, then the Shufang, or library, and then the Houyuan or Back Yard, with a pavilion. The layout of the buildings has remained unchanged since the Song dynasty.

The Yanqing Temple, with its Jade Ruler Tower, is situated in the south-west of town. As with the Pota, the grounds of the temple were taken over by a neighbouring factory and the temple buildings used as storerooms. It has now been returned to the city of Kaifeng and repairs are being carried out.

The Dragon Pavilion (Longting), in the north-west corner of the walls, once stood in the palace of the Song capital. Earlier buildings were destroyed by the 1642 floods and this one was rebuilt during the Kang Xi era (1662-1723). It used to be called the Wanshou Gong (Palace of Longevity) and was where local officials presented birthday gifts and greetings to the emperor. The large five-bays-wide building with its double golden roof stands on a high terrace at the top of a long flight of white marble steps. The centre of the steps is carved with a motif of intertwined dragons, worn smooth by generations of children sliding down on their cloth shoes and padded trouser bottoms. Inside the pavilion, a large marble slab, decorated on four sides with dragons, was where the birthday tablet of the emperor and the birthday gifts sent by the local officials were placed. Four crouching lion-looking animals guard the four corners of the hall. Their curly manes cover their eyes and they can hear everything, hence their name, *tingting* (*ting* means 'to hear').

Looking south from the terrace, one can see the Yang lake on the right (west) and the Pan lake on the left (east), both dug in 1734. The Yang lake is named after a royal marshal whose reputation was spotless, and is said to contain clean water; the water in the Pan lake, dug by a corrupt local official by the name of Pan, is muddy. The area of the Dragon Pavilion has been converted into a public park dedicated to Sun Yatsen whose small figure on an enormous pedestal stands at the bottom of the terrace.

LUOYANG 洛阳

Luoyang (North of the Luo River) lies between the Mangshan (Mang Hills) to the north and the Luo River to the south, in the northwest of Henan province. The plain around Luoyang is fertile but dependent on a good irrigation system. In many places west of Luoyang, curious loess and sandstone hills rise above the plain like ruined fortresses, and the peasant population lives either in well-built farm houses or primitive cave dwellings. The landscape is dotted with numerous kilns producing mainly bricks and tiles. The climate is of the North China plain continental type, with dry and cold winters and hot and humid summers.

Luoyang now has 1.1 million inhabitants and its industries have all but a few been developed since 1949, in particular mechanical engineering. Luoyang has always been famous for its craftsmen and is still known for its pottery, lanterns and silk flowers. The city has grown considerably since 1949, mostly west of the old city which is very small and busy.

Luoyang is about thirteen hours by train from Beijing, on the Beijing-Xi'an railway line. Foreign guests at present stay at the *Friendship Hotel* (tel. 2139) in Tangyuan Road, in the west of the new town. The hotel was built for Soviet experts in the 1950s and is one of the most hospitable of its kind. It is in the area known as the Canton Market, patronized by the large Cantonese community which came to Luoyang after 1949 to work in industry. A new hotel for tourists is being planned.

Luoyang itself can be visited in one to two days but two neighbouring counties, Gongxian and Dengfeng (see below), have a wealth of sites of interest. Although the weather may still be fairly cold, the first fortnight of the Chinese New Year is a particularly good time to visit Luoyang. The Longmen caves south of the city are still crowded at that season with visitors (mostly old ladies) who come to make offerings to the Buddhas; the White Horse Temple receives many pilgrims on the eighth day of the New Year, and the

Lantern Festival (two weeks after the New Year) in Luoyang is a particularly lively event.

History. Like Kaifeng and Xi'an, Luoyang has been a capital on several occasions, and is sometimes called 'the ancient capital of nine dynasties'. The area has been settled since the neolithic age and first became a capital in the Xia dynasty in 2100 B.C. Three dynasties, the Zhou, the Han and the Tang, moved their capital from Xi'an to Luoyang after having been driven east by Western 'barbarian' people. The great Taoist philosopher Laozi is said to have been the historian in charge of the imperial archives in Luoyang in the Eastern Zhou dynasty, around the end of the sixth and beginning of the fifth century B.C. Buddhism came to Luoyang in the first century A.D. during the Eastern Han dynasty and the carving of the caves of Longmen began in the fifth century A.D. under the patronage of the Wei dynasty emperors. The founder of the Sui dynasty had the capital rebuilt with an imperial city at the centre. During the Tang dynasty it was the second official capital of the empire, but only the last emperor lived there permanently. Empress Wu Zetian had several palaces built in Luoyang; it became an intellectual and artistic centre and the Fengxian Temple caves at Longmen were carved. During the period of the Five Dynasties, the capital was moved to Kaifeng (937) and Luoyang was never again chosen as a capital.

Places of interest. In its golden days during the Tang dynasty Luoyang had many temples, but few remain today and none are open to the public. The Chenghuangmiao (Temple of the Town Gods), inside the old town, is very dilapidated and used as a school. The Zhougongmiao, near the river Luo, at the foot of Dingding Road, is a radio station.

The Working People's Park is still known as the Wangcheng (Royal Town) Park because it is built on the site of the palace of the Zhou emperors. The park is famous for its tree peonies, also called the 'king of flowers'. Two Han dynasty tombs can be visited in the park: the Western Han Tomb was unearthed when the railway station was built and moved to its present site. The murals of the burial chamber are particularly beautiful: cosmic decorations on the ceiling and mythological scenes on the walls. The carved sheep's head above the entrance is a propitious symbol. The Eastern Han Tomb has two pairs of carved stone doors, a main burial chamber for the coffins of the husband and wife, and a smaller chamber on the left for the concubine.

The Luoyang Museum has moved to a new building in Zhongzhou Road. Among the exhibits is a model of the palace of a Xia dynasty capital which was discovered in the eastern suburbs of Luoyang, the oldest capital of China as yet discovered (around 2100 B.C.). There is also a very large (80 cm in diameter) bronze bowl which filled with water was used as a mirror. It was cast during the Western Zhou dynasty as part of the dowry of the daughter of a marquis of Qi. Several collections of bronze money show the evolution of the coins, from little spades with wooden handles to round pieces with a square hole, between the Spring and Autumn period (770-476 B.C.) and the Han dynasty. The museum also has some very representative pieces of Tang dynasty three-coloured glazed pottery.

Several old buildings which are not at present open to the public are worth mentioning: the Wenfeng Pagoda, in the south-east corner of the old town; the Shanxi-Shaanxi Merchants' Hall, south-east of the walls; and the Luzaihuiguan, east of the walls, a residence built by a rich merchant in the Ming dynasty.

Environs of Luoyang. The Guandimiao (Temple of the God of War), east of the road to the Longmen caves (see below), which used to house the Luoyang Museum, is under repair and will reopen with a display of archaeological finds. The temple takes its name from Guan Yu, general and companion of Emperor Liu Bei of the Three Kingdoms period, who was raised to the status of God of War during the Ming dynasty, and whose tomb is there, marked by a clump of cypress.

The Baimasi, or White Horse Temple, about 15 km east of town, is one of the oldest Buddhist temples in China (A.D. 68). In the Western Han dynasty, two Indian monks, Matanga and Zhu Fanlan, arrived in Luoyang riding white horses and carrying the Buddhist sutras; they founded the temple and their remains are said to be buried there. Two short stone white horses and two lions stand outside the gates. Most buildings in the courtyards date from the Ming or Qing dynasty and the temple was extensively restored in 1935.

The first hall, or Hall of the Heavenly Kings, has, apart from the four guardians, a main figure of Maitreya Buddha which is relatively new, and a statue of Wei Tuo at the back, holding a mountain in his hand, which is probably from the Ming dynasty. The next hall is the Dafodian (Big Buddha Hall), with a gilded clay statue of Sakyamuni in the centre and Wenshu on the right and Puxian on the left, with the usual disciples, and two unexpected maidens painted with bright colours. A Guanyin seated on a throne floating in the clouds at the back is the only deity still apparently worshipped in the temple. To the right of the entrance, a large bell cast in 1546 (Ming) has a top piece in the form of two helmeted heads.

The Daxiongdian, or Hall of the Great Heroes, has a very ornate main altar with a gallery above supporting another altar. The most interesting statues in this hall are the eighteen Lohans made of *tuotai* or dry lacquer, of the Yuan dynasty. They are all sitting on chests, each of them rendered in a vivid manner, some with their shoes off, one accompanied by a cat.

The Jieyingdian, or Reception Hall, smaller than the others, was specially reserved for visiting monks from India. The Qingliangtai, or Cooling Terrace, is alleged to have been built under Emperor Ming Di of

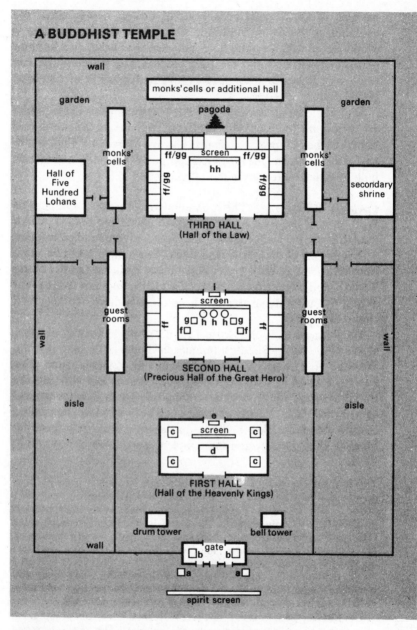

A BUDDHIST TEMPLE

wall

garden

garden

monks' cells or additional hall

pagoda

monks' cells

monks' cells

Hall of Five Hundred Lohans

secondary shrine

ff/gg   screen   ff/gg

ff/gg   hh   ff/gg

THIRD HALL
(Hall of the Law)

guest rooms

guest rooms

wall

wall

i
screen

ff   g□ h h h □g   ff
f□   □f

SECOND HALL
(Precious Hall of the Great Hero)

aisle

aisle

e
c   screen   c

d

c   c

FIRST HALL
(Hall of the Heavenly Kings)

drum tower

bell tower

wall

gate
□b   b□
□a   a□

spirit screen

a stone or bronze lion (or other animal)
b Celestial Guardian
c King
d Maitreya Buddha
e Weituo
f Disciple (Lohan)
g Bodhisattva
h Buddha

i Guanyin (Kuanyin)

ff   row of Disciples
ff/gg   row of Disciples and/or Bodhisattvas (and/or library of sutras)
hh   one Buddha or a group

the Han dynasty. It is shaded by cypress about one thousand years old. The hall contains the sutra library.

A few monks belonging to the Chan, or Dhyana sect (also called Zen in Japan), still live in the temple.

The Qiyunta, or Pagoda Which Reaches to the Clouds, is a square-based, thirteen-storey pagoda, built at an unknown date but restored in the Song and Jin dynasty, which is now some distance east of the Baimasi. It was probably originally built inside the temple walls.

The Longmen caves. The road to the caves, south of Luoyang, starts at the Luoyang Bridge over the Luo River. A small pavilion stands alone on the sandy river bank, on a high platform, the only vestige of a Tang dynasty bridge that once spanned the river. The small Anlewo (Happy) village, just across the river, was given this name by the philosopher Shao Kezi who led a very happy life there. When Luoyang was the Tang dynasty capital, foreigners used to live in this village, then a suburb.

The Longmen caves are some 12 km south of Longmen, on the north bank of the river Yi, in a very pleasant setting. At this place, the cliffs on both sides of the river are positioned like gate towers, hence the name Longmen (Dragon Gate). The caves are hollowed out of the cliff over a distance of about 1 km; warm water (about 24°C. throughout the year) streams run through cracks in the limestone and gather in basins built at the bottom where the local people do their laundry. A narrow road winds between the cliff and the river, busy with local traffic of man-drawn wheelbarrows taking the family to the next village.

The caves were started in A.D. 494 when Emperor Xiao Wen of the Northern Wei dynasty moved from Datong in northern Shanxi to Luoyang. The work continued for four centuries, and only a few caves were added after the Tang dynasty. There are over 1,300 caves, some of which are almost inaccessible, and 750 niches.

Starting from the north: The Qianxi Temple, also known as the Zhaifutang, was carved in the early Tang dynasty; it has a large figure of Buddha seated on a lotus throne and flanked by two Lohans (disciples) and two particularly good examples of full-bodied, feminine-looking Tang dynasty Bodhisattvas. The two celestial guardians, inside the cave, either side of the wall have fierce foreign faces, and their dress has a sweeping movement which suggests that they have just marched in. They stand on beasts with human faces.

The Three Pingyang caves, or caves which 'greet the sun', were all begun in the Northern Wei dynasty. The central cave is the most even in style because it was built in a short period of time, between 500 and 523. The work was commissioned by Emperor Xuan Wu of the Northern Wei in memory of his parents. The serene smile and heavy body of the seated

Sakyamuni, 8.40 m high, as well as the formal heavy draping of his robe, are very typical of the Northern Wei style. The carvings are very close in style to some of those in the Yungang caves in Shanxi province, but, limestone being more durable than sandstone, the carving is crisper and better preserved than at Datong. The adoration processions which used to decorate the walls by the entrance were removed to the United States in 1935. The ceiling is one of the finest in the caves, carved with flying *apsarah* (angels) and ten musicians.

The south Pingyang cave was started in the late Wei dynasty and completed at the beginning of the Sui. The style is uneven, the central Buddha figure being very plain and massive by contrast with the two standing Bodhisattvas, wearing flowing robes and ornate beads and belts. The north Pingyang cave took even longer to carve, from the end of the Wei to the Tang, and has the same mixture of styles.

The Wanfotong (Ten Thousand Buddha) cave, carved in the Tang dynasty (A.D. 680), takes its name from the 15,000 small Buddhas carved in niches on the north and south walls which are also decorated at the base by a pattern of dancers and musicians. The entrance is decorated outside and inside by standing figures, including a very fine Avalokitesvara holding a whisk in her right hand and a water jug in her left hand. Two high-relief lions used to guard the entrance; one is now in Kansas City, the other one in Boston.

The Lianhua (Lotus Flower) cave, named after the large and richly carved lotus flower on the ceiling, dates from the end of the Northern Wei dynasty. The Sakyamuni Buddha figure is standing, a rare instance in the Longmen Caves. The south wall is decorated with small niches (most of them around 60 cm high) with small Buddhas seated on lotus thrones, the pleats of their skirts arranged in an opulent and formal pattern.

The Fengxiansi, completed in the Tang dynasty, in 675, and now completely exposed to the outside, is the most photographed cave in Longmen, with its giant statues of a standing Vairocana Buddha (17.14 m high), his disciples, two Bodhisattvas and four fearful figures of Heavenly Kings. Young visitors climb to the feet of the guardians and try to embrace their ankles; anyone whose fingers can meet will have good luck for the year.

The Guyang cave, built around 494, is the oldest, and because the emperor, his family and many other noble families contributed to the carving, one of the richest caves at Longmen. The main statue of Buddha sits on a particularly high throne. Amongst the many niches decorating the walls are pieces of calligraphy engraved on steles; nineteen out of the twenty famous calligraphic inscriptions of Longmen are in this cave. More niches were carved over a period of nearly a hundred years after A.D.494 until hardly a bare space was left.

The Kanjing Temple of the East Hill was carved in the Tang dynasty during the reign of Empress Wu Zetian. The lower part of the walls is decorated with high-relief figures of 24 Lohans, carved in a particularly realistic manner.

The small town of GONGXIAN (34) is about 65 km east of Luoyang. It can be reached by train (it is on the Zhengzhou-Luoyang railway line) or by car (two hours' drive from Luoyang). There is a guesthouse where foreigners can stay, south of the town, within walking distance of two important Song dynasty tombs, but as yet (1979) no permanent CTS staff or transport.

The Song Tombs. The Song dynasty tombs are scattered in the Mangshan, all in the county. There were nine Song emperors, seven of whom are buried in Gongxian; the first emperor buried his father there, and the last two emperors died in exile in the Northeast, prisoners of the Jin. There are therefore eight imperial tombs. More than a hundred members of the imperial family are said to be buried in the Mangshan, not including young children for whom there is no record. The peasants in the area are constantly ploughing up steles, some of which have been gathered in a sort of makeshift museum in Gongxian.

One of the largest and best preserved is the Yongding tomb, of the third emperor who died in 998. The bricks and tiles of the building have vanished and all that remains are several mounds of earth and the magnificent alley of the animals, set in a landscape of rolling fields. In Song times all the carvings had to be completed within seven months of the emperor's death, and were therefore done by a number of sculptors; the results are highly individual, and of uneven quality. First come the two Wangzhuang, or pillars with linear carving, then two elephants with their keeper, then two steles engraved in bas-relief with a mythical animal which has the body and feet of a dragon, a horse's head, bird's wings and a peacock's tail: it is supposed to be able to turn into a dragon and fly away. Its head is as high as the mountains in the background and its feet planted deep in a cave. The next pair are also mythical animals, called Jiaoduan, which can walk a thousand *li* in a day and eight hundred *li* in a night, on the ground, in the air and on the water, know everything and can report to the emperor. Then come the two pairs of horses with two keepers each, the guard of honour. The next animals are two tigers carved in naturally striped stone, two rams for good luck, two sets of three foreign envoys bearing presents, and two sets of four Chinese officials (taller than the foreign envoys), including two pairs of generals with long swords, and two pairs of official holding tablets. Two crouching lions lead the procession and two guardians stand by the gate.

The square wall around the tomb had four gates, the south, east, north, and west Spirit Gates, each having a pair of crouching lions. The tomb itself, now just a mound, used to be faced with bricks and is 46.8 m in circumference. To the north-west, one can see the tomb of the third emperor's empress, smaller and accompanied by a smaller guard of honour of stone statues.

Each of the Song tombs used to be guarded by 500 to 1,000 soldiers who were quartered in buildings outside the wall of the tomb, to the north. Two other tombs can be visited on foot from the guesthouse: those of the fourth and fifth emperors, and their empresses.

The Gongxian caves. About 9 km north-east of Gongxian, on the north bank of the Yiluo River (downstream from the confluence of the Yi and Luo Rivers), in the production brigade of Siwan (Temple Bend), are the Gongxian caves. Carved out of the Dali (Atlas) Hill in the Mangshan, these are among the most famous Buddhist cave temples in China. They are rather small, and were all built after the Longmen caves, the earliest in the late Northern Wei period (517-534); like the Yungang caves at Datong, they are carved out of soft sandstone and often very damaged. The caves are now partly below ground; they were originally dug at ground level, but in the fourteen hundred years since, the ground has been raised by silt brought by the river.

There are five caves: No. 1 has some giant carvings chiselled on the face of the cliff outside. Inside the cave the entrance wall is decorated with fine scenes of the adoration of Buddha, with a row of musicians at the bottom and 'thousand' Buddhas in niches above the doorway. The main decoration is a central pillar with a Buddha carved on each of its faces; seated on a throne, he is supported by Dali (Atlas) and with a carved canopy hanging over his head. The Buddhas are of the late Wei transitional period: their heads are square and their chests flat in the Northern Wei style, but the folds of their robes announce the Tang period. The two side walls and back walls are adorned with niches — four on each wall — depicting scenes of Buddha teaching. The lower part of the back wall is carved with eighteen *xu*, mythical creatures representing the constellations.

No. 2 is small, was begun during the late Northern Wei period but left unfinished; more carvings were added in the Tang dynasty. The earliest carving is a bust of Buddha on the left side; the seated Sakyamuni on the right was begun in the Eastern Wei period and finished (the lower part) in the Tang dynasty. No. 3 is fairly large and now well below ground. The decoration is arranged around a central pillar. Some finely carved low-relief *apsarah* fly above the south-facing seated Sakyamuni. The high-relief lions either side of its throne are characteristic of the late Northern Wei period, being almost free-standing. As in No. 1, there is a scene of the adoration of Buddha on the inside of the entrance (south) wall, but not as well preserved.

No. 4 is also fairly large, and the plan is traditional. The main figures are carved on the four faces of a central pillar, the west face of which shows the Buddha of the North and the Buddha of the South discussing. No. 5 is very small. The ceiling is decorated with a lotus flower central motif and flying *apsarah*. One of the Bodhisattvas on the west wall is missing, now in an American museum. The wall outside the cave is decorated with a thousand Buddhas in niches.

Enjoy the bumpy ride back to Gongxian. Look at the villages with a mixture of poor dwellings dug out of the cliff and prosperous houses with tall gatehouses. Some of the villages are still fortified, with a mixture of man-made and natural walls.

The town of DENGFENG is about 80 km south-east of Luoyang and can be reached by road (nearly three hours' drive) from Luoyang. Dengfeng county is exceptionally rich in ancient monuments but permission to visit is not often given.

The Shaolinsi, or Temple of the Small Forest, about 20 km northwest of Dengfeng, has a long tradition of martial arts training which is still in force. The temple was founded during the Northern Wei dynasty and tradition says that an Indian monk named Boddhidarma, Damo in Chinese, came to live in the temple about A.D. 520 and died there, having spent several years in motionless meditation. He brought the Chan (Zen) tradition to China. The temple has been enlarged and rebuilt several times and is at present under repair. The main temple hall, the Hall of the Thousand Buddhas, is well known for its frescoes. The monks were buried in an area called the Forest of Stupas, each grave being marked by a stone stupa.

The Zhongyuemiao, or Temple of the Central Peak, in the Song mountains about 10 km north of Dengfeng, is dedicated to one of the five sacred mountains of Taoism, also known as Gaoshan (High Mountain). The temple as it stands now was designed during the Tang dynasty; it was considerably enlarged during the Song dynasty, when the capital was at Kaifeng and the emperors used to offer sacrifices at the temple, and was rebuilt again under the Qing.

Emperor Wu of the Western Han dynasty visited the Song mountains in 110 B.C. and had some small stone monuments erected in memory of his visit. Two of them stand just south of the Zhongyuemiao, and there are two others in the vicinity of Dengfeng.

Other buildings of interest in Dengfeng county include the Songshan temple, with a brick pagoda erected in 520, the oldest still standing in China. South of the Zhongyuemiao, there is an observatory built during the Yuan dynasty, inside a temple, the Zhougongmiao. Built of bricks in the shape of a truncated pyramid, it too is the oldest still standing in China. Also near the Zhongyuemiao, there is a small Buddhist temple, the First Ancestor's Nunnery, which is the oldest wooden structure in Henan province.

MIANCHI is about 75 km west of Luoyang on the Luoyang-Xi'an railway. About 6 km north of the town, in the village of Yangshao, some important neolithic remains were uncovered in 1921. They date from about 4000 B.C. and the name Yangshao Culture has been used since for all other middle-neolithic cultures which made and used painted pottery. (Another major site of Yangshao culture is Banpo village, near Xi'an in Shaanxi province.)

In Tiemen (Iron Gates), about 25 km west of Mianchi, on the Luoyang-Xi'an railway, there are some cave-temples dating from the Northern Wei dynasty. The Hongqing Monastery was built outside six of these cave temples. I was told that the sculptures have been obliterated by natural erosion and that the caves cannot be visited.

SANMENXIA (Three Gates Gorges) (**35**), about 125 km west of Luoyang on the Luoyang-Xi'an railway, takes its name from the Yellow River gorges east of it. At the point where the river divides into three streams when it cuts through the mountains, a dam and a hydro-electric station have been built since 1948, and this is what tourists are taken to see. But the area has other attractions. Over the centuries the rock has been carved with inscriptions in many inaccessible places. A temple dedicated to Yu the Great, who was credited with having divided the waters into three streams, was built in the gorges. Traces of wooden overhanging paths used for towing the boats upstream can still be seen on the rocks.

III
THE SOUTH

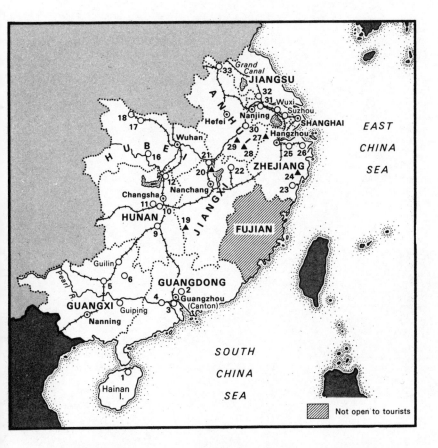

1	Haikou	16	Shashi	26	Ningbo
2	Conghua	17	Xiangfan	27	Moganshan
3	Foshan	18	Danjiang (Junxian)	28	Huangshan
4	Zhaoqing	19	Jinggangshan	29	Jiuhuashan
5	Liuzhou	20	Lushan	30	Wuhu
6	Yangshuo	21	Jiujiang	31	Zhenjiang
9	Hengyang	22	Jingdezhen	32	Yangzhou
10	Xiangtan	23	Wenzhou	33	Xuzhou
11	Shaoshan	24	North Yandangshan		
12	Yueyang (Lake Dongting)	25	Shaoxing		

1 The Lower Yangzi Basin: Anhui and Jiangsu

The basin of the lower Yangzi (Yangtze) River is dotted with lakes and traced by canals and rivers on which the greater part of the local freight is carried. Rice is grown and water buffaloes munch placidly in the flat land around the waterways; you often see junks sailing through the mosaic of the paddy fields. On the gentle green hills are tea and mulberry plantations, amidst lush forests and cascading streams. The climate is mild in winter and the summer season generously watered by monsoon rains. This area produces a wide range of manufactured goods, from traditional silk and brocade to large and sophisticated machinery.

HEFEI 合肥

Hefei (Union of the Fei), since 1949 the capital of Anhui province, lies north-east of Lake Chao, the largest body of water in this well-watered province. The city is served by a branch of the Beijing-Shanghai railway (Hefei is eighteen and a half hours from Beijing), but there are few through trains; if you want to go on from Hefei to Shanghai or in a southerly direction, you must travel back along the line to the junction at Bengpu. Hefei is linked to Beijing, Jinan and Shanghai by air, but flights are infrequent.

The *Hefei Guesthouse* is small, clean, and tourists are usually given suites. The food is excellent.

Hefei, a 2,000-year-old city built at the confluence of the North and South Fei Rivers (hence its name), has traditionally been a centre for trade. Industries have been developed since 1949. The old city is surrounded by a moat which has been turned into parks, making a ring of greenery round the city centre, but there is little in Hefei to interest the tourist, except for a Buddhist temple, recently restored, which is now open to visitors, and the provincial museum. In the latter is displayed a reproduction of a jade burial suit unearthed in the province, one of a collection of cultural relics which toured Europe and North America in 1974-5. Tourists can also visit the university, and the suburban East is Red commune. Hefei, though not worth a detour, is included in several package tours.

The principal attractions of Anhui province are in the south-east, which is effectively cut off from the rest of the province by the wide and meandering Yangzi River over which no bridge has yet been built in the area.

JIUHUASHAN (Nine Blossoms Mountain) (29), one of the four sacred mountains of Buddhism, is accessible by train from Nanjing to Tongling, and then by car — a drive of 75 km — to the village of Jiuhuajie. Its name comes from a poem by the Tang poet Li Bo (Li Bai), who compared the peaks to nine hibiscus flowers. The highest of these peaks rises 1,342 m above sea level. Because the area is on the border between the temperate and sub-tropical zones, the vegetation is varied and includes many Alpine species, and temperatures stay cool during the summer.

The best time to visit Jiuhuashan is on the last day of the seventh lunar month, which falls between the first and third weeks of September. This is the time when Di Zang, the patron saint of the mountain, is honoured and worshipped. Di Zang, whose name in Sanskrit is Ksitigarbha, is the ruler of the netherworld and also the protector of little children. He has the power to open the gates of hell and rescue the miserable sufferers. In a Buddhist temple, his statue is usually found in the second hall. Jiuhuashan has several Buddhist temples, some of which are dedicated to Di Zang, and Buddhist rock carvings.

Another famous mountain range in southern Anhui province is HUANGSHAN (28), 30 km south of Jiuhuashan. Its highest peak, the Guangming Ding, rises 1,841 m above sea level. The ascent starts from the village of Tangkou to the south of the mountains, at a place famous for its hot springs.

These mountains, with their vertical rock formations shrouded in mist and pine trees (*cathaya*) clinging to the rock face, spreading their branches out over the abyss, comprise some of the most beautiful scenery in China. Together with the sugar-loaf-shaped mountains of Guangxi province, they have inspired Chinese landscape painters over the centuries.

NANJING (Nanking) 南京

Nanjing (Southern Capital), situated on the south bank of the Yangzi River and bordered on the east by the Zijin (Purple) Mountains, is the capital of the coastal province of Jiangsu, and now has a population of more than 2.4 million. The climate is mild in winter — the temperature seldom goes below freezing — but summer can be lethal: Nanjing (with Wuhan and Chongqing) is one of the 'three furnaces of China', with very high humidity and temperatures of above 27° centigrade from July to mid-August.

Nanjing has a modern and diversified industry, with steel and automobile factories, petrochemical plants, refineries and coal mines; scientific instruments and textiles are also manufactured. It is a handsome city with elegant tall buildings topped with traditional-style roofs, dating from the Kuomintang period. The south of the city is picturesque, with narrow streets, canals and wooden houses. Nanjing is well worth two days of your visit to China, but will be competing for your time with a dozen interesting places in the

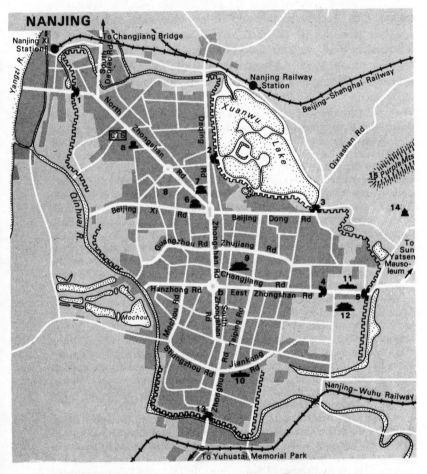

Hotels and amenities			6	Drum Tower
a	Nanjing Hotel		7	Bell Tower
b	People's Bazaar		8	Nanjing University
			9	Palace of the Taiping emperor
Landmarks and places of interest			10	Museum of the Taiping
1	Yijiang Gate		11	Nanjing Museum
2	Xuanwu Gate		12	Ming Palace ruins
3	Taiping Gate		13	Zhonghua Gate
4	Wuchao Gate		14	Ming Tomb
5	Zhongshan Gate		15	Observatory

area. The train journey from Beijing, some 1,000 km away, takes about twenty-four hours.

Most foreign tourists stay at the *Nanjing Hotel* (**a**) in North Zhongshan Road (tel. 34-121). Set in a garden, it is one of the quietest and most pleasant hotels in China. The food is good, but few rooms are air-conditioned. A new tourist hotel is being built and and should be completed by the early 1980s.

Gastronomic specialities of the city include Nanjing Duck, also called 'Flat Duck', cherries and watermelon. The mildly spiced local cuisine can be sampled at the *Sandayuan Restaurant*, 40 Zhongshan Road, and the *Jiangsu Restaurant*, 126 Jiankang Road; and Cantonese food and local dishes at the *Old Guangdong Restaurant*, 45 Zhongshan Road, opposite the Sandayuan.

History. Bronzes found in the area attest that Nanjing was populated during the Xia dynasty from around 2400 B.C. After the break-up of the Han dynasty, the city, then called Jianye, became the second capital of the south-eastern state of Wu, protected by the wide Yangzi River from attacks by the northern state of Wei. Between the Three Kingdoms period (third century A.D.) and the establishment of the Sui dynasty (end of the sixth century) it was the capital of six successive dynasties ruling over the lower Yangzi basin and the south. During the Tang dynasty it was a provincial town but continued to attract artists, among them the poet Li Bo (Li Bai); during the Southern Tang it became a capital again. In 1368, when the former Buddhist novice whose reign title was Hong Wu, having driven the Mongols out of the northern provinces, declared the new Ming dynasty, he made Nanjing his capital, and 'invited' 20,000 rich families to settle there and contribute to its construction.

The layout of the city, unchanged since then, was dictated by the natural boundaries formed by the river and the hills and its shape is uncharacteristically asymmetrical. The Imperial Palace was to the east. The 35-km-long city wall enclosed a large expanse of land under cultivation. Hong Wu's intention had been to install the capital permanently in Nanjing, but Yong Le, when he became the third emperor, chose to move the capital to Beijing, from which he could control the northern provinces. Nanjing remained a secondary capital and continued to expand, unaffected by the change of dynasty in 1644.

In 1842, in the first Unequal Treaty, Nanjing became an open port. In the middle of the nineteenth century, when corruption and unrest had spread to most of the country, the Taiping (Great Peace) movement broke out in Guangxi, led by a religious fanatic who proclaimed himself to be the Younger Heavenly Brother of Jesus Christ. In 1851, the Taiping captured Nanjing and two years later set up their capital there. They built palaces and ran their southern 'empire' until 1864, when Nanjing was recaptured by the Qing armies after a very destructive battle.

Nanjing was briefly the capital of the first (provisional) Republican government in 1912 and, from 1928 to 1937, the capital of the Nationalist government of Chiang Kaishek. The Japanese occupied the city in 1937 and stayed until their defeat in 1945. Once again during the Civil War (1945-9), the KMT set up their government there.

Places of interest. Nanjing is one of the very few large Chinese cities whose ancient city wall and gates have been preserved. Large sections of the wall, built at the beginning of the Hong Wu era (1368-99) with bricks from Hubei province made in many different kilns but all of exactly the same size, remain around the city as well as several gates: the Yijiang Gate (**1**) in the north-west, near the west (Nanjing Xi) railway station; the Xuanwu Gate (**2**), in the north-east, leading to the Xuanwu Lake; and the Wuchao (**4**) and Zhongshan (**5**) Gates in the east, near the Nanjing Museum.

Both the Drum (**6**) and Bell (**7**) Towers were built at the same time as the walls but have been repaired several times since. They stand at the end of the long north-south axis which was the Imperial Way of the Ming capital (Zhonghua and Zhongshan Roads). To the west of the Drum Tower is Nanjing University (**8**), which was founded in 1902. North Zhongshan Road which goes through the former consulate area is planted with plane trees imported from France in the 1930s, and lined with tall buildings.

The palace of the Taiping emperor (**9**), later used as offices by the Nationalist government, is on the north side of the Changjiang Road, east of Xinjiekou Square. South of Jiankang Road, in the south-east quarter of the city, is the Museum of the Taiping (**10**), in the remains of the palace of the Eastern King of the Taiping, with exhibits tracing the history of the Taiping rebellion which, because it introduced agrarian reforms, is considered by the present government to have been a peasant rebellion. Near the Taiping Museum, on Meiyuan (Plum Garden) New Road, are the houses where the Communist delegation led by Zhou Enlai and Dong Biwu stayed in 1946-7 when negotiating an agreement to end the civil war.

The Nanjing Museum (**11**) is near the site of the ancient Ming Palace (**12**), covering a large area in the east of the city, to the north and south of East Zhongshan Road. The large Wuchao Gate, with five archways, leads to the site. Five partly destroyed marble bridges can still be seen and also the stone base of some of the pillars of palace halls and a stele put up in memory of Fang Xiaoru, an official who died protesting against the *coup* led by the future emperor Yong Le.

The Nanjing Museum, which is also the provincial museum, contains exhibits from about 5000 B.C. to the Taiping rebellion, among them Xia dynasty bronzes, fine Han dynasty glazed pottery, iron agricultural tools, printed works by the philosopher Sun Zi (Zhou dynasty), exhibits of printed works and reproductions of paintings spanning the period of the Six Dynasties, handicrafts from the Ming and Qing dynasty, and furniture.

In the north-east, outside the city wall and the Xuanwu Gate, is Xuanwu Lake, with its five small islands, recently connected by causeways, each named after a continent. The Imperial Archives used to be kept on 'Australia'. The lake is surrounded on three sides by hills and on the west by the city wall. In a park to the south of the lake, in an area used as an execution ground during the Yuan dynasty, are the buildings of the Jimingsi (Cock's Crow) Temple.

Changjiang Bridge, north-west of the city, is one of three bridges across the Yangzi River, known in China as Changjiang (Long River); the others are at Wuhan (1957) and Chongqing (1959). Completed in 1969, the Nanjing bridge is the longest of the three (6.7 km). Its construction posed difficult engineering problems because of the width of the river, its shifting bed and fast current. The bridge is high enough to allow the passage of 10,000-ton vessels; it has an upper deck for road traffic and a lower deck for the railway, whose carriages had formerly to be ferried across the river.

Environs of Nanjing. A few miles east of the city, in the Purple Mountains (also called the Eastern Hills), are a number of places worth a visit. If you leave by the Zhongshan Gate, a road to the left leads to the Ming Tomb (Mingxiaoling) (**14**), where the Hong Wu emperor, founder of the Ming dynasty (known posthumously as Tai Zu, Great Progenitor), is buried. His consort, who died sixteen years after him, in 1415, is buried there as well.

The tomb is approached by the traditional Spirit Way, which starts at Dahongmen (or Dagongmen), the Great Gate, near which is a tortoise bearing a stele. After a turn of the path to the west, and a marble bridge, begins the Guard of Honour, pairs of standing and crouching animals followed by pairs of officials. A gate leads into the first courtyard of which a terrace in the centre is all that remains of the original structure. On it a recent building houses steles. In the second courtyard, the main hall is also of recent reconstruction (post-Taiping era), erected on the old marble base of the original hall. A newly rebuilt gate leads to the third courtyard, the largest, bordered on the north by a canal spanned by a marble bridge. The entrance to the tumulus is through a passage sloping up under a stone tower with slanted sides, and leading to a terrace.

Further to the east, on a southern slope of the Purple Mountains, is the Sun Yatsen Mausoleum, in a setting worthy of an imperial tomb. The great Nationalist leader Dr Sun, who died in Beijing in 1925, had expressed a wish to be buried here. His body remained in Beijing until the mausoleum was finished in 1929. It covers an area of 8 *ha* (19.75 acres), and a flight of 392 steps leads from the triple gateway at the entrance to the memorial hall at the top. A second gateway is inscribed with the words *Tianxia wei gong* (the world belongs to everyone). A way paved with white stones leads to the stele pavilion, built of white stone and covered with blue-glazed tiles, blue and white being the colours of the KMT flag. In the mausoleum itself, a seated statue of Sun Yatsen, carved in white marble by the French sculptor Landowski, occupies the centre of the hall. The walls are decorated with stone tablets inscribed in gold letters with the 1912 constitution and the National Charter. Unfortunately, cordons keep visitors too far from the tablets to be able to read them. Behind the statue is the entrance to the vault which holds the coffin, on top of which is a reclining figure of Sun Yatsen.

To the east of the mausoleum, also on a southern slope of the mountains, is the Linggu Temple, or Temple of the Valley of the Spirits; it once stood on the present site of the Ming Tomb, and was moved east when Emperor Hong Wu chose the site for his tomb in 1381. The only remaining hall is the Wuliangdian, named after a large statue of Buddha which has now disappeared, called Wuliang-shoufo (Buddha of Infinite Longevity). Because it is built without any wood beams, it has become known as the Hall Without Beams. The sixth-century Linggu pagoda is a stone tower 61 m high, rebuilt in steel and concrete under the Kuomintang, with a spiral staircase leading to the top floor roofed with blue-glazed tiles. Near by are a stone stele engraved with a poem by the great Tang dynasty poet Li Bo and the tomb of the monk Bao Zhi who died in the sixth century.

Leaving the city by the Taiping Gate (3), to the north-east, you take the Qixiashan Road, south of which is the Observatory (15) founded in 1934 during the KMT government, and one of the major astronomical research institutes in China. It has two armillary spheres designed in 1427 by the Yuan dynasty astronomer Guo Shoujing, which used to stand on the Beijing Observatory and were removed to Nanjing in 1933.

The Qixiashan (Mountains Resting on Rosy Clouds) are some 28 km east of the Taiping Gate. In one of the valleys is the Qixia Temple, founded during the Southern Qi dynasty in 483, and still in activity. The temple buildings show a Southern influence in their sharply upturned roof ends; almost entirely destroyed after the Taiping defeat in Nanjing, they have been restored several times. One hall is devoted to a Japanese monk who lived in the temple during the Tang dynasty. To the east of the temple is a six-storey pagoda built under the Song which has fine carvings of the life of Buddha on its base and a bas-relief of the Four Celestial Kings above. Next to the pagoda is a 'Thousand Buddha' cliff with carvings from the Qi, Tang and Song dynasties.

A short distance south of Nanjing, past the Zhonghua Gate (13), is the Yuhuatai, Terrace of the Rain of Flowers. A legend tells that the monk Yun Guang was preaching from the terrace when Buddha, moved by his eloquence, caused a rain of flowers to fall from the sky. The terrace is covered in multi-coloured pebbles which look very pretty when immersed in water, and are collected by the many visitors. The Yuhuatai was an execution ground for Communists and revolutionaries during the KMT government and a monument to the martyrs of the revolution was erected on the spot in 1949. In April 1976, during the Qingming Festival (Festival of the Dead), the people of Nanjing brought wreaths to honour the memory of Zhou Enlai who had died three months before; when the Nanjing municipality ordered the wreaths to be removed, riots were sparked off — precursors of the more highly publicized Tiananmen Incident in Beijing — which were branded as 'counter-revolutionary' by those who later became known as the 'Gang of Four'.

West of the Yuhuatai is the tomb of the king of Borneo who died in Nanjing in 1408 while visiting emperor Yong Le. He was buried under a mound with a Guard of Honour of stone statues, like a Chinese ruler.

About 18 km south of Nanjing is the Bull's Head Hill (Niutoushan), which used to have many temples and where the tombs of the first and second emperors of the Southern Tang dynasty (923-34) have been excavated.

In the western suburbs of Nanjing, outside the Shuixi Gate, is the Mochou (Light-Hearted) Lake, named after a heroine of the Liang dynasty, one of the famous scenic spots of the city. In the Chess Hall, Emperor Hong Wu is supposed to have won a game of chess against his counsellor Xu Da (the latter's tomb is north of the Qixiashan road, about 3 km east of the Taiping Gate). The Yujin Hall is furnished with antique redwood pieces and decorated with ancient paintings and calligraphy.

YANGZHOU (32) 扬州

The pretty town of Yangzhou (Yang Country) is on the north bank of the Yangzi River, near its junction with the Grand Canal; several locks and sluice gates regulate the flow of water between the canal and the river. The Grand Canal, built to transport the tax grain from the lower Yangzi to Luoyang, was extended under the Yuan dynasty to Beijing. This portion of the canal was first dug during the Sui dynasty (completed by 605) and at that time Yangzhou was called Jiangdu, the River Capital. During the Ten Kingdoms period which followed the collapse of the Tang dynasty, it was the capital of the Southern Wu dynasty (903-37). Yangzhou has attracted scholars and painters over many centuries and one of the seven original sets of the Complete Library of the Four Treasuries of Emperor Qian Long (see p. 80) was deposited there; it was destroyed during the Taiping rebellion. Yangzhou was also the home of a prestigious school of painting, and its story-tellers were well known in the whole empire.

As yet little industrialized, this small provincial town has retained a quiet charm. Its narrow streets are lined with old whitewashed houses. It can be visited from Nanjing within one day. Avoid the summer season.

Places of interest. The Grand Canal, which skirts the town to the east and south, used to be spanned by many stone bridges. Overlooking it is the Baota (Precious Pagoda), a seven-storey octagonal pagoda built of brick and wood. In the northern suburbs, on the shore of Lake Shuxi, is a park with the Lianhuasi (Lotus Flower) Temple, named after its white dagoba shaped like a lotus flower. It is topped by a bronze cap with bells hanging from the rim. Behind the temple is a bridge, built during the Qian Long era in 1755, whose central portion is in the shape of a terrace with five pavilions, one at each angle and one in the centre. It is known as the Wutingqiao (Five Kiosk Bridge).

Also in the vicinity of Lake Shuxi is a Buddhist temple, the Fajingsi, founded during the Wu dynasty of the Ten Kingdoms (902-37), destroyed during the Taiping rebellion and rebuilt during the Kuomintang era (1934). The Pingshantang, a hall to the east of the main courtyard, was built in 1048 by Ou Yangxiu, philosopher and painter of the early Song dynasty (1007-72) who was prefect of Yangzhou. Recently rebuilt, its simple and forceful structure of brown pillars and beams is enhanced by whitewashed walls; the shape of its roof is reminiscent of Japanese temple architecture. Behind the hall is a small temple dedicated to Ou Yangxiu.

In the town, the He Garden is a typical southern garden with rockeries and ponds. It has a two-storey house with a gallery on the upper floor, built entirely of wood.

WUXI 无锡

Wuxi (Without Tin) lies in the south of Jiangsu province, a short distance north of the Taihu (Great Lake). It is in what is known as the 'land of fish and rice' but is also a major silk-producing area. Its name refers to the vein of tin which was exploited during the Zhou dynasty but became depleted in the Han dynasty. Wuxi is perhaps the most industrialized of the smaller cities in the area, though it has mainly light industry. The population is now around 700,000.

Wuxi is about 120 km north-west of Shanghai and 180 km south-east of Nanjing and can be reached by rail from either of these centres. The city attracts many tourists, Chinese and foreign, and has four hotels. Foreign guests usually stay at the *Taihu Hotel,* on the lake shore, or at the modern air-conditioned *Lihu Hotel* which is more expensive. Both hotels are pleasant and serve good food. Wuxi is encircled by canals, and its narrow streets have great charm. One day is enough for a visit; it is best to avoid summer.

History. Wuxi was founded at the beginning of the Zhou dynasty by the son of Prince Tai, who made it the capital of the state of Juwu. The section of the Grand Canal which runs through the city was completed during the Sui dynasty in 610. The Donglin (Tung-lin) Academy, founded in Wuxi during the Song dynasty, was reorganized in 1604 by a few dismissed officials who tried to rally support from the scholars against the villain eunuch Wei Zhongxian (see p. 68); they failed and the movement was destroyed. Wuxi remained a dormant city until the creation of a textile industry (silk and cotton) during the Kuomintang administration.

Places of interest. Visitors come to Wuxi to see the Taihu, the third largest lake in China (after the Poyang and Dongting lakes, in Jiangxi and Hunan respectively). There are lotus farms in the lake waters, and many fish; flat boats with square sails animate the smooth surface. A boat tour of the lake will give you a panoramic view of its shores and islands, of which there are seventy-two. The Turtle-Head Islet (Yuantou Zhu) — in fact a peninsula, linked to the shore by a bridge — takes its name from its shape. Its shores are graced with pavilions and the view from the top of the hill is said to be the best that can be had of the whole lake. At the point of the islet, a rock is engraved with the inscription *Embracing Wu and Yue*, carved in the Ming dynasty, which recalls that during the Warring States period, the lake was between the states of Wu and Yue.

The Liyuan (Li Garden), on the north shore of the adjoining small lake, Lihu, next to the Lihu Hotel, features the Pavilions of the Four Seasons, erected on four sides of a pond and planted with flowers and shrubs characteristic of their respective season. East of them is the Long Causeway planted with peach trees and willows. There is also a covered promenade with eighty-nine flower-shaped windows and facing it the Mid-Lake Pavilion with a tiny five-storey pagoda. A path between the rockeries leads to the Cave of Returning Clouds, at the top of the garden.

Along the roads leading from the city of Wuxi to the lake are two parks, the Xihui Park and the Plum Garden (Mei Yuan). In the centre of the Xihui Park — located in the western suburbs between the Hui and Xi mountains, hence its name — is a hill topped by a pagoda visible from a long distance, the Longguang Pagoda, built in the Ming dynasty. In the park rises a spring which has been famous since the Tang dynasty for the purity of its water. A temple used to stand near the spring. The Jichang (Ease of Mind) Garden, designed at the beginning of the sixteenth century by a scholar when he retired from an official post at the court in Beijing, fell into decay at the end of the nineteenth century but in recent years has been restored to its former splendour.

Wuxi has been famous since the Ming dynasty for its clay figurines. They used to be models of opera characters sold to the peasants in the market places. Today the range of figurines has been greatly expanded but they have very little artistic value. The factory, situated near the Xihui Park, can be visited.

SUZHOU (Soochow) 苏州

Suzhou (Su Country) is situated south of the delta of the Yangzi River and to the east of the Taihu (Great Lake). The Grand Canal runs to the west of the city, which is itself criss-crossed by a network of canals. Once important arteries, many of these canals have now been filled in and surfaced to carry road traffic; but if you leave the main streets and take any small alley, you are sure to come across a canal. The houses are whitewashed, often with the front on the main street and the back overlooking the canal, each with its small embankment. The countryside around Suzhou is mainly flat, to the east, with vast expanses of water and paddy fields, and has green undulating hills to the west, planted with orchards, mulberry and tea bushes.

A popular proverb says, 'Above there is paradise, and on earth there is Suzhou and Hangzhou'. Apart from its scenery — it is often called 'the Venice of China' — Suzhou is famous for the beauty of its women and the harmonious sounds of its dialect: another proverb contends that 'An argument in Suzhou is more pleasant than praise in Guangzhou' (Canton). The traditional Suzhou Opera is one of the most prestigious in China.

Suzhou is a stone's throw from Shanghai (60 km) and serviced by hourly commuter trains. You can sample Suzhou's gardens in one day, retaining your hotel room in Shanghai; or you can stay at the *Suzhou Grand Hotel* (**a**), quietly situated in a garden off Youyi Road, and spend two to three days exploring. The hotel is old-fashioned but solidly built and relatively cool in summer. The cuisine is excellent and includes a great variety of fresh fish and vegetables. The newer *Nanlin Hotel* (**b**), also in Youyi Road, offers equally peaceful surroundings, spacious rooms and good food. It is partly air-conditioned.

Two good restaurants are the very old *Songhelou*, 141 Guangqian

Street — try their delicious Xiangsuya (Fragrant crispy duck) — and the *Xinjiufeng*, 657 Renmin Road. A local speciality is the hairy crab, a freshwater crab fished in the many lakes in Jiangsu province, usually served steamed with a sauce of soy and ginger. The best season for them is the autumn, indeed they are seldom available at any other time. The first direct flights from China to Hong Kong were the seasonal 'crab planes' from Shanghai carrying a cargo of live Jiangsu hairy crabs.

Suzhou is a good place for buying silk, silk embroidery — it is one of the embroidery centres of China — baskets, bamboo, and antique hardwood furniture. The antique shop, 344 Renmin Road, will only ship furniture north during the spring and autumn, when the humidity in the north and south of the country is relatively the same.

History. Suzhou was founded in the sixth century B.C. by the king of

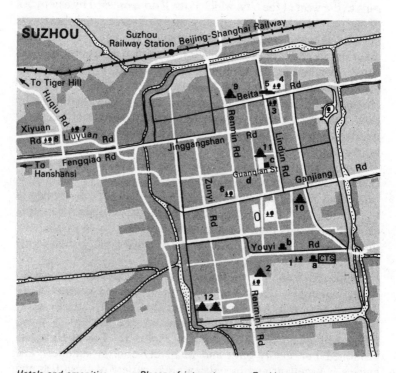

Hotels and amenities	Places of interest	
a Suzhou Grand Hotel	1 Wangshiyuan	7 Liuyuan
b Nanlin Hotel	2 Canglangting	8 Xiyuan
c Friendship Store	3 Shizilin	9 North Pagoda
d People's Bazaar	4 Zhuozhengyuan	10 Twin Pagodas
	5 History Museum	11 Xuanmiaoguan
	6 Yiyuan	12 Kaiyuansi and Ruiguangsi

the state of Wu, He Lu, who made it his capital. He is buried on Tiger Hill. Historical records show that there were already iron foundries at that time. Suzhou acquired its present name during the Sui dynasty in 589.

Although the silk industry was already well developed during the Tang and Song dynasties, it was only in the fourteenth century, during the Ming, that Suzhou became the most important centre for the manufacturing and trading of silk. As such it contributed its share of the taxes sent to Beijing via the Grand Canal. Suzhou was the home of a rich and powerful class of merchants and also a favourite retirement place for wealthy officials, who had beautiful gardens laid out and surrounded themselves with poets and painters.

The city suffered a great deal during the Taiping rebellion and was retaken in 1863 by a Chinese army headed by General Gordon. The late nineteenth century brought some changes to Suzhou, which was drawn into the foreign-dominated Shanghai orbit. It was opened to foreign trade in 1896, that trade centring almost exclusively around the silk industry.

The gardens. Suzhou's gardens are celebrated throughout the country; there used to be about a hundred of them, but now only seven can be visited. These gardens were built by wealthy scholars or merchants, as peaceful retreats, to be enjoyed in solitary contemplation or in the company of a few chosen friends; the fact that they are now public tends to destroy their atmosphere, and it is left to one's imagination to recreate the original ambience.

Two gardens can be visited on foot from the Youyi Road hotels:

Wangshiyuan, or Garden of the Master of the Nets (1), was laid out in 1140 by a retired official from Yangzhou, and fell into decay after his death; in 1770 it was bought and restored by another retired official. It has a main pond in the centre and one artificial hill. This garden, one of the smallest in Suzhou, shows a particularly good use of walls to create multiple perspectives and an illusion of space. Just over half the grounds, on the east and north, are occupied by buildings, designed in the Song dynasty but restored at the same time as the garden.

Walking west along Youyi Road and taking the first major turning south (left) into Renmin Road, one comes to the Keyuan, now abandoned, and the larger Canglanting (Surging Waves Pavilion) (2), both on the east side of the street. These were originally designed as one garden. Made in 1044, it passed into several hands, including a general's in the Song dynasty and a monk's; it was destroyed during the Taiping rebellion and restored in 1873. The garden is bordered on the south by a stretch of limpid water crossed by a bridge immediately inside the gate. The Pavilion for Viewing the Water, to the east, and the Pavilion for Watching the Fish, to the west, both overlook the water. The main part of the garden is occupied by a hill crowned by the Pavilion of the Surging Waves.

In the northern quarter of the city are two other gardens:

Shizilin (Lion-rock Forest) (3), with its strangely shaped rocks brought from the Great Lake, is on the south side of Beita Road, approached through a long corridor. Rockeries were very popular in Chinese gardens;

not only were rocks hauled out of lakes and the sea, some were even sub-
merged for years in the hope that they would weather interestingly. This
garden was designed by a monk, with the help of artists and painters, in
1350. It was originally part of a monastery and was named after the place —
the Lion Cliff — where the abbot of the temple had lived. (Another
explanation for the name is that many of its rocks are shaped like lions.)
The former residential buildings are to the east and north, and an expanse
of water divided by causeways and islands into four lakes occupies the
greater part of the garden.

The Zhuozhengyuan (Humble Administrator's Garden) (4), north of
Beita Road, was laid out in the Ming dynasty (1522) by a retired censor, and
seems to be built entirely on water. The main feature of the Central Garden
is a large lake with two islands contributing to an impression of space; on
the south shore is the Hall of Distant Fragrance, of sober and classical
design. A wall with an undulating top and the head of a dragon at the end
separates the Central Garden from the West Garden, smaller and more
intimate, and formerly overlooked by the private residential buildings
which are no longer part of the grounds. The History Museum (5) is to the
west of the garden. The Beiyuan (North Garden) east of the Zhuozhengyuan, has fallen into ruin and cannot be visited at present.

In the centre of Suzhou, only one garden is open to the public, the
Yiyuan (6), near the intersection of Ganjiang and Renmin roads. It
is not very large and was laid out recently (late nineteenth century).
Some of the rocks came from older abandoned gardens.

There are several gardens in the north-west outskirts of the city,
beyond the former city walls, now only marked by a moat which is
difficult to distinguish from the many canals.

The Liuyuan (Tarrying Garden) (7) was made during the Ming dynasty,
at the turn of the sixteenth century, and was then called the Green Country
Villa; it was owned by a civil servant, Xu Shitai, who also owned and
designed the neighbouring West Garden. The Liuyuan was extensively
rebuilt in 1876 and given its present name. Most of the halls and studios are
in the East Garden, which consists of orchards and a walled garden where
miniature landscapes are grown in flat pots, recreating lake views and hills,
and planted with miniaturized trees and shrubs. The Central Garden is laid
out around a pond surrounded by covered walks.

The Xiyuan or West Garden (8), across the Huqiu Road, was given to a
Buddhist community by the son of Xu Shitai, and the Xiyuan Temple was
built shortly thereafter. It was destroyed during the Taiping rebellion and
rebuilt at the end of the nineteenth century.

The temples.   The Beita or North Pagoda (9), is one of the first
landmarks you see when you enter the city from the railway station.
It was part of a temple called the Baoensi (Temple of Gratitude),
founded in the third century A.D., rebuilt in the tenth century, destroyed in the twelfth century, rebuilt, destroyed again by fire and
rebuilt after 1570. The nine-storey pagoda is octagonal and built of
wood; it is at present under repair, and will eventually be opened to
the public.

The Shuangta or Twin Pagodas (**10**) are in the east of the city, south of Ganjiang Road. The temple was originally founded during the Tang dynasty and the two brick pagodas added during the Song. The last restoration dates from 1860; and they cannot be visited but only seen from the street.

The Xuanmiaoguan (Monastery of Mystery) (**11**) is a large Taoist monastery situated in the centre of town in Guanqian Street (the Street to the Front of the Monastery). Founded in the third century A.D. but destroyed and rebuilt several times, the last time after the Taiping rebellion, the monastery is dedicated to the Three Pure Ones of the Taoist pantheon: Yuhuang, the Jade Ruler and supreme deity; Dao Qun, a mysterious character who controls the opposite influences of Yin and Yang; and Laozi, the earthly founder of Taoism. The temple is no longer used for worship but has been turned into a library.

There are two temples (**12**) in the south-west corner of the city: the Kaiyuansi, built during the Tang dynasty when Emperor Xuan Zong took the reign title of Kaiyuan (713-42), and ordered that each town build a Kaiyuan temple in honour of his reign; and the Ruiguangsi (Temple of Auspicious Brightness), founded in the third century A.D. but of which only a Song dynasty brick pagoda remains.

Outside the city wall, to the north-west, are two temples, the Hanshansi or Temple of the Gold Mountain, named after the hermit Han Shan who was also a poet. The temple was immortalized in some lines by another poet, the eighth-to-ninth-century Zhang Ji, engraved on a stele in the main hall of the temple. Anchored at the Maple Bridge,

> The moon was down, the crow cawed and the frost was sharp;
> With sadness in my heart I fell asleep,
> While maple leaves and fishing lights could be seen dimly.
> Soon the bell of Han Shan temple beyond Suzhou sounded
> And its deep booming was carried to my boat,
> Yet it seemed midnight.*

The temple, approached by the Maple Bridge over the canal, is enclosed behind gorgeous saffron walls. The bell tower in the forecourt now holds a replica of the original bell which was taken to Japan. The second hall contains three statues of Buddha and a statue of Guanyin (Kuanyin) behind the screen against a background of the tortures of Hell, traditional in a Buddhist monastery but seldom seen today. The temple, destroyed during the Taiping rebellion, was almost entirely rebuilt and contains few buildings or statues of interest. In the Hall of the Five Hundred Lohans, dating

---

*101 Chinese Poems, trans. Shih Shun-liu (Hong Kong , 1967).

from the late Qing period, it is fascinating, however, to see these realistic and often vulgar Buddhist images, all of the same period and constituting a complete iconographic set. In the north-west of the temple grounds is a garden, now open to the public but difficult to find.

Tiger Hill (Hushan) is said to be the burial place of He Lu, the king of Wu who died in the sixth century B.C. The seven-storey brick pagoda built in 961 A.D., called the Tiger Pagoda, is all that remains of the original Yunyuan temple; the present buildings date from after the Taiping rebellion. The pagoda, which has a definite slant to the south-east and cannot be climbed, stands on top of a hill 36 m high. On this hill are several rock formations of interest: the Thousand Stone Men, said to be the petrified remains of the retinue of King He Lu, sacrificed during the funeral; the Stone Where the Swords are Tried, a rock with a long crack said to have been made by He Lu's sword, and to the left the Stone Pillow, said to have been used by the monk Shen Gong. On the eastern slope is the Tomb of the Good Wife, a virtuous lady who committed suicide when she was sold as a concubine after the death of her husband.

Near Suzhou, on the hills rising on the eastern shore of the Great Lake, are several places of interest, including the ruins of the Palace of the Wu kings on Divine Cliff Hill (Lingyan) and the Zijinsi (Purple Gold Temple) on Dongting Hill, which contains eighteen statues of Lohans in painted clay.

2 Shanghai and its Environs

Shanghai (Above the Sea), with Beijing and Tianjin one of the three municipalities directly under the central government, is situated halfway down the coast, south of the Yangzi River delta and on the border between Jiangsu and Zhejiang provinces. It is the largest city in China and one of the largest metropolises in the world, with a population of over 10 million, 5.4 million of whom live in the 54-square-mile urban area. It is also the largest industrial centre in the country, with metallurgy, mechanical engineering, electronics and chemical manufacturing, shipyards, paper mills and printing presses, refineries, textile factories and light industry.

Two rivers run through the city: the Huangpu or Yellow River (distinct from the Huanghe, Yellow River, the major river which waters the North China plain) and the Wusong River, also known as Suzhou Creek. Shanghai harbour, which extends more than 60 km along the Huangpu, is the largest port in China, handling half its export trade and navigable all the year round by ocean-going ships of 10,000 tons and over.

The left bank of the Huangpu in the city centre is a promenade which used to be called the Bund. It is very popular with those who enjoy watching the colourful river traffic or who like to practice *taiji* (shadow-boxing) in the early hours of the morning. The Bund is also the place for young men to show off their turtle-neck sweaters, 1950s air force leather jackets or army greatcoats. and young women their curly hairdos and tight miniskirts. They walk along holding plastic carrier bags from shops in Hong Kong or Singapore, or meet at the Donghai restaurant in Nanjing Road for coffee, ice cream and pastries. Everyone will agree — the Shanghainese them-selves first of all — that the people of Shanghai belong to the twentieth century, even if the rest of the country does not. They belong too in their bustling metropolis and retain a particular kind of self-confidence and a businesslike attitude which distinguishes them from their compatriots, even when they are transplanted to another part of the country.

The streets of Shanghai, with their overwhelming preponderance of early-twentieth-century European-style buildings, without a doubt feel like home to us foreigners. The gigantic façades of the former foreign banks and trading houses, blackened by pollution and with their window frames unpainted for thirty years, overlook the busy and muddy Huangpu which carries its fetid smell to every street during the hot and sticky summer. The crowds are thick in Nanjing Road, the busiest shopping street in Shanghai (east-west streets are named after cities and north-south ones after provinces), and eager to purchase the latest fashions in the many department stores or just to look at the window displays, still rarely seen in Chinese cities. Even advertising billboards — taken down in the 1950s or sometimes replaced by political slogans — are coming back.

The resident foreign community in Shanghai is small — a few dozen persons including students — but the city has an increasingly large transient population of foreign businessmen and tourists.

Even though it has little traditional Chinese architecture, you must not miss a visit to Shanghai, which you can conveniently use as a base for short trips to Suzhou and Wuxi. The best seasons for visiting Shanghai are the spring and autumn. Winters are grey and can be cold, and summer is very wet and hot.

PRACTICAL INFORMATION

Hotels. Shanghai hotels alone are worth a visit to the city. You will get the best service and comfort (old-fashioned) in the whole of China. Unlike their colleagues in the Beijing Hotel, the hotel staff in Shanghai have some idea of what service is all about and are proud of running these palaces of former times.

Jinjiang Hotel (a), formerly the Cathay Hotel (tel. 53 4242), comes top of the list but is usually reserved for official delegations. It is situated near the former French Park, rebaptized Fuxing Park, in Maoming Road South, at the intersection with Shandong Road. It has polished parquet floors, and glass-leaded windows, and is centrally air-conditioned. The dining room on the eleventh floor serves excellent meals, both Chinese and Western-style. It has a Telex service and a 'coffee shop' which also serves wine and spirits. In a new building at the end of the courtyard the 1972 Shanghai communique was signed by Zhou Enlai and President Nixon.

Peace Hotel (b), formerly the Palace Hotel (tel. 21 1244), is on the Bund, near the beginning of Nanjing Road. Its main entrance on the Bund is no longer in use and the lobby has the air of an abandoned opera house, but the rooms are spacious (with a day bed in an alcove). The dining room, on the eighth floor overlooking the harbour, is decorated with gold dragon motifs on a red background and serves excellent food. This is the hotel most often selected by CTS for tourists and businessmen.

Shanghai Mansions (c) (tel. 24 6260), north of Suzhou Creek and dominating the confluence of the Huangpu and the harbour, were formerly the Broadway Mansions and you can see the former Astor House Hotel across the road. The décor is not as glamorous as in the Peace and Jinjiang. The service is excellent and the rooms spacious, but there is no escape from the sirens in the harbour which go on all night.

International Hotel (d), formerly the Park Hotel (tel. 56 3040), is at 170

Nanjing Road West, overlooking the Renmin (People's) Park. The restaurant is on the twelfth floor and serves good food, both Chinese and Western.

Overseas Chinese Hotel (**e**) (tel. 53 6444) is at 104 Nanjing Road West, next to the International Hotel, and receives Chinese tourists from abroad, as its name suggests.

Hengshan Guesthouse (**f**) (tel. 37 7050) is in Hengshan Road, in the south-west of town, far from everywhere. It is a second-class hotel which receives foreign tourists when the other hotels are full.

Shopping. Browsing and shopping will be two of your main occupations while staying in Shanghai. Most shops are situated in Nanjing Road, where you can find almost anything from paper cut-outs to TV sets. The old Nanjing Road Universal Shops (Sun, Sincere and Wingon Department Stores) are just south of the new No. 1 Department Store (**g**), at 800 Nanjing Road, near the People's Park. The Friendship Store (**h**), 33 Zhongshan Road East (at the northern end of the Bund), has been enlarged and is one of the largest in the country. It has a curios and antiques department. There is a foreign language bookshop in Fuzhou Road, and an antique shop at 694 Nanjing Road. The old shopping district is near the Yu Garden (**1**).

Restaurants. Shanghai serves the best European food in the whole of China and it can be tasted in the dining rooms of the Peace, Jinjiang and International Hotels, and of Shanghai Mansions. In addition, the International Club, the former Country Club, at 63 Yan'an Road, has a small restaurant, as well as tennis courts and a swimming pool.

The *Hongfangzi*, or Red House, at 37 Shanxi Road South (tel. 56 5748, 56 5220), is run by a cook trained in the art of French cuisine when the restaurant was called Chez Louis. It serves Sole Meunière, Crêpes Suzette, and Soufflé au Grand Marnier.

The *Donghai*, 143 Nanjing Road (tel. 53 5202), is a favourite rendezvous for the *jeunesse dorèe* of Shanghai. It serves pastries, sundaes and coffee on the ground floor, and Western food upstairs.

The *Xinya Restaurant*, also known as the Canton Restaurant, in Nanjing Road East (tel. 28 1393), is famous for its cuisine from Guangzhou province.

The *Yangzhou Restaurant*, in Nanjing Road East (tel. 22 2779), serves the regional cuisine, and so does the *Luyangcun*, 763 Nanjing Road East (tel. 53 7221), near the No. 1 Department Store. Shanghai cuisine has two characteristics: abundance of seafood and refined presentation.

HISTORY

Shanghai already existed in the Song dynasty (960-1280) but was part of the county of Songjiang, some 40 km to the south-west. By the seventeenth century, Songjiang had become the major centre for weaving and trading cotton which was produced in Shanxi, Shaanxi and Hebei provinces. In 1553, the town of Shanghai had to build walls pierced with nine gates and dig a moat to keep the Japanese pirates at bay. Its harbour was developed in the Kang Xi era (1662-1723) and it became a county town during the Jia Qing era (1696-1821), with a population of about 50,000.

In 1839, the British, barred from trading in Canton after their refusal to surrender sailors to Chinese justice, established a base in Hong Kong, and the next year seized Zhushan Island, south of Shanghai and facing Ningbo. The ensuing Opium War ended in 1842 with the signing of the treaty of Nanjing, opening five ports to trade: Guangzhou (Canton), Amoy, Fuzhou, Ningbo and Shanghai. Hong Kong was ceded to the British crown.

The foreigners maintained neutrality during most of the Taiping era, but in 1853, when the Taiping took Nanjing, 1½ million refugees swamped the new concessions in Shanghai; about 100,000 of them stayed. Meanwhile the city had its own internal troubles: members of the Dagger Society, entrenched in the old city, raided the foreign settlements until they were beaten in 1854 by the combined foreign forces including British gunboat crews, at the Battle of the Mudflats, a swamp west of the British concession. In 1862 the foreigners joined with the imperial armies to wipe out the Taiping.

The treaty ports not only provided a base for trading, their extra-territoriality enabled foreigners to live outside the Chinese law and avoid Chinese taxation. The former British concession, which in 1863 became the International concession, had a population of about 2,000 British and Americans, and adventurers of all nationalities soon gathered in the other foreign concessions. With the expansion of foreign trade, the old and complicated Chinese customs system became obsolete and a new Maritime Customs Service was created, with its head office at Shanghai, in the 1860s, with a foreigner as its Inspector General.

Chinese capitalism began in the late nineteenth century; a cotton mill was opened in Shanghai in 1878 to fight back foreign imports. In 1868, the first Chinese steamship had been built in Shanghai at the Jiangnan Arsenal, which in a few decades became the largest in China and one of the major ones in the world, producing not only ammunition but also tools and machinery.

After 1900, when the Boxer Rebellion inflicted losses on the lives and property of a foreign population by then numbering about 350,000 in the whole of China, the foreign concessions in Shanghai became a centre of anti-Manchu reaction. Schools and colleges in the city bred a number of revolutionaries who were going to catch the foreigners at their own game, demanding justice and national integrity. The Chinese Communist Party was founded in Shanghai in 1921 and held its first congress there. When Chiang Kaishek took over the KMT in 1925, after the death of Sun Yatsen, he began a drive against the Communists, starting with the Shanghai massacre in April 1927. The 1920s also saw the beginnings of foreign withdrawal from Shanghai; in 1927 the Shanghai Mixed Court, which had been created in 1911, was replaced by a Chinese court.

Shanghai was occupied by the Japanese from 1937 until their defeat in 1945. In May 1949, the Red Army took Shanghai and the new government undertook a clean-up of the city which after eighty years of foreign domination and twenty years of war and civil war had become the capital of vice and crime.

CENTRAL SHANGHAI

People who revisit Shanghai after a gap of thirty years or more will

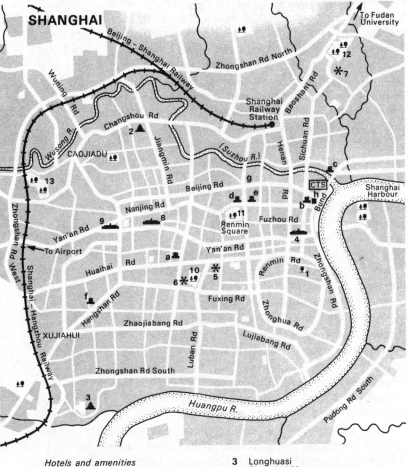

Hotels and amenities
a Jinjiang Hotel
b Peace Hotel
c Shanghai Mansions
d International Hotel
e Overseas Chinese Hotel
f Hengshan Guesthouse
g No.1 Department Store
h Friendship Store

Places of interest
1 Yuyuan
2 Yufosi

3 Longhuasi
4 Shanghai Museum
5 Site of First National Congress
   of the CCP
6 House of Sun Yatsen
7 House of Lu Xun
8 Shanghai Industrial Exhibition
9 Children's Palace
10 Fuxing Park
11 Renmin Park
12 Hongkou Park
13 Zhongshan Park

be struck by how little it has changed. Indeed, though some new dormitory towns have mushroomed on the outskirts since 1949, downtown Shanghai has very few new buildings. Even the brass plumbing and red carpets of the former Palace Hotel (now the Peace Hotel) are the original ones. The former head offices of banks and trading houses have been taken over by various administrative departments of the municipality, which for lack of funds have not been able to remodel or even repaint the buildings, and are merely functioning in a wilderness of makeshift partitions and closed-off doors and windows. The glamour has vanished but sometimes you can recapture a glimpse of it, for instance when you walk in the garden of the former British Consulate, now the Seamen's Club and Friendship Store, and you notice that the sweeping lawn and mixed border are still kept with loving care and pride by an old gardener and his young helpers.

If you want to discover the fabulous metropolis of the early part of this century, explore the city on foot and by taxi. A tour of Shanghai should include the Nanjing Road, the main shopping street; a walk on the Bund and its southern extension, formerly called the Quai de France, as it ran through the French concession, created in 1847; a visit to Renmin Park, which was once a race course, and to the two former entertainment centres, the New World, in Nanjing Road north-east of the park, and the Great World, in Yan'an Road (once the Avenue Edward VII) south-east of the park.

Do not miss seeing the old walled city which was once such a labyrinth that foreigners were advised not to enter it without a guide. The walls were taken down in the 1920s and streets built over them: Renmin Road to the north and Zhonghua Road to the south.

Gardens and temples.   Yuyuan, the Yu Garden (1), is perhaps the most visited place in the old Chinese city. It is situated in the north-east of the former walled city, at the intersection of Fuyu and Anren streets. Built in the mid-sixteenth century by a high-ranking official from Sichuan, Pan Yuntuan, in honour of his old father, Pan En, it originally covered twelve acres. The famous landscape artist of the late Ming, Zhang Nanyang, contributed to its design. The fortunes of the Pan family declined and the garden changed hands several times until it was acquired in 1760 by Shanghai merchants, who restored it on a smaller scale and added the West Garden.

In the mid-nineteenth century the garden served as headquarters for the Dagger Society, and later, in 1860-2, the combined Manchu and foreign forces which drove the Taiping out of the Shanghai area were quartered there. The site was left half-ruined at the end of the fighting. The Guilds of Shanghai bought it and restored it about a hundred years ago, but in the early twentieth century, the south-western part was used as a market and a school occupied the central buildings. At last, a major restoration took place in 1956.

The garden is divided into three parts separated by dragon-spined walls, built of whitewashed masonry and their undulating top covered with tiles simulating the scales of a dragon. The Huxinting, or Pavilion in the Heart of the Lake (in Shanghai dialect Wuxingting, which has been mistranslated as Five-Star Pavilion), is linked to the shore by the Nine Zig-Zag Bridge. It was once part of the Yu Garden but is now in a separate enclosure. For many years, it was a famous teahouse called the Willow Pattern, and an outline of the Huxinting is the central motif of the well-known blue-and-white Willow Pattern underglaze porcelain, which is still made today and was for a time a symbol of Shanghai.

The Yu Garden contains about thirty halls built in fine Southern style of the Ming period. The large Hall for Heralding the Spring, in the north-east, was the headquarters of the Dagger Society from 1853 and contains a small museum where daggers, coins and a map of the uprising are displayed. Just north of it is the very old (sixteenth century) Hall of the Three Ears of Corn, a name which expresses a wish for good harvests.

The Chenghuangmiao (Temple of the Town Gods) is just north of the Yu Garden, built in front of a garden known as the Houyuan (Back Garden). The temple is not easy to visit but the small garden, in traditional Suzhou style, is open to the public.

The Temple of the Jade Buddha (Yufosi) (2) in the north-west of Shanghai, near the intersection of Changshou and Jiangning Roads, is still in use and has about ten resident monks. Its bright saffron walls can easily be spotted from the street. In the third hall are two white 'jade' (actually alabaster) statues of Buddha, one seated and a smaller one, reclining, brought from Burma by a monk in 1881.

The Longhua temple (Longhuasi) (3), at the south-west corner of Shanghai, is situated in a park planted with peach trees which bloom in April. The temple was originally founded in 345 A.D.. during the period of the Three Kingdoms, but a fire destroyed it entirely in 880. It was reconstructed in 977 and a pagoda built to the north of the compound which is still standing today — the only pagoda in the area, 40.4 m high, built of brick with a roof and a balcony on each of its seven storeys. The temple was enlarged, in 1147, under Emperor Gao Zong of the Song dynasty. The buildings, with their saffron walls, red-lacquered pillars and sharply upturned roof-ends, although greatly restored, are a fine example of Southern architecture of the Song dynasty. There are the traditional four halls: the Hall of the Four Celestial Kings has a statue of Maitreya Buddha 9 m high; the Hall of the Great Hero, with a triple roof and richly decorated coffered ceiling, has a large statue of Sakyamuni and eighteen Lohans. The temple is in very good condition, and the pagoda which is leaning has been reinforced and refurbished with care, down to the bronze bells hanging from the angles of its roofs.

The Shanghai Museum (4), at the corner of Yan'an and Henan Roads, occupies a building which was once a bank. Although the collection has for the most part been built up since 1949, it is one of the richest in the country, particularly outstanding for its bronzes and paintings. Every autumn, the Shanghai Museum puts together a special exhibition of ancient paintings, rotating the exhibits from one year to the next with the Palace Museum in Beijing.

Revolutionary and post-1949 sites. The first National Congress of the Chinese Communist Party was held in July 1921 in a two-storey house (5) at 76 Xingye Road, near Huaihai Road, east of the Jinjiang Hotel. The original building, damaged during the Shanghai massacre of 1927 and again during the Japanese occupation, has been rebuilt since liberation (1949). Twelve founding members of the Party attended, including Mao Zedong and Dong Biwu who died in 1975. The meeting was interrupted by the concession police and continued in Jiaxing, 60 km south-west of Shanghai, on the South Lake (where the beautifully panelled pleasure boat they used is still anchored on the shore, and can be visited).

Sun Yatsen's house (6) is also in Shanghai, in the former French concession, near Fuxing Park (10). The house, where he lived intermittently after his return from exile in 1911, has been turned into a museum.

You can also visit, in a north-eastern suburb of the city, the house and tomb of Lu Xun (1881-1936; real name, Zhou Shuren), a writer of great courage and talent who was born in Zhejiang province. His stories, including the remarkable 'Diary of a Madman', have been translated into English and other Western languages. A Communist sympathizer, Lu Xun never became a party member. His tomb and memorial statue are in Hongkou Park (12), north of the railway station. His house (7), not far south of the park, has been turned into a museum.

The Shanghai Industrial Exhibition (8), in Yan'an Road West, is the former Sino-Soviet Friendship Palace, and not unexpectedly built in Soviet Russian style. It houses a permanent exhibition of industrial products, mostly manufactured in the Shanghai area.

Several mansions formerly owned by Shanghai's business tycoons have been turned into Children's Palaces, offering tutoring in extra-curricular activities to children aged between seven and seventeen. The one (9) most often visited by foreign tourists is west of the Industrial Exhibition Hall in Yan'an Road. If you think you can stand being taken round by the hand and called *shushu* (uncle) and *ayi* (auntie) while listening to young children 'singing' in falsetto voices with all their strength, or seeing very nimble young acrobats, or young artists being taught to draw in depressing socialist academic style, by all means let your CTS guide take you there. My two daughters were very impressed by the children's performances and so pleased to be called *meimei* (little sister.)

Fudan University, formerly the Catholic Aurora University, was founded in 1905 and ranks with Beijing and Xinhua Universities in Beijing as among the most prestigious in the country. It has nearly 5,000 students and a teaching staff of over 2,000. Its campus, built in the early 1950s, is in Handan Road in the northern suburbs. In spite of its poorly maintained buildings and crowded conditions — a plight shared by all Chinese universities — it offers a high level of education in the sciences (two-thirds of the enrollment), humanities and the arts.

The harbour and shipyards. A two-hour tour of Shanghai harbour can be arranged by China Travel Service or your host organization and, if you can afford the time, I highly recommend it. Traffic on the muddy Huangpu and Suzhou rivers appears as congested and chaotic as it is in downtown Shanghai streets and your guide's voice will be drowned in a cacophony of horns and sirens. Slow junks with patched brown sails and frail sampans criss-cross the paths of unyielding tugboats and crowded ferries, while often rusty ocean liners are being loaded and unloaded. You will also see the Shanghai Shipyard, formerly known as the Machine Shipbuilding Plant, capable of producing 10,000-ton ocean-going vessels. Repairs and building of smaller ships occupy the greater part of its shipyards which have been greatly expanded since the early 1950s and are the most important in the country.

A wide variety of other industries can be visited in the Shanghai municipality, including the Shanghai No. 1 Machine Tool Plant, which manufactures precision grinding equipment and employs 6,000 workers. It earned the status of model factory in 1968, after it created the 21 July Workers' College, which educates within the factory student-workers from its own ranks as well as from other factories.

Visitors with a sweet tooth may enjoy a visit to a chocolate factory, in the northern quarter of Shanghai, where they will be invited to sample the products at each stage of processing. Clad in white coats, hats, masks and rubber boots, visitors are taken to various departments, including, at the end of the tour, the sterile room where ice cream is packed — long after the white garments have ceased to be sterile. In addition to ice cream, chocolate wafers and sweets, the factory processes other foodstuffs such as meat, vegetables and fish.

ENVIRONS OF SHANGHAI

If you are going to be in Shanghai for a few weeks, and are interested in ancient architecture, you might like to explore the outlying counties under the municipality.

JIADING county, 20 km north-west of Shanghai, in the Song dynasty was by the sea but is now inland. In 1217, during the Southern Song dynasty, a temple of Confucius was built there, on the north shore of the Wusong River (Suzhou Creek). About two-thirds of the original buildings remain, enclosed behind a saffron wall and approached through a triple archway guarded by two stone lions.

In QINGPU county, about 25 km west of Shanghai, south of the Wusong River, there is a Tang dynasty temple, the Longfusi, built between 821 and 824. Its pagoda and the temple were destroyed by fire and rebuilt in 1041-8. Today the temple is much smaller than it once was, and the seven-storey octagonal brick pagoda, pierced by two windows on each floor, though still standing, is in great need of repair.

SONGJIANG county, 20 km south-west of Shanghai, a centre for the trade and manufacture of cotton in the seventeenth century, has a few remains of its prosperous past. A very unusual old stele, 9.3 m high, octagonal, and crowned with a lotus throne with the celestial guardians carved round the base, was erected in the Tang dynasty (859) and carved with the Dharani sutra. In the former Xingsheng-jiao temple (1008-16), west of the Gushiqiao (Grain Market Bridge), is a square pagoda, 48.5 m high, built of red brick with wooden balconies and roofs on each of its nine storeys.

3 Zhejiang and Jiangxi

Zhejiang, a coastal province south of Shanghai, Jiangxi, a largely mountainous area inland and to the south of it, and Fujian, also on the coast (facing Taiwan, and not at present open to tourists), form a geographical unit of southern China, with several important cities and some spectacular scenery.

HANGZHOU (Hangchow) 杭州

Hangzhou (Country across the Stream), the capital of Zhejiang province, is situated inland from the Qiantang River estuary, at the

HANGZHOU

9 Tiyuchang

To Airport

Rd

Zhongshan Bei

Jianguo Bei

Shanghai-Hangzhou Railway

8

7

Qingchun

Rd

Jianguo Zhong

Bai Causeway

a

2

3 4

Jiefang Rd

Zhongshan Zhong

b

To the Lingyinsi

West Lake

Su Causeway

Railway Station

Hang-Hu Highway

5

Qinjian Rd

1

To the Dragon Well

6

Hangzhou-Nanchang Railway

Hang-Fu Highway

To Qiantang River and Bridge and to Liuheta

Hotels and amenities
a Hangzhou Hotel
b City Department Store

Places of interest
1 Wushan
2 Gushan

3 Zhongshan Park
4 Provincial Museum
5 Three Pools Mirroring the Moon
6 Huagang Park
7 Baochu Pagoda
8 Yellow Dragon Spring
9 Provincial Exhibition Hall

southern extremity of the Grand Canal. The West Lake — to the west of the city — used to connect with the estuary, but the natural build-up of silt over the centuries and the construction of causeways combined to cut it off. The city itself is built on reclaimed land, with green hills covered with luxuriant forests rising in a crescent to the west and south-west of the lake. Rice and vegetables are grown in the low-lying irrigated areas, and there are tea plantations and mulberry farms on the lower slopes of the hills. Silk brocade weaving is one of the major industrial activities in the area. Hangzhou has a population of nearly one million.

Whereas Suzhou is a beautiful town in an indifferent setting, Hangzhou — like Wuxi — is an indifferent city in a sumptuous setting. If you arrive there after several days of touring the north of the country, you will be delighted and overwhelmed by so much greenery. Hangzhou is perhaps at its best in the spring when the magnolias, camellias and azaleas (both wild and in gardens) burst into bloom. The summer, even in this setting, is really too hot and humid.

Hangzhou is much enjoyed by the Shanghainese as a resort town, and a favourite honeymoon spot — hence the large number of young couples you will surely notice. It is about 200 km south-west of Shanghai, a journey of approximately four hours on the Shanghai-Guangzhou railway line. There are flights from Beijing, Shanghai and Guangzhou. Two days are enough for visiting the scenic and ancient sites of Hangzhou.

Most foreigners stay at the *Hangzhou Hotel* (a) (tel. 22 921), a large Kuomintang-style building, not without grace, on the shore of West Lake. The bedrooms are large and the corridors endless. The dining room overlooks the lake and the food is fairly good. The staff was as unhelpful when I revisited Hangzhou in 1977 as during my stay in 1969. The comfortable *Xihu Hotel* is also open to foreigners.

Hangzhou is a good place for dining out. The *Louwailou Restaurant,* on the south shore of Gushan island, near the entrance to Zhongshan Park and the departure dock for tours of the lake, is a charming old building where you can enjoy delicious Zhejiang cuisine, featuring fish from the lake and fresh-water shrimp. Another very good restaurant, the *Tianwaitian,* is situated west of the city, near the entrance to the Lingyin Temple.

Hangzhou is also quite a good place for shopping. Local handicrafts include basketware, fans, chopsticks, parasols, brocade and other silks, embroidery and green tea. There is a good antique shop, the Hangzhou Painting and Calligraphy Company, in Hubin Road not far from the City Department Store (b), which specializes in paintings and ancient inkstones.

History. Hangzhou and the area around it were settled at the beginning of the Qin dynasty, 2,100 years ago, but it grew into an important city only during the Sui dynasty when the Grand Canal linking Chang'an (Xi'an) with the rich Southern provinces was dug (605-10). Hangzhou was already the 'home of silk and satin' in the seventh century. As the city developed, the need to protect it from the damaging equinoctial tides in the Qiantang River grew, and sea walls were built — first of mud, then later of stone and a primitive form of cement — upstream from Hangzhou, as well as dykes (now causeways) in the West Lake. In 824, Bai Juyi (Bo Juyi), one of the greatest Chinese poets, was appointed governor of Hangzhou and continued the building of dykes, one of which, leading from Gushan to the north shore, is named after him. A century and a half later, another great poet, Su Dongpo, was governor of Hangzhou, and he too built a causeway which bears his name, protecting the west shore.

When Kaifeng was invaded and looted by the Jin in 1126, the emperor and the heir apparent were taken prisoner, but a younger son of Emperor Hui Zong took refuge first in Nanjing and then, in 1135, established his capital in Hangzhou, where it remained for the latter part of the Song dynasty, known as the Southern Song. The population of Hangzhou suddenly swelled to about one million and, to accommodate the influx, multi-storeyed houses were built, a departure from the traditional 'bungalows' of north China. An imperial palace was built to the south of the city, at the foot of Wushan, and the presence of the court attracted entertainers of all kinds as well as many poets and painters. One of the most important schools of painting in the country was founded there. Hangzhou under the Southern Song was a fabulous city, and the gardens of the imperial palace were decorated with silk flowers in the winter. During the Mongol invasion the palace was destroyed, but when Marco Polo visited Hangzhou, it was still one of the most beautiful and lively cities in the empire. With houses built mostly of wood, fires were frequent in the crowded streets, and when in the mid-nineteenth century the Taiping invaded Hangzhou, they set it alight and destroyed it entirely. It suffered a second time during the Japanese invasion and this explains why today next to nothing is left of the twelfth-century capital, save a few temples in the hills.

Places of interest. The city itself, on the eastern shore of the lake, is not particularly attractive. Hangzhou suffered great disruptions in 1976 and the town has a general air of neglect. A small mountain rises to the south, Wushan (**1**), which is reputed to have twelve peaks. The cobbled road to the top goes through a picturesque quarter and emerges near a group of pavilions which serve as a teahouse.

In the city centre, you can visit the Hangzhou silk and brocade mill, which specializes in the production of brocade, quilt covers, silk pictures and silk fabrics. From a small factory with 17 hand looms in the early 1950s, it has grown into a large plant with 300 automatic looms and employing 1,700 people. Much of the production caters for Chinese taste, but silk fabrics are increasingly designed for export. Like most large Chinese factories, it runs a clinic, a crêche, dormitories, and a school.

West Lake is divided into a large central and two smaller sections to the north and west, separated by the Bai and Su dykes respectively. There are four islands in the lake, the largest, to the north, called Gushan, or Solitary Hill (**2**), is linked to the shore by a bridge and you can explore it easily on foot from the Hangzhou Hotel.

The first group of buildings at the western end of the island is the Xiling Seal Engravers' Society, founded in the early twentieth century by a group of scholars. Like calligraphy, seal engraving is inseparable from the art of painting; many scholars were not only poets, but also calligraphers, painters and often engravers of seals. The Society's buildings include a small stone pagoda of the Song dynasty and a small stone house, said to date from the Han dynasty, containing an exhibition of stone drums and a very valuable stele, bought back from a Japanese collector by a member of the Society. The former headquarters of the Society contains an exhibition of prints from old seals and modern ones in different styles. Old and new seals can be bought in the Chop Shop at the bottom of the hill.

The next building along the shore is the provincial library, then come the Zhongshan Park (**3**), on the site of the garden of Emperor Qian Long's palace, and next to it the Provincial Museum (**4**) which occupies what is left of the Wenlange, a library created by Qian Long which used to have a set of the Complete Library of the Four Treasuries (see p. 80) and which was destroyed during the Taiping rebellion. Past the museum, the shore is adorned with several pavilions, the oldest and best known being the Autumn Moon on the Calm Lake, built in 1699 during the reign of Kang Xi.

Tours of the lake leave from a dock outside the Zhongshan Park. The flat-bottomed boats used to be poled by women, and although the poles have been replaced by motors, women still operate the boats. A tour of the lake usually includes a look at the Mid-Lake Pavilion, made from silt dredged out of the lake in recent years, and a visit to the famous Three Pools Mirroring the Moon (**5**) and the lake within the lake. In the water are three small stone stupas, each about 1.2 m high, with little windows at the top in which candles were placed during the Moon Festival. The island has four inner ponds and is pleasantly landscaped, but after the peacefulness of the boat ride, fighting one's way along the tortuous and crowded paths to feed enormous golden carp is something of an anticlimax. The tour continues by boat to the Huagang Park (**6**), more spacious than the island but equally crowded and of no great interest.

North of the lake rises the Baochu Hill (Hill of the Precious Beginning), on whose southern slope is the Baochu Pagoda (**7**), on the site of a tenth-century temple of the Great Buddha. The present brick structure, not of great interest, is a recent reconstruction (1933), standing on a terrace at the top of many steps from which there is a good view of the lake towards the south. Near by is the

Yellow Dragon Spring (8) and above it on the hill an old Taoist monastery with a small garden in which grows a variety of square bamboo.

South of the lake, the Liuheta (Pagoda of the Six Harmonies) dominates the Qiantang River, upstream from a modern bridge. It is a large octagonal pagoda with thirteen storeys, and pierced by three windows on each of the eight faces, on each floor, and can be climbed to the top. Built in 970 during the Song dynasty to protect the city from the dangerous tides at the spring and autumn equinox, its core is of brick and the outer structure of wood; the thirteen roofs outside correspond to only seven levels inside.

Every year after the Mid-Autumn Festival, between 15 and 21 September, people gather along the Qiantang estuary to watch these equinoctial tides, even more spectacular here than the *mascaret* in the estuary of the Seine River in France. A single gigantic wave rides up the estuary growing in height and force as it is compressed between the narrowing shores of the estuary. This first wave, having hit the sea wall, turns back and collides with successive incoming waves, sending up columns of water several metres high (record height, 8.6 m). These tidal waves constantly change the outline of Hangzhou bay and, when combined with typhoons, can cause extensive damage.

A little way east of the Pagoda of the Six Harmonies, at the top of a steep path, are the Tiger Spring and the Hubaosi (Temple of the Running Tiger). The spring itself rises inside a cave where a gaudy plaster tiger welcomes the visitors. The water has strange properties: it can support aluminium coins because of its high surface tension. The spring takes its name from the legend of a monk who came to this place in the ninth century and like the peaceful prospect so much that he decided to build a hermitage there. But he could find no water. In the night he dreamed he saw two tigers clawing the ground until they found water, and the next morning he found a spring. The Hubaosi is still there: its charming courtyards have been turned into a teahouse and a sort of summer camp for young pioneers. You can try a cup of Longjing tea brewed with Tiger Spring water.

West of the lake is a very attractive area, with several places of interest.

The Lingyinsi (Temple of the Divine Mystery) was founded in the fourth century by an Indian monk, was destroyed and rebuilt during the Sui dynasty (596), and took its present name during the Tang dynasty. It suffered major destruction during the Taiping rebellion and was not restored until the beginning of this century, so that most of the building of this very ancient temple are fairly recent.

During the Cultural Revolution the two main halls were bricked up to prevent depredation by the Red Guards, and have only recently (1977) been refurbished.

The first hall contains a statue of Maitreya Buddha in gilded camphor wood with a gilded Wei Tuo guarding the rear. The four Celestial Kings, so recently repainted, flash their bright colours at the visitors. Traditional guardians of the sacred Mount Sumeru, they each stand on the body of a monster. The Guardian of the East has a white face and carries a jade ring, a spear and also a magic sword called Blue Cloud with the four characters for earth, air, fire and water marked on its blade. The Guardian of the West, also known as the Far Gazer, has a blue face and carries a four-stringed guitar (*pipa*), the Guardian of the South a red face and an umbrella. The Guardian of the North has a black face, two whips and a panther-skin bag in which lives a mysterious demon-eating creature sometimes represented as a dragon, a white-winged elephant or a rat.

The second hall, a tall building topped with a three-tiered roof, contains the statue of a giant Buddha (20 m high) and behind a screen, the statue of Guanyin (Kuanyin). This hall dates from the late Qing dynasty; the statues were damaged when a main beam caved in and fell on them in the 1930s.

Two very old *chung* (stone pillars) carved during the Wuyue kingdom in 969 stand near the gate, engraved with the Dharni sutra and small figures. Two steles embedded in the temple wall commemorate the visit of Emperors Kang Xi and Qian Long.

Near the temple is the Feilaifeng (The Peak which Came A-flying), a rock so named by the Indian monk who founded the Lingyinsi because he thought it resembled the sacred Mount Grdhrakuta in India. Behind the rock is a sixteenth-century stupa and two figures of Celestial Guardians carved in the Yuan dynasty. The cliff which runs alongside a small torrent is also carved with Buddhist images, 280 no less, though compared with those in the Wei dynasty cave temples in Henan and Shanxi, they seem rather inferior. They were carved from the tenth to the fourteenth century, many of them during the Yuan dynasty.

You must be prepared to get your feet wet in the torrent if you want to examine them closely. There are three caves, the first containing statues of the Indian monks who introduced Buddhism to China and of the monk Xuan Zang who went to India in the Tang dynasty to collect the sutras and bring them to China. Inscriptions engraved on the walls by visitors include one by the poet Su Dongpo. The next cave, often called Yixiantian (A Thread of Sky) because of a crack in its ceiling, is decorated with small carvings of Lohans and Bodhisattvas carved in the Five Dynasties and the Song. The hills above the cliff are covered in wild azaleas which people pick in the spring and sometimes give as offerings to the stone buddhas.

The Longjing (Dragon Well), in the hills south-west of West Lake, gave its name to one of the finest green teas in China. The road to the top of the hills starts near the Huaguang Park and you can visit a plantation on the way, at the Shangwang brigade. It is very interesting to observe the picking and drying of tea. The well itself is carved under a rock which is supposed to have the shape of a dragon; at any rate, the dragon is the genie protector of underground water. An old temple which used to stand near the Dragon Well has been turned into a teahouse where you can also buy some Longjing tea.

The road down is very bumpy but so attractive, and to me, the best part of a visit to Hangzhou. It is cut by nine creeks and eighteen brooks and winds through a luxuriant forest where you may be lucky enough to meet a few men carrying old shotguns, and some brightly coloured birds. It is an ideal place for a walk and a picnic, if you can persuade your guide. At the Nine Creek hamlet you see people washing their clothes or a freshly caught fish in the stream, while others simply sip their tea outside the teahouse. Eventually, the road emerges from the hills in sight of the Qiantang River.

There are other places of interest in the Hangzhou area, not at present shown to the public but worth enquiring about if you have the time: the tomb of General Yue Fei of the Southern Song dynasty, in the hills above the Hangzhou Hotel; the Temple of the Big Buddha at the foot of the Baochu Pagoda; the Taoguang Nunnery, above the Lingyingsi to the west; and the ruins of three little Indian temples to the east.

From Hangzhou, you can make an excursion 60 km to the north, to MOGANSHAN (27) (Mogan Mountain), named after a famous swordsman of the Spring and Autumn period (770-476 B.C.). Bamboo groves and waterfalls abound, and wealthy Shanghainese had villas built there to escape the summer heat. One beautiful spot is the Cataract of the Pond of Swords, where Mogan and his wife used to make their swords.

SHAOXING (25) 绍兴

Shaoxing (Continued Prosperity), a pretty city off the south coast of the Bay of Hangzhou, is on the Hangzhou-Ningbo railway, and linked to Hangzhou by a canal built during the early Tang dynasty. It lies in a well-watered plain, with the Guiji mountains rising to the south and the foothills of the Longmen mountain range to the west. Like Suzhou and to a lesser extent Wuxi, Shaoxing, with its tight network of canals, can be called a Venice of China.

Shaoxing can be visited in one day, and combined with a visit to Hangzhou and Ningbo, provides an alternative to the tourist 'milk run' of the lower Yangzi region (Hangzhou, Suzhou and Wuxi). The only way to get there is by train from Hangzhou (50 km, 40 minutes' ride).

Always a secondary provincial town, engaged chiefly in trading in rice and silk, Shaoxing nevertheless has several claims to fame. It is the home of Shaoxing wine, deservedly considered the best yellow wine in the country, and famous, according to historical records, as far back as A.D. 502. It is brewed from high-quality glutinous rice and water from the near-by Lake Jian. After a fermentation process, the wine is kept for several years in sealed earthenware jars and then blended with freshly distilled wine. It has a rich and mellow flavour and, like all yellow rice wines, is served warm from a porcelain jug, in porcelain cups which hold little more than a few drams. There are several varieties of Shaoxing wine, ranging from dry to sweet One of the well-known ones is Nu'er Hong, or Crimson Daughter, so called because it should be buried in the ground when a daughter is born and opened when she gets married (red being the colour of a bride's clothes).

Shaoxing also claims to be the place where the mythical emperor of the Xia dynasty (2205-1766 B.C.), Yu the Great, also known as the Jade Emperor, died while on a water-taming tour of the South. His tomb and a temple dedicated to him, both in the foothills of the Guiji mountains, can be visited. The tombstone itself is a rock with a hole at the top which legend says was his boat. The temple was probably founded during the period of the Warring States (476-221), when Shaoxing was the capital of the kingdom of Yue and the cult of Yu the Great became popular.

In the south-west of the town, on the Tashanling Hill, is another old temple, the Yingtiansi, founded under the Song, restored in the Ming dynasty, and burned down during the Taiping rebellion. A pagoda still stands, restored in the late nineteenth century. In addition, Shaoxing has a Southern Song dynasty pagoda, restored in the Yuan dynasty, the Dashan Temple pagoda, right in the centre of town.

Shaoxing was the birthplace of China's greatest modern writer, Lu Xun (see p.162), whose house is still standing; a small museum dedicated to his life and works has been opened in the town. The renowned scholar and calligrapher of the Ming dynasty, Xu Wenzhang (Xu Wei), was also born in Shaoxing, in 1521, and his home, the Green Wine Study, can be visited.

NINGBO (26) 宁波

Ningbo (Gentle Waves), a city of half a million people on the coast of northern Zhejiang province, is at the end of the eastern Zhejiang railway, 150 km southeast of Hangzhou. At the confluence of two rivers and served by a network of canals, it is a major seaport, protected from the sea by a stretch of salt marshes and dykes. It has food processing as well as silk industries.

History. During the late Tang dynasty a system of lakes and canals was devised to offset the effects of the tides, and Ningbo was enabled to grow; by the beginning of the Ming dynasty, it was one of three Superintendencies of merchant shipping, trading mainly with Japan but also with Manchuria, Korea and north China. In 1374, Hong Wu closed the Superintendency, boycotting exports to Japan, in retaliation against Japan's refusal to pay tribute to China; but in 1403 trade with Japan was resumed — as well as raids by Japanese pirates who by the end of the Ming dynasty were plaguing the Chinese coasts. Trade brought foreign contacts: as early as the 1520s the Portuguese had maintained a fort downstream from Ningbo to protect their trade at Zhenhai, the harbour of Ningbo. The British traded at the island of Zhushan, but attempts by the East India Company to maintain trading links with Ningbo itself failed in the face of imperial opposition. When the Opium War broke out in 1841, the British invaded Zhushan, Ningbo and Amoy. The treaty of Nanjing, signed in 1842, opened Ningbo to foreign trade and the British set up their consulate there in 1843, and were followed by missionaries. By 1863, the Customs Service at Shanghai had been extended to Ningbo, which had a resident Customs commissioner. Ningbo escaped the first Taiping invasion, but in 1861 the rebels entered the town. They were driven out the following year by a combination of British and French gunboat crews and a troop of Chinese and foreign mercenaries paid by the merchants.

Ningbo, three hours by train from Hangzhou, can be visited in a day. Places of interest include the Tianfeng pagoda, built in the late fourteenth century, and the Tianyige library. Started in the eleventh century by the Feng family and bought and increased in the sixteenth century by Fan Qin, a retired official, this library was well known and when Qian Long ordered the compilation of the Complete Library of the Four Treasuries (see p. 80) Fan Qin's descendants had to present it to the emperor. It is by now totally dispersed but the original buildings are still standing, south of Zhongshan Road, on the western shore of the lake.

Also in Zhejiang province are two important Buddhist centres: TIANTAISHAN (Mount Tiantai), about 100 km south-west of Ningbo, is the home of a sect founded by the monk Zhi Yi in the sixth century which popularized the Lotus sutra; the small town of Tiantai, at the foot of the mountain, can be visited. PUTUO ISLAND, a mile or so off the coast of Zhejiang, to the north-east of Ningbo, is one of the four sacred mountains of Buddhism; its patron saint is Guanyin (Kuanyin), the goddess of mercy. Its full name,

Putuolajia, derived from the Sanskrit Pataloka, means 'the mountain from the top of which Guanyin contemplates the world'.

The island, at the southern tip of the larger Zhoushan Island, was settled exclusively by monks and nuns; it claims to have three hundred temples. The Pujisi (Temple of Universal Rescue), also known as the Monastery in Front of the Hill, is reached after a climb; in front of it is a lotus pond and pavilions. Its walls are painted orange and its roofs covered with blue or yellow tiles; in the main hall is a large gilded statue of Sakyamuni Buddha. The Fayusi (Temple of the Rain of the Law), also called the Temple behind the Hill, is of palatial proportions. Its Hall of Guanyin, which contains a delicate white marble statue of Guanyin carved in the Ming dynasty, is the finest building on the island. From the Fayusi, several hundred steps carved out of the rock lead to the Summit of Buddha. The Huijisi (Temple of Intelligent Rescue) is at the top of the Truncated Summit (Jueding). Guanyin is said to have jumped into the whirlpool at the bottom of a rock inscribed with the characters *Guanyin Pao*, Guanyin's Leap.

WENZHOU (**23**) is an important port on the southern Zhejiang coast, situated in a sheltered estuary at the mouth of the Ou River. The town is almost entirely industrial, specializing in food processing. About 50 km north of Wenzhou are the NORTH YANDANG mountains (**24**), a popular summer resort with forests, springs and strangely shaped rocks.

JIUJIANG (**21**) 九江

Jiujiang (Nine Rivers), known as the gate to Jiangxi province, is situated on the south bank of the lower Yangzi River, a few miles north-west of the Poyang Lake. It is a very old city, founded during the Han dynasty, which served as a trading centre for tea, bamboo, wine, foodstuff and porcelain produced in the region. The Tang dynasty poet Bo (Bai) Juyi (772-846) held the post of sub-prefect in Jiujiang at the beginning of the ninth century, when the town was known as Xunyang. In a poem called 'The Lute Song'; he tells of his sorrow at being banished to this small place, 'a town without music', where 'not stringed or bamboo instrument is heard / Throughout the years'. During the Song dynasty, the leading neo-Confucian philosopher of the Zhejiang school, Zhu Xi (1130-1200), taught in Jiujiang. In 1862, it was opened as a treaty port and the British built a concession to the west of town, with a resident Customs Superintendent. In 1927, the concession was overrun by angry demonstrators and the British gave it up.

Jiujiang is at the end of the Changsha-Nanchang railway line, about two hours from the provincial capital Nanchang. Most visitors only pass through on their way to Lushan, a short distance to the south. This is a pity, for the town is very attractive, spreading around two lakes, Gantang and Nanmen, separated by a causeway built in 821. In the middle of Lake Gantang is the Yanshui Pavilion which covers the whole of a small island now linked to the shore by a bridge. It is an exquisite succession of halls, pavilions and courtyards with trees and potted plants. Tourists can also visit the Nengren Temple with its ancient brick pagoda, the Dasheng Pagoda, and also the Suojiang Tower. Local specialities include Jiujiang wine, crisp sweetmeats and cakes.

LUSHAN (20) 庐山

A dirt road leads from Jiujang south to the pretty village of Guling at the foot of Lushan (Black Mountain). Situated on the boundary between the temperate and sub-tropical zones, generously watered all the year round and, because of its elevation (highest peak: 1,474 m), cool and pleasant in the summer, Lushan in the late nineteenth century became popular as a summer resort, and a sanatorium was built there for foreigners from Shanghai and Wuhan. It now receives about 10,000 model workers every year as well as patients recovering from lung disease.

Foreigners stay at the Lushan Guesthouse (tel. 2252), built of rough stone with patios and wicker chairs. Local restaurants serve eel, goose, fish and the local wine. A bugle sounds in the early morning and again after the siesta to rouse people from their beds, a custom which is not especially popular with foreign guests.

The town has an Alpine atmosphere, with its colourfully painted villas. Several walks lead to the five peaks and there are beautiful views of the Poyang Lake below. The hills are dotted with pavilions and inscriptions carved in the stone by illustrious visitors, including one by the Ming emperor Hong Wu in memory of a Taoist monk who cured him of an illness. A cave of the Immortals has a statue of Lu Tongping, a scholar who lived around A.D. 750 and was one of the Eight Immortals.

Lushan abounds not only in cedars, pines and bamboo, but in large bright butterflies. The Lushan Botanical Garden, one of the largest in China, is on the Peak of the Nine Strange Things, 1,100 m above sea level, at a place which overlooks the lake. The garden was started in 1834 and most of the original plants came from England. It now has a rare collection of 'relics' or living fossil plants, exchanges specimens with sixty countries of the world, and in particular, sends Chinese plants to Kew Gardens.

The Kuomintang held numerous meetings at Lushan from 1928 to 1938, to which Chiang Kaishek always insisted on being carried in a sedan chair. The resort was the scene of some dramatic political confrontations in the recent past, as when General George C. Marshall met Chiang Kaishek there in 1948-9, after the KMT armies, which had received massive military aid from the Americans, surrendered to the Red Army in Manchuria. At a CCP plenum held at Lushan in 1959, Marshal Peng Dehuai, then Minister of Defence, had the temerity to criticize Mao Zedong's handling of the Great Leap Forward, which had caused economic disruption — the first time Mao's leadership had been questioned since he assumed the leadership of the Party. At another plenum in 1970, it was the turn of Marshal Lin Biao, who by then had replaced Peng in the Defence post, to criticize Mao — this time for the *rapprochement* with the U.S. Today, Peng Dehuai has been rehabilitated (posthumously), but Lin Biao's seat on the podium of the meeting hall has been removed.

JINGDEZHEN (22)　景德镇

Jingdezhen (Market Town of Prospective Virtue), in northeast Jiangxi on the banks of the Chang River, which flows into the Poyang Lake, is the most important centre in China for the manufacture of porcelain. To the north-east of Jingdezhen rises a mountain, Gaoling (High Ridge), made of white clay which became known as kaolin; when fired at 1400° centigrade, this clay becomes vitrified, translucent and very hard. Pottery was made at Jingdezhen as early as the second century B.C. and during the Northern and Southern dynasty period (420-589), when Nanjing was the capital of six successive Southern empires, the kilns produced ceramics for the imperial palace. In the Ming dynasty, the imperial kilns began also to supply wealthy households and even the export market, as 'Chinaware' or porcelain became known and appreciated in Europe. In the eighteenth century, Jingdezhen had about 500 kilns. It is still a major porcelain producer, but the modern designs made there have little aesthetic value; it appears that the creativity and originality of the Chinese ceramists died in the early nineteenth century.

NANCHANG　南昌

Nanchang (Glory of the South), capital of Jiangxi province and an important industrial centre for the region, has a population of about 700,000. It is located in the north of the province, in a plain south of the Poyang Lake and on the Gan River which flows into the lake. It is linked by air to Shanghai, Changsha and Guangzhou and on the Shanghai-Guangzhou railway.

Nanchang is a revolutionary city and since 1949, ten hotels have been built to accommodate visitors on a revolutionary pilgrimage. Foreign visitors stay at the *Jiangxi Hotel*, in the centre of town near the East Lake and Bayi Park.

Nanchang, a very old city, was founded under the Han, and was a trading centre for the porcelain produced in the region. In 1927, Chiang Kaishek established his headquarters at Nanchang and from there moved to control the rice-growing area of the lower Yangzi. He set up his own government in Nanjing, and started a purge of Communists in KMT-controlled areas. On 1 August 1927, the Communists rose against the KMT, starting an open war between the two parties. The first of August (in Chinese *Bayi*) is celebrated every year as the date of birth of the Red Army.

Revolutionary sites in Nanchang include the headquarters of the Nanchang uprising in Shengli Road, the site of the Officers Training Corps led by Zhu De, in Jiujiang Road, and the Museum of the Revolutionary History of the Province.

There is also a museum dedicated to the hermit-painter of the early Qing dynasty, Badashanren, a precursor of the early-twentieth-century painters Qi Baishi and Wu Changshi. South of Nanchang is the Qinyunpu, the temple where he spent twenty-seven years of his life; it has been turned into a small museum where the rooms used by the painter and some of his paintings can be seen.

South-west of Nanchang, on the border between Jiangxi and Hunan, the JINGGANGSHAN (Jinggang mountains) (**19**) rise about 1,000 m above sea level. It is a place of great natural beauty, accessible only after a long journey by road. This is where the Communists set up their base after having been driven underground by the KMT in 1927, and it remained a sanctuary for the Red Army until the first anti-Communist campaign of the KMT in 1931. The revolutionary sites include Mao Zedong's former residence, the headquarters of the Fourth Army and a Revolutionary Museum.

4 The Middle Yangzi Basin: Hubei and Hunan

The eastern two-thirds of Hubei province, in the centre of China, is a low-lying alluvial plain, criss-crossed by rivers and dotted by large and small lakes. Western Hubei is mountainous, cut through by the Yangzi River which enters the plain at Yichang, after flowing through precipitous gorges. The main crops are winter wheat and summer rice grown in rotation. Stone quarries and deposits of iron and coal are the mainstay of industry, in which this province is one of the leaders in the country. The climate is temperate: sheltered from the north winds by the Huaiyang Mountains, the province has January temperatures averaging 4°C., but summers are very hot, averaging 29°C. in July.

WUHAN 武汉

Wuhan, capital of Hubei province, situated at the confluence of the Han and Yangzi Rivers, is a complex of three cities: Wuchang, on the south bank of the Yangzi; Hankou, on the north bank of the Han; and Hanyang, on the south bank of the Han. A bridge across the Yangzi helps to integrate the separate cities. Wuhan has an overall population of about 3 million and is one of the main industrial centres of China.

The Yangzi at Wuhan is more than 1 km wide, and its muddy waters flow very fast. The city is surrounded by flat, low-lying land, under constant threat of floods. The dykes along the banks of the river have been greatly reinforced, particularly in Hankou which used to be most menaced by the Yangzi's periodic rampages. The Wuhan bridge, completed in 1957, is one of only three bridges which span the Yangzi (the others are at Nanjing and Chongqing); it is 1.16 km long, 18 m wide and 80 m high, with a lower deck for the railroad and an upper deck for motor vehicles.

Wuhan, less than twenty hours by train from Beijing, is not the most fascinating of cities, but there is plenty to keep you occupied if you should spend a day or two there. The city is notorious as one of the 'three furnaces' of China, so avoid the summer if possible. During June and early July heavy tropical storms occur, known as 'plum rains' because that is also the ripening season for plums, and the skies are often overcast.

Each of the three cities has its own railway station on the Beijing-Guangzhou line; the Yangzi ferry pier is in Hankou, near the foot of Jianghan Road. Accommodation and shopping facilities are concentrated in Hankou, the largest and most westernized of the three cities.

There are several hotels for foreigners in Hankou: The *Victory Hotel* (Shengli Fandian) (**a**), in Shengli Road, in the former French concession, is pre-1949, old-fashioned, and some rooms have air-conditioners. The *Xuangong Hotel* (**b**), in Jianghan Road, near the main CTS office, is also a pre-1949 building. The *Wuhan Hotel* (**c**)

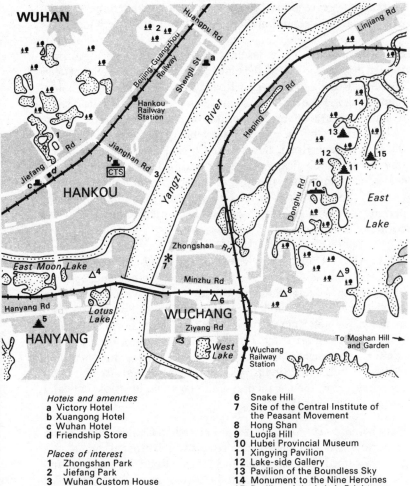

Hotels and amenities		Places of interest
a Victory Hotel		6 Snake Hill
b Xuangong Hotel		7 Site of the Central Institute of the Peasant Movement
c Wuhan Hotel		8 Hong Shan
d Friendship Store		9 Luojia Hill
		10 Hubei Provincial Museum
Places of interest		11 Xingying Pavilion
1 Zhongshan Park		12 Lake-side Gallery
2 Jiefang Park		13 Pavilion of the Boundless Sky
3 Wuhan Custom House		14 Monument to the Nine Heroines
4 Tortoise Hill		15 Pavilion of the Lake's Brightness
5 Yanguisi		

is in Jiefang Road, opposite the Friendship Store (**d**). *The Hotel for Foreign Experts*, in Wuchang near the Iron and Steel Works, north of the East Lake, was built by the Russians for their own engineers and is quite comfortable.

HANKOU (Mouth of the Han River) became a flourishing centre for trade in the nineteenth century. In 1861, the British obtained a concession there; other countries soon followed suit, and by the end of the century, the concessions stretched along the north bank of the Yangzi, the 'Hankou Bund', for about 3 km. In 1911, the town was almost entirely destroyed by fire during the heavy fighting between the revolutionaries (mainly railwaymen) and the imperial troops, and has been rebuilt largely with western-style houses.

Places of interest. It is fascinating to walk through the former foreign concessions along the embankment of the Yangzi, between Jianghan Road and Huangpu Road: first the British concession, then Russian, French, German and Japanese, each with its distinctive architectural characteristics, set in pleasant tree-lined streets.

The former Chinese city is on the bank of the river Han. West of the long Jiefang Road, the former Chinese race course is now a stadium and zoological gardens (**1**); and further north off the left side of the same road, the former European golf course is now a park (**2**). Few buildings in the city are worth mentioning, except perhaps the Wuhan Custom House (**3**), on the river front at the corner of Jianghan Road.

HANYANG (Upper Han River) already existed in the Tang dynasty, but remained small until the end of the nineteenth century. In the 1890s, Zhang Zhidong, viceroy of the province of Hubei, decided to try and modernize Hanyang by following Western methods. He built China's first iron and steel plant north of Tortoise Hill (**4**) on the river front, and by the beginning of the twentieth century, an arsenal and several factories were in operation. Hanyang's burgeoning industry was all but destroyed after the 1930s economic crisis, then again during the Japanese invasion, and later during World War II.

Places of interest. The old, formerly walled, Chinese city is south of Tortoise Hill and its two main streets which cross at right angles are now named Hanyang Road and Yingwu Road. The area around the Lianhua (Lotus) Lake used to be a quiet residential suburb for retired officials. In the north-west of Hanyang, the area south of the Xiyue (East Moon) Lake is a park with the Workers' Cultural Palace and the Lute Terrace. In the south-west quarter, the Yanguisi (5), a temple founded relatively recently, in the Qing dynasty, is well known for its Hall of the Five Hundred Lohans, which are said to be the best in this part of China.

WUCHANG (Military Glory) is the oldest of the three cities; historical records show that there was a Yellow Crane Tower built on Snake Hill as far back as the Han dynasty. In the Yuan dynasty (twelfth century), Wuchang became the administrative centre of the former Huguang region comprising the provinces of Hubei, Hunan, Guangdong and Guangxi. It is now the centre of Hubei province administration and of a large military region.

Places of interest.   Snake Hill (6), on which the eastern approach to the Yangzi River bridge is built, used to separate the old city into two distinct areas, and the building of the bridge has perpetuated this division. A Yuan dynasty pagoda, the Shengxiangbaota, which used to stand on Snake Hill facing the river, was moved south of the approach to the bridge when it was constructed. The Site of the 1911 Revolution Headquarters is near by, at the foot of Snake Hill. Wuhan was the first city to rise against the Manchus and the dynasty fell within a year of the uprising.

North of Snake Hill, in the north-west corner of the old town, is the site of the Central Institute of the Peasant Movement (7) which was headed by Mao Zedong in the 1920s. The Zhongshan Road follows exactly the boundaries of the old walled city of Wuchang.

The main tourist attraction in Wuchang is the East Lake (Donghu) and its shores. Two pagodas stand on Hong Shan (Great Hill) (8), south-west of the East Lake: the Xingfusita, a Song dynasty stone pagoda, which is about 10 m high, and east of it, the Hongshansita, rebuilt in the Qing dynasty; both are in Hongshan Park. Two hills rise south of the lake: the Luojia Hill (9), and the Moshan Hill, south-east of the lake. Moshan Hill now has a botanical garden. The western shore of the lake is a public park which has several noteworthy buildings.

The Hubei Provincial Museum (10) is at the end of Donghu Road. The Xingying Pavilion (11), a traditional-style building with a three-tier roof, has a little museum dedicated to the memory of the poet and statesman Qu Yuan. Subjected to a false accusation by a prince of the court, Qu drowned himself in protest, on the fifth day of the fifth moon, in 295 B.C. in the river Miluo north of Changsha in Hunan province. A search party went out in boats to look for his body. The event has been commemorated through the centuries with the Dragon Boat Festival, until the Cultural Revolution when it was forbidden. The festival is being revived, in particular in Chengdu, Sichuan, and in Nanning, Guangxi.

Still further north along the west shore of the lake is the Lake-side Gallery (12) and then the Changtian Pavilion or Pavilion of the Boundless Sky (13), also a traditional-style building. Past the Changtian Pavilion, after a short walk, one comes to the Monument to the Nine Heroines, the Jiunüdun (14), erected in memory of nine women fighting in the ranks of the Taiping who were left behind when the rebels retreated and who fought to their deaths rather than surrender to the Manchu armies. Past the monument, a bridge leads to a small elongated island at the southern tip of which stands the Pavilion of the Lake's Brightness (Huguang Pavilion) (15).

Most of the institutions of higher education are located south of the West Lake, including the Survey and Cartography College, and the Physical Education Institute — Wuhan being the home of one of the best acrobatic troupes in the country. The very large Wuhan University, with its early-twentieth-century traditional-style buildings, is on the shore of the West Lake.

The Wuhan Iron and Steel Company, north of the East Lake, is often visited by foreign groups and prides itself with having been inspected in 1958 by Chairman Mao himself.

Finally, one cannot fail to mention that it was in Wuhan on 16 July 1966, that Chairman Mao, then aged seventy-three, swam about 15 km down the Yangzi River. He was in the water for nearly an hour. If you find yourself in Wuhan on the anniversary of the Chairman's swim, you will see thousands of people with rubber rings and red flags attempting the crossing of the fast-flowing river.

The province of Hunan lies, as its name (South of the Lake) indicates, south of Dongting Lake, the second largest in China after Poyang Lake in Jiangxi province. Dongting Lake, which is part of the drainage basin of the Yangzi River, plays a major role in preventing flooding by acting as a reservoir. A series of small lakes connected to one another and to the Yangzi River, it is the main feature of the north of the province. The Xiang River flows north through most of the province into Dongting Lake, and its valley is bordered to the east and the west by mountains.

Hunan's climate varies from temperate in the north to sub-tropical in the south. The temperatures in winter seldom go below zero in the plains but the summers are very hot and humid; the annual average is 16-18°C.

Hunan province is one of the granaries of China, the main crop being rice. Another major crop is tea.

CHANGSHA 长沙

Changsha (Vast Sands), the capital of Hunan province, is situated on the east bank of the Xiang River, some 80 km south of Dongting Lake. Greater Changsha has a population of 2.2 million. The average annual temperature is 17°C. and the yearly rainfall, falling mostly in the spring and summer, 1300 mm.

Changsha is a distribution centre for the agricultural produce of the province, and is famous for its traditional handicrafts and light industry: ceramics, embroidery, bamboo carving, the making of fireworks and eiderdowns. Modern industries have been developed since liberation, including steel mills, machine tools, and textile plants.

Changsha is about twenty-two hours by train from Beijing and twelve hours from Guangzhou. There is now a new railway station on the eastern outskirts of the city, built at the same time (1972) as the bridge over the Xiang River.

There are several hotels in Changsha. The *Hunan Guesthouse* in the Martyrs Park, in the north-east quarter of the city, is a relatively modern building in a quiet setting. The *New Changsha Hotel* is near the new railway station, in Wuyi Dong Road.

Hunanese cuisine, spiced with small red peppers, is, with that of Sichuan, the hottest (most peppery) in China.

History.   Changsha was already in existence in the eighth century B.C. and was then called Chingyang. In the third century B.C., during the Qin dynasty, it became Changsha. Three roads in the centre of the city, and the river on the west, mark the limits of the old walled city. Until the beginning of the Qing dynasty (1644) it was part of the Huguang region, administered from Wuhan; after that it became the provincial capital of Hunan. In the 1850s, when the south was being swept by the Taiping rebels, Changsha and Guilin (in Guangxi province) were the only two southern cities to resist a siege. In the late nineteenth century, under the leadership of a provincial mandarin, Changsha achieved a degree of modernization: modern colleges were opened, the city acquired street lighting and the telegraph. At the same time, it remained hostile to foreign missionaries, until in 1904 it became a treaty port.

The city is associated with the early career of Mao Zedong (Mao Tse-tung), who was a student there and later, in the early 1920s, a teacher. Changsha was badly damaged by fire in 1938 when the KMT armies retreated before the Japanese.

Places of interest.   Changsha has no building of architectural interest, but visitors are taken to places where Mao Zedong studied and worked. The Hunan First Teacher Training School, where Mao studied from 1913 to 1918, is a European-style building of some elegance in the south of town. The original building was destroyed by fire but faithfully rebuilt after 1949; it has a museum with photographs and publications related to Mao Zedong's early revolutionary activities. In 1920 and 1921 Mao was superintendent of the primary school attached to the Teacher Training School and then taught a course in Chinese Literature; at the same time, he founded the first local branch of the Communist Party, a Socialist Youth League, and organized evening classes for workers and the Hunan Society of Russian Studies.

The site of the former Xiang District Committee of the Chinese Communist Party, to the east of Jiangxiang Road central, used to be in the suburbs of Changsha but has been engulfed by the urban area. The place was called Qingshuitang (Clear Water Pond), and the small house which Mao Zedong used to rent there has been turned into a museum called the Qingshuitang Memorial Hall. Here Mao lived until 1923, when he left for Shanghai, and here was held the first meeting of the Hunan branch of the CPC. The site of the Teach Yourself College, near the Qingshuitang, west of Jianxiang Road, can also be visited.

In the northeast quarter of the city is the large Memorial Park to the Martyrs, with two lakes and a small zoo. The Hunan Provincial Museum, near the north entrance to the park, has exhibits mainly pertaining to local revolutionary history.

Orange Island, in the middle of the Xiang River, is sometimes known as Long Island because of its shape — it is about 5 km long and 300 m wide. It is called Orange Island because of its abundant crop of mandarin oranges. Ferries carried passengers and goods from the city to the island, and from the island to the west bank, until the Xiang River bridge was completed a few years ago. A small pavilion at the southern tip of the island overlooks the beach to which Mao Zedong used to organize 'Sunday Club' swimming expeditions.

On the west bank of the river, covered with trees and overlooking Hunan University, is Yuelu Hill, which Mao used to climb and where he sometimes slept overnight. In 1918, he founded with a few friends the Xinmin Society which often met at the Aiwan (Loving Dusk) Pavilion, on Yuelu Hill. The pavilion, originally built in 1792 and named Hongye (Red Leaves) or Aifeng (Loving Maple) pavilion, was later renamed Aiwan Pavilion after a poem by the Tang dynasty poet Tu Mu, 'A Trip to the Hills':

> A stony path winds far up cool hills
> Toward cottages hidden deep among white clouds.
> Loving the maple woods at dusk I stop my cart
> To sit and watch the frosted leaves redder than February flowers.

The pavilion was rebuilt in 1952 and bears an inscription by the hand of Chairman Mao.

The Han Tombs at Maowangdui are by far the most interesting historical site in the Changsha area. Situated 4 km east of the city centre, they were excavated in 1972 (tomb No. 1) and late 1973-early 1974 (tombs No. 2 and 3). The three tombs date from the early Western Han dynasty (*c.* 193 to 140 B.C.). Tomb No 1 is that of Xi Zhui, wife of Li Cang, first Marquis of Tai; tomb No. 2, that of the Marquis himself; and tomb No. 3, that of his son. A museum has been opened on the site of the excavations.

In one hall of the museum can be seen the structure of No. 1 tomb, which was covered by a mound 16 m high and itself built of wood and carefully insulated with layers of charcoal and white clay. The body of the nobleman's wife and the objects found in the tomb with her were in a perfect state of preservation after having been in this air-tight chamber for more than 2,000 years; doctors were even able to determine the lady's blood group, and what she had eaten before her death.

The body, shrouded in twenty layers of clothing and covers, was found inside four coffins fitting tightly into one another. In the second hall of the museum are displayed these coffins and covers, and some of the objects found in the burial chambers: a unique polychrome painting on silk, T-shaped, perhaps a banner used in the funerary procession; many garments and rolls of silk, including polychrome and pile brocade of very fine workmanship which are the earliest specimens found; lacquerware (184 pieces altogether found in No. 1 tomb), so well preserved that the pieces look like new, though again, some of them are the earliest yet found in China; a total of 162 wooden figures, some of them wearing silk costumes; three models of musical instruments; and smaller objects including baskets, mats, bamboo cases, food, coins and seals.

The excavation of the Maowangdui tombs has been one of the most rewarding in the history of Chinese archaeology. The quality of the lacquerware and the fabrics cannot fail to amaze and delight visitors. Surprisingly, almost no objects made of silver, gold or precious stones were found.

SHAOSHAN (11) 韶山

Shaoshan (Shao Hill — Shao is the music of the legendary emperor Shun), 104 km south-west of Changsha in the green hills of eastern Hunan province, is the birthplace of Mao Zedong (Mao Tse-tung), and visitors, mostly Chinese, flock there by their thousands every day. There is a rail link with Changsha, but transport for foreign visitors is usually by road through the paddy fields and the tea plantations; because of the distance, it is worth enquiring in Changsha about the possibility of joining a tourist group or finding companions to fill up a taxi. A visit can be completed in one day from Changsha, but one can also stay overnight at the guesthouse.

Mao Zedong was born in 1893 into a family of 'middle peasants', who owned 2½ acres of land and eventually a small business. He began working in the fields when he was six. He attended the village school, and stayed in Shaoshan until he was twenty, when he went to Changsha to study at the Teacher Training School.

Mao's family house, where he lived with his parents, two brothers and a sister, is typical of a Hunanese middle peasant house, with several buildings arranged around a courtyard and overlooking a pond. It is built of unbaked bricks, with a 'cock loft' under the overhanging roof. A wing of the house has been converted into a reception area and the walls are hung with photographs of Chairman Mao visiting his own house.

The Museum, in a modern building near Mao Zedong's house, contains family photographs, books which Mao liked to read as a child, and documents and photographs relating to the founding of the Communist Party and its early history.

The former ancestors' temple of the Mao clan (there are still many families named Mao in Shaoshan) has been turned into a memorial hall to Mao's investigations, on his return to Shaoshan in 1927, into the possibilities of organizing the peasants' societies into a revolutionary movement. Another former temple where Mao set up evening classes for the peasants in 1925 is open to the public.

5 Guangdong Province and Guangzhou (Canton)

Guangdong province, one of the southernmost coastal provinces of China, lies in the sub-tropical to tropical zone, and its lush banana trees, clumps of bamboo and venerable banyans growing on the edge of manicured paddy fields make it one of the prettiest regions in the country. The population is concentrated in the deltas and coastal plains, while the hills rising in a crescent to the north are almost empty. The building of the Beijing-Guangzhou railway, the busiest line in the country, put an end to the relative isolation of the province, though communication with Guangxi to the west and Fujian to the north-east is still easier by sea.

Agricultural production in the province is abundant and varied, and there are three harvests of rice per year, not to mention the infinite range of vegetables, citrus, tropical and other fruit. Guangdong is also a major centre for the production of silk. Industry, concentrated around Guangzhou and a few other cities, includes mainly food-processing, textiles, electronics, light industry and traditional handicrafts (bamboo).

Because of its remoteness from the centre and its orientation towards the sea, there has been a steady flow of emigration from the province, so that Cantonese — the second most important dialect of China, after the Northern dialect (Mandarin) which is now the official language — is the most widely spoken language among Chinese overseas.

GUANGZHOU (Canton) 广州

Guangzhou (Wide Country), the capital of Guangdong province, is situated in the delta of the Pearl (Zhu) River. The Baiyun Mountains rise to the north-east of the city, which is built on a gentle slope descending towards the river. It is a pleasant city, with several attractive parks filled with tropical vegetation; the downtown streets are lined with arcades of open-fronted shops which stay open after dark. The population of the city and suburbs is around 3 million, including 2 million in the city proper.

Guangzhou is in the monsoon and typhoon zone and this means that it rains all the year round and more particularly in the spring, summer and early autumn. Summer is suffocating because the sea breezes do not reach the city, but spring and autumn, between showers, are delightful.

Guangzhou is linked by air with several major Chinese cities, including Shanghai, Beijing, Changsha, Wuhan, Guilin, etc. The journey by train to Beijing (about 2,000 km) takes forty hours.

PRACTICAL INFORMATION

Entering and leaving China via Guangzhou. Guangzhou is the point of entry and exit for the largest number of visitors to the People's Republic of China. Though you can make the journey from Hong Kong by plane or by hydrofoil and bus (see below), the most common means of entering China via Guangzhou is still by train.

There is now (1979) an express train service, non-stop from Kowloon station (Hong Kong) to Guangzhou in less than three hours; but you must book a place on this train two or three days in advance, at an office of China Travel Service in Hong Kong.* Customs and immigration formalities are at the respective railway stations, and you can change money in the Guangzhou station, at a branch of the People's Bank of China which is open during the period of traffic to and from the border.

If you fail to get a seat on the express train, you can travel by the slow train which leaves Kowloon station in the early morning, and will reach Guangzhou (180 km away) as much as seven hours later — having crossed the border on foot, over the Lowu railway bridge, been greeted by the People's Liberation Army and channeled through customs and immigration at Shenzen (Shumchun), and been given lunch (included in the fare) while you wait to board the 1 p.m. Chinese train for Guangzhou. The return journey is equally arduous, but you can have breakfast on the early morning train bound for the border, if you are lucky enough to get a seat in the restaurant car; if not, and you change your *yuan* into foreign currency in the station or on the train, remember to keep a few pennies to buy a cup of green tea on the train.

As an alternative to the train journey, charter flights operate daily in the morning from Hong Kong's Kaitak Airport to Guangzhou and back during the tourist season. There is also a regular hydrofoil

---

*Tourists will be urged to purchase a return ticket on this train when booking in Hong Kong, but it is more economical to pay the outward fare in Guangzhou. You can also book the journey, by the express train or by plane or hydrofoil, by post from China Travel Service (HK) Ltd, 77 Queen's Road Central, Hong Kong, enclosing a photocopy of your visa (on your passport) and a cheque or money order.

service between Hong Kong and Huangpu (Whampoa), which carries passengers three times a day in less than three hours; but you pay an expensive surcharge for excess baggage on the hydrofoil, and the 25 km journey onward by bus to Guangzhou takes a further hour.

Whether you arrive in Guangzhou by train, plane or hydrofoil, you are met there by a CTS escort and taken by taxi or bus to your hotel, or to the airport if you are flying onward the same day. (You can confirm your onward plane booking in Hong Kong, at the CTS office, and save a detour to CAAC office in Guangzhou and the risk of a missed connection.) If you feel very tired and the weather is unbearably hot, you can take a hotel room for part of the day (always possible in China) and have a rest rather than sitting in a waiting room or touring the city. When leaving Guangzhou by train for Hong Kong, it is possible to dispense with CTS escorts, but you will then have to carry your own luggage at the station, the border and at Kowloon station.

Hotels. Accommodation in Guangzhou is so much in demand at the height of the business and tourist season that strangers are sometimes even asked to share a room. To date, only two hotels accommodate tourists from western countries:

Baiyun (White Clouds) *Hotel* (a), Huanshi Road East, tel. 67 700. Situated in a quiet area in the north-east of the city, near the Mausoleum of the Seventy-two Martyrs, the Baiyun is the most recent (1977) and the pleasanter of the hotels for foreigners, affording such luxuries as air conditioning, and with a charming inner rock garden with a waterfall and some old trees. The usual range of services and facilities is available: laundry, barber and hairdresser, bank, post and telegraph office. Telex, and a particularly well-supplied lobby shop. The hotel has a Chinese dining room on the second floor, open all year round, and a Western dining room on the first (ground) floor which is open during the Canton Fairs and the high season for tourists. A bus service is available from the hotel to the Exhibition Hall during the time of the Fair.

Dongfang Binguan (Eastern Guesthouse) (b), North Renmin Road, tel. 69 900. This hotel, where tourists and Fair-goers traditionally put up, is conveniently located across the road from the Fair Exhibition Hall. The old part has larger but poorly lit rooms, and is theoretically air-conditioned; a large new wing, noisy and cheaply built, was added in the early 1970s, with open corridors leading to the rooms. There are the usual services and facilities, and a dining room which serves both Chinese and Western food, located on the eighth floor of the old wing. During the Fair, a vast dining hall on the ground floor of the old wing serves meals to Fair-goers and other guests; the 'Top of the Fang', the cafeteria on the eleventh floor of the new wing, is open from 8 p.m. to midnight and serves alcoholic drinks and meals.

A number of other hotels, including the Guangzhou (c), Overseas

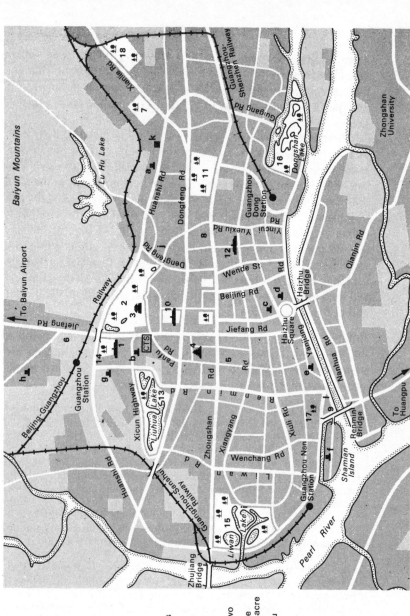

GUANGZHOU

Hotels and amenities

a Baiyun Hotel
b Dongfang Guesthouse
c Guangzhou Hotel
d Overseas Chinese Hotel
e Renmin Hotel
f Shengli Hotel
g Lihua Hotel
h Guanquan Villa
j Banxi Wine House
j Beiyuan Wine House
k Friendship Store
l Nanfang Department Store

Places of interest

1 Chinese Export Commodities
  Exhibition Hall
2 Yuexiu Park
3 Zhenhai Tower and Museum
4 Liurong Temple
5 Huaisheng Mosque
6 Sanyuanli Monument
7 Monument of the Seventy-two
  Martyrs
8 Peasants' Movement Institute
9 Monument of the Shaji Massacre
10 Sun Yatsen Memorial Hall
11 Monument to the Guangzhou
  Uprising
12 Lu Xun Museum
13 Liuhua Park
14 Orchid Garden
15 Liwan Park
16 Dongshan Park
17 Cultural Park
18 Guangzhou Zoo

Chinese (**d**), Renmin (**e**), Shengli (**f**), Liuhua (**g**), Guanquan Villa (**h**), and others, receive Chinese from overseas or from Hong Kong.

When staying in Guangzhou be prepared for mosquitoes and midges, which thrive all year round and can find their way through window screens and mosquito nets. A small electronic, battery-operated mosquito repellant can be purchased in Hong Kong; or, if you have failed to pack the usual repellants and lotion, you can burn the local incense coils and rub Tiger Balm into your bites.

Restaurants. Guangzhou is a gastronome's paradise. At the main hotels listed above, most of which serve both Western and Cantonese food during the busy Fair and tourist season, there is usually no need to book a table unless your party is very large. At the restaurants given below you should book in advance (through your interpreter), stating a cash limit per person (drinks excluded), and any special instructions, such as no dog or no snake.

GUANGZHOU RESTAURANTS

Name	*Specialities/Comment*	*Address/Location*	*Tel. no.*
PRESTIGIOUS RESTAURANTS			
Banxi (Pond and Cascade) Wine House (**i**)	Cantonese: dried scallop and crab soup, pigeon, quail eggs, Dim Sum. Beautiful setting in a garden with a pond, pavilions and a three-storey old wine house.	Xiangyang Rd. One/ Liwan East Rd. In south-west of town.	85 655 20 350
Beiyuan (North Garden) Wine House (**j**)	Cantonese: sharksfin, Shaoxing chicken, fish, Dim Sum.	Dengfeng Rd. North, No. 318. Near the Renmin Stadium. Beautiful setting.	32 471 31 154
Nanyuan (South Garden) Wine House	Cantonese: Maotai chicken, steamed fish with pine nuts, jade sauce on fish soufflé. In a tropical garden in the southern suburbs: most private rooms are in pavilions.	Qianjin Rd., No. 120. Head south, cross Haizhu Bridge.	50 532 50 542
Guangzhou (Canton) Wine House	Cantonese and Chaozhou dishes: winter melon soup, quail, goose, boned chicken and frog's legs. In an old wine house.	Wenchang Rd., No. 2. South end of the road, near Shamian Island.	87 136 87 840 23 493 21 139

Name	Specialities/Comment	Address/Location	Tel. no.
PRESTIGIOUS RESTAURANTS (contd.)			
Datong (Great Togetherness) Wine House	Cantonese: winter melon soup, peacock chicken, straw-mushrooms with crab, Dim Sum. Top floor of modern building with view over Pearl River.	Yanjiang Rd. (The Bund), No. 63, at Changdi, between Haizhu and Renmin Bridges.	24 902 20 318 88 697 86 983 24 764 etc.
GOOD CANTONESE RESTAURANTS			
Yuyuan (Happy Garden) Restaurant	Cantonese and Northern: sliced pigeon meat with bean sprouts, Peking Duck. New building with small inner garden.	Liwan Road North, No. 90	88 552 88 689 24 362
Jianghai (River and Sea) Restaurant	Cantonese: all kinds of fish and seafood.	Shisanhang St.	25 760
Dongjiang (East River) Restaurant	Cantonese and Hakka: salt-baked chicken, crab with black bean sauce. Simple setting. Good food.	Zhongshan East Rd., No. 337	32 493 33 343 32 473
Dongshan (East Mountain) Restaurant	Cantonese: prawns, quail, Dim Sum. Dining rooms for foreign visitors upstairs.	Guigang Rd./Dongshan, North of Dongshan Lake and Park.	70 556
SPECIALITY RESTAURANTS			
Shahe (Sandy River) Restaurant	Cantonese: Shahe Noodles (different kinds) are the speciality, served at the end of the meal after a variety of Cantonese dishes. Steep stairs to dining rooms.	Shahe Street. North-east of town.	70 956
Dumpling Restaurant.	All kinds of Dim Sum.	35 Renmin Rd., opposite Nanfang Department Store.	
Vegetarian Restaurant of Fragrance	All vegetarian: flavours and textures imitate meat and fish. Bamboo furniture and decoration.	Zhongshan Road Six, No. 167	86 836 23 733
Snake Restaurant	Cantonese: speciality of snakes which are skinned live before guests if they wish.	Jianglan Rd., No. 43	24 679

Name	Specialities/Comment	Address/Location	Tel. no.
SPECIALITY RESTAURANTS (contd.)			
Wild Fragrance Restaurant	Cantonese: game, dog and cat meat.	Beijing Rd.	30 33/ 30 997
NORTHERN RESTAURANTS			
Beijing Restaurant	Northern	Xihaokou	21 186
North China Restaurant	Northern.	Zhongshan Rd. Five.	33 837
Huimin Restaurant	Moslem: Lamb, chicken, beef, fish. No pork. Kebabs, Hot Pot.	Beijing Rd.	30 475
INEXPENSIVE RESTAURANTS			
Taiping (Great Peace) Restaurant	Cantonese and Western: simple and inexpensive.	Beijing Rd. North.	32 599
Economical Restaurant	Cantonese and Western.	Shamian Island	20 763
Beixiu (Northern Elegance) Restaurant	Cantonese: inexpensive. Meals served in upstairs dining room or on upstairs terrace.	Jiefang Rd./Dabei St. Within walking distance of Dongfang Guesthouse.	31 154 30 941
Liuhua (Stream of Flowers) Restaurant	Cantonese: freshwater fish. Upstairs dining room for foreigners with pretty view of park.	Liuhua Park, within walking distance of Dongfang Guesthouse.	68 800
Liwan (Bay of Lichee) Restaurant	Cantonese.	Xiangyang Rd. Two. Near Liwan Park.	26 165
Donghe (East River) Restaurant	Cantonese: snacks. In shaded patio.	In Dongshan Park.	
Sanru (Three Alike) Restaurant	Cantonese: turtle.	Nanhua Rd. East.	50 844

If you are in Guangzhou on business (see below), you will probably be hosting a banquet at one of the hotels or restaurants for your Chinese business contacts. Book a table early through your interpreter, take advice from old hands about the current average cash limit per person for a good meal, and remember that as a host you will be expected to help your guests to at least a first sampling of each dish brought to the table. There are special serving chopsticks and spoons provided in front of the host(s)' seat(s), and you will surely have mastered the art of using chopsticks after a few days and a few banquets. Should you use your own chopsticks by mistake when serving a guest, do not worry: it used to be considered a special favour in the traditional code of behaviour. Your Chinese hosts will seldom make the mistake themselves because they fear foreign guests would take offense. Chinese negotiators in these business affairs come from all parts of China and, whereas snake, dog and cat meat are considered delicacies in the South, Northerners are every bit as reluctant to eat them as Westerners are.

Shopping. The new Friendship Store (**k**) is in Huanshi Road, just east of the Baiyun Hotel in a modern four-storey building. First (ground) floor: foodstuffs, beverages, bicycles and appliances. Second floor: clothing, luggage, fabrics, knitted goods, toys and blankets. Third floor: antiques, jewellery, chinaware, embroideries and other handicrafts. Although cotton goods are available elsewhere in town, visitors, who are not issued with ration coupons, can only purchase them at the Friendship Store.

Several retail stores are located in the Exhibition Hall. Items which can be purchased include silk, embroidery, antiques, furs, tea and foodstuffs, books and prints, down products. Have your Foreign Currency Declaration form which you will have to present at the bank in the fairground together with your invoice, and pay there before picking up your purchase. This is one of the few places in China where credit cards are accepted. Some other shops:

Canton Antique Shop, 146 Wende Street North, sells ceramics, paintings and small carvings. Expect no bargain.
Canton Antique Warehouse, Huangshu Road, has four rooms filled with a jumble of antiques but is reserved for large purchases (5,000 *yuan* minimum). Payment is by letter of credit and purchases are sent directly abroad from the shop.
Arts and Crafts Shop, 393 Beijing Road, has a selection of cloisonne ware, carvings and bamboo furniture, including small tables, chairs, bookshelves and screens.
Jiangnan Native Product Store, 399 Zhongshan Road, sells basket and bamboo articles.
Department stores: *Nanfang Department Store* (**l**), Yanjiang Road, No. 1 and *Beijing Road Department Store*, Beijing Road, No. 2.
First Cultural and Antique Supply Store, Beijing Road, No. 322, sells art supplies, brushes, ink and ink stones.
Lantern shop: 55 Renmin Road.

If you are in Guangzhou for more than a week, you can try to have clothes made by a local tailor. The Guangzhou Tailor (suits, shirts, dresses) and the Nanfang Tailor (shirts only) are both in Xiuli Road Two, which runs east-west between Renmin and Liwan Roads. Results are not guaranteed.

Renmin Road is one of the busiest shopping streets in the city and is well worth exploring on foot.

Business visits. The Chinese Export Commodities Fair, more often called the Canton Fair, was a bi-annual event, in the spring and autumn, until the autumn Fair of 1979; in 1978 some 25,000 businessmen attended the Fair. It has now (1980) been announced that the exhibition halls will be open the year round and that services previously available only during the Fair will be maintained continuously; business negotiations formerly conducted at the Fair will be carried on throughout the year.

The Canton Fair Exhibition Hall (**1**) is situated on Xicun Highway opposite the Dongfang Guesthouse. Even if you are not in Guangzhou on business, it is interesting to visit the exhibition, which promotes Chinese exports and therefore displays a complete range of products.

If you come to China as a tourist, do not expect to be able to make any kind of business contact. You need a special visa to visit China on business, obtainable only through being invited by one of the Chinese State Import-Export Corporations with which your firm has had prior contact.

Negotiations are sometimes drawn out over a long period, so you should come prepared professionally (bringing very detailed information on the products about which you will be dealing) and personally (have your favourite tapes, a good wireless, reading material, your favourite drinks and cigarettes, etc.). The main hotels provide special services for businessmen, including a Trade Fair Liaison Office, medical service, shuttle bus services between distant hotels and the exhibition halls, and post, cable and Telex facilities; and will arrange visits to the opera and cinema and Sunday outings and excursions.

Any business visit always leaves some time for sightseeing, even to places to which you have no business reason to go, if you apply in time (at least one week's notice) and your visa does not expire during the planned excursion. Should you want a break in Hong Kong, you must plan ahead because transportation and hotels get very booked up.

HISTORY

Chinese civilization did not penetrate the Guangzhou area until the unification of the empire: in 214 B.C., the Qin armies reached the south of modern China and the north coast of modern Vietnam, arriving by boat. In the Han dynasty (206 B.C.-A.D. 220) Guangzhou, then called Nanhai and capital of the autonomous state of Nanyue, developed as a centre for maritime commerce, importing glass, wool, and linen fabrics from the western Roman Empire, from southern and western Asia, and exporting silks and handicrafts. A Regional Commandery was created in Guangzhou during the Tang dynasty, and by the seventh century, there was already a fairly large foreign community residing there, including Moslems who built a mosque. In 758, Islamic groups even seized the city. Guangzhou was sacked in 879 by the rebel Huang Chao and his men and it was reported that 120,000 foreigners were killed — no doubt an exaggeration.

During the interregnum between the Tang and the Song, Guangzhou was briefly (907-971) the capital of the Southern Han dynasty and expanded greatly over the next two centuries. During the Ming, industrial activity increased: ship-building, textiles, ceramics and manufacturing of iron pans which were sold in the empire and also exported to the whole of Asia. In 1514 the first European envoys, the Portuguese, landed in Guangzhou, and Macao was ceded to them in 1553. The Manchu conquest of the south was difficult: it was only forty years after the establishment of the Qing dynasty that the southern provinces were brought under control. A permanent garrison of Bannermen was stationed in Guangzhou, 4,000 men strong and quartered with their families in a fortified section within the walled city.

In 1699, the East India Company ship *Macclesfield* opened the first British trading post, known as a 'factory', dealing mainly in tea and silk; the provincial administration was reorganized to control trade with the foreigners, with a Governor-General, known as the Viceroy, at its head. The old East India factories were situated on the north bank of the Pearl River, to the west of the walled city, between today's Nanfang Department Store and Renmin Hotel. The city walls ran along modern Haizhu Road to the west, Panfu Road to the north, Yicui and Yuexiu Roads to the east, and along the river to the south. Anchorage for the Company ships was at Whampoa (Huangpu), 15 km downstream.

Opium had been known in China for a long time and was used as a medicine; in the seventeenth century the Chinese began smoking it. In 1729, selling and smoking opium, and in 1796, growing it, were prohibited by imperial edict without much result. In the late eighteenth century, opium imports stood at 1,000 chests per year and until 1821 they averaged 4,500. But a combination of availability of opium and apathy and corruption of the administration increased opium addiction amongst the lower grades of the civil service and the soldiers, until by 1838 imports — paid for with silver which heretofore the British had had to disburse for their own imports of tea — had reached 40,000 chests a year and the burden on the Chinese economy grew intolerable.

In 1839, the energetic Lin Zexu was sent to Guangzhou as Viceroy, and, within a few days of his arrival, demanded the surrender of the stocks of opium. The foreigners were confined to their factories until they complied. The opium, 20,000 chests of it, was destroyed. In the same year, some drunken sailors killed a Chinese and the Viceroy demanded the surrender of the culprits. The British never found out who they were and in any case refused to commit one of theirs to Chinese justice; as a result they had to withdraw first to Macao and then to the island of Hong Kong which became a base for the British community. Full-scale hostilities, known as the Opium War, broke out in the summer. The British broached the antiquated Qing defenses along the coast from Guangzhou to Shanghai and even landed at Tianjin. The first Unequal Treaty, signed in Nanjing in 1842, granted five treaty ports to the British and ceded them the island of Hong Kong.

Guangzhou was occupied only briefly during the Taiping rebellion. However, it had to deal with a rebellion of its own, led by Li Wanzhong, in 1854-5. The 'factories' were the target of the angry mobs and in 1859, when the dust had settled, the British, along with the French, obtained the lease of Shamian Island where they were granted extra-territoriality.

Guangzhou, which had been the earliest and most important point of entry for foreigners and where anti-Manchu feelings had always been high, became a centre for anti-imperial and revolutionary movements at the beginning of the twentieth century. The dynasty collapsed in 1912, thanks to the efforts of a native of Guangdong province, Dr Sun Yatsen. He attempted to set up a military government in Guangzhou in 1917, but it counted for little in the face of the warlords' power. Eventually a socialist government, the Guangzhou Commune, was set up but suppressed bloodily by Chiang Kaishek in 1927.

Guangzhou, along with Hong Kong and much of southeast Asia, was occupied by the Japanese from 1938 to 1945. The city was one of the last ones held by the KMT armies on the eve of the Communist take-over.

PLACES OF INTEREST

Downtown Guangzhou. The Yuexiu Park (2), one of the most popular in Guangzhou, is east of the Dongfang Guesthouse, within walking distance. It has a lake, sports facilities, and a hill which gives its name to the park. As in other parks of the city, flower exhibitions are held in the spring and autumn. The most attractive

feature of the park is the Zhenhailou (Tower for Guarding the Sea)
(**3**), a five-storeyed structure from the top of which armed guards
once kept watch for attacks from the river. It used to stand at the
highest point of the northern city wall which no longer exists. Built
in 1380, the tower suffered during the Manchu conquest of the
south and was extensively rebuilt in 1686 after the Qing gained
control of the region. There is a teahouse on the top floor and the
Guangzhou Museum occupies the rest of the building. On display is
a collection of art objects and ceramics from the neolithic culture to
the products of today's kilns, particularly interesting for the Ming
and Qing Southern blue and white underglaze wares, so attractively
decorated with lively and informal patterns.

The Liurongsi (Temple of the Six Banyan Trees) (**4**) was founded
in 479 and takes its name from a poem by the eleventh-century poet
Su Dongpo. When he visited the temple his attention was drawn to
six old banyan trees growing outside; they are no longer there, but
the name remains. The Liurongsi, situated in a street which bears its
name, north of the intersection of Chaoyang and Zhongshan
Roads, has been restored several times since the Song dynasty. It is
the headquarters of the Guangzhou Buddhist Association and can
be visited with special permission. The Huata, or Ornate Pagoda —
so named in contrast to the Guangta (Plain Tower) of the mosque
near by — stands just north of the main temple hall. It was founded
in 537 but was entirely rebuilt in the Song dynasty. Its nine storeys
conceal seventeen inner storeys; it is about 57 m high.

The Huaisheng Mosque (**5**) is in Guangta Street, south-east of the
intersection of Zhongshan and Renmin Roads. It is almost certainly
the oldest in the country, traditionally believed to have been
founded by an uncle of the prophet Mohammed in 627, but was
destroyed and completely rebuilt in the early twentieth century.
Visitors should ring the bell on the right, outside the iron gates. The
prayer hall is at the far end of a large courtyard shaded with trees
and enclosed in whitewashed walls. The minaret is a modern tower
(Guangta), 28 m high, with a balcony from which there is a good
view of the town. Guangzhou has a sizeable Moslem community
and the mosque is still in use. A school in the compound is attended
by Moslem children.

The Roman Catholic Cathedral is behind the Renmin Hotel, off
Haizhu Road. It is a Gothic-style granite building with twin spires
53 m high which was consecrated in 1863. It is now used as a
warehouse.

The memorials. A visit to Guangzhou's memorials will give the
visitor an illustrated account of the city's revolutionary tradition.

The Sanyuanli Monument (**6**), on the way to Baiyun Airport, commemorates the attack by local militia, in May 1849, on Captain Eliott and a troop of 24,000 men; he was withdrawing after having seized the city and extracted a ransom of 6 million Chinese dollars in compensation for the destruction of the stocks of opium ten years before (see HISTORY).

The Monument of the Seventy-two Martyrs (**7**), near the Baiyun Hotel, commemorates the 1911 revolution, when in one attack in May on the palace of the viceroy, seventy-two people lost their lives. The final revolutionary assault took place on 10 October 1911, which is celebrated on Taiwan, though not in the People's Republic, as a national holiday.

The Peasants' Movement Institute (**8**), created in 1924, was really the first Communist Party school for the training of its cadres. Mao Zedong was its director in 1926, but the Institute was closed the following year when the Guangzhou Commune was crushed. It is located in a former Temple of Confucius built in the sixteenth century, an elegant but somewhat austere building, sparingly and simply furnished.

The Monument of the Shaji (Sakee) Massacre (**9**) is a stone stele erected after the Sakee incident in 1925, when demonstrations against the Unequal Treaties took place opposite Shamian Island where the foreigners were barricaded. They shot into the crowds trying to force the bridge, killing scores of Cantonese but with only one casualty on their side. The island was subsequently under siege for some weeks, having to be provisioned from Hong Kong.

The Sun Yatsen Memorial Hall (**10**), built after Sun Yatsen's death in 1925, is a large auditorium which can seat 5,000 people, roofed with bright blue tiles.

The Monument to the Guangzhou Uprising (**11**), in a park in the east of the city, was erected in 1957 to commemorate the crushing of the Guangzhou Commune by the KMT in 1927, when 5,000 people died in the fighting.

The Lu Xun Museum (**12**), in Yan'an Street, near the intersection with Lixin Street, is on the site of the former Guangzhou University where the writer (see p.162) taught in 1927. The buildings also house the provincial museum.

The Parks. Guangzhou boasts several beautiful parks. The Liuhua Gongyuan, or Park of the Stream of Flowers (**13**), in the north-west, has several lakes, shaded walks and a small restaurant. Like the Yuexiu Park, described above, it is easily accessible from the Dongfang Guesthouse. The Orchid Garden (**14**), a very pleasant small park opposite the southern entrance to the Yuexiu Park, is more intimate than the other parks and well cushioned from traffic noise by its tropical vegetation. Over a hundred varieties of orchids are grown there. The Liwan Gongyuan, Park of the Bay of Lichees (**15**), in the west of the city, is the largest in Guangzhou. The prestigious Banxi Restaurant is located on its edge. The Dongshan Gongyuan (East Mountain Park) (**16**) is near the old Guangzhou Railway station in the east of the city. It is on the edge of the river and of the built-up districts, and it, too, has a small restaurant

The Cultural Park (17), in the south-west, at the bottom of Renmin Road, is a sort of funfair ground with teahouses, exhibition halls, open-air stages and fish ponds. Guangzhou Zoo (18), the north-east, is one of the best in the country. It even has pandas, native to the province of Sichuan, who were first brought to the zoo in 1957.

Shamian Island. Should you have only a little time to spend in Guangzhou, I would recommend that you visit the Zhenhai Tower (see above) and Shamian Island. When the latter became a foreign concession in 1859, following the burning of the 'factories' during the second Opium War, the British and French reclaimed some land around it with silt dredged from the river and built stone embankments. There used to be only one bridge linking the island to the north bank of the river, but since 1949 the new Renmin Bridge, which spans the whole river, has been built. Two streets cross the island at right angles. The former French consulate was at the eastern tip and the British built theirs in the main street. The style of the buildings is Mediterranean, very like those of the Portuguese colony of Macao, with stucco balustrades and balconies covered with red-tiled roofs. Underneath their present neglected appearance, their romantic charm, enhanced by the shade of the venerable banyans growing on the embankments, strikes the European visitor.

The Baiyun (White Cloud) Mountains rise to the north-east of the city. Their wooded slopes used to shelter a number of hermitages and monasteries. They are only about 450 m high but command a good view of the Pearl River delta. It takes only about twenty minutes by taxi to drive to the foot of these mountains, and if you feel energetic and in need of escaping the steaming city, a couple of hours is all you need to walk up and down the trail.

Communes. In the attractive countryside surrounding Guangzhou a number of communes can be visited. The Huadong Commune, some 30 km due north of the city, is watered by the Liuxi River and its main feature is a complex network of dams, reservoirs, embankments and irrigation canals. The major crop is rice. The Luodong Brigade in Shaoguan county, some 70 km north-east of Guangzhou, specializes in citrus fruit.

The Logang Commune, in Dongguan county, about 20 km east of the city, is by far the most attractive. It is a fruit-growing commune set in a spectacular mountainous landscape where tourism is taken seriously as an additional source of income. The half-day long visit is highlighted by an opulent lunch, the opportunity to purchase fruit, to take a ride in a buffalo-drawn cart and shoot balloons with an air gun. Apart from the commune's agricultural produce, paintings in traditional style by local artists are sold in the village shop and a temple complex featuring some very old fruit trees is open to the public.

FOSHAN (3) 佛山

Foshan (Buddha Hill) is a medium-sized city, 18 km to the southwest of Guangzhou. A day's excursion from Guangzhou will usually include a lunch break at the Foshan Guesthouse, a large, old-fashioned hotel. Up until the Ming dynasty, Foshan's claim to fame was its hill carved with three large statues, giving the town its name. By the middle of the Ming dynasty, it had developed into an important centre for the making of pottery and iron pans which were exported as far as southern Asia and Persia, and the population grew to about 1 million. Foshan was still called a village, however, because it did not have a wall and was administered from Guangzhou. In the nineteenth century, it declined as Guangzhou's importance in the province increased, until today the population is only around 500,000.

The Zumiao (Ancestral Temple), a Taoist temple founded in the Ming dynasty, serves now as a museum, displaying some of the original statues of Buddha as well as archaeological finds from the area, where Song dynasty kilns were discovered recently. The buildings, restored in the Qing dynasty and also in the 1970s, are a classic example of the gaudy Qing dynasty style of the south, very ornate and with sharply up-turned roof-ends in the shape of horns.

At the Shiwan Pottery Works to which visitors are usually taken, three kinds of products are made: bricks and tiles for the building industry, ordinary ceramics for everyday use and ornamental ceramics, including reproductions of old styles. The pottery has a display room for its non-industrial products which can be bought locally. The miniature ornaments are a particularly attractive and practical buy for visitors from abroad.

CONGHUA (2) 从化

Conghua (Trace of Flowers) is a small city about 70 km north-east of Guangzhou, two hours by road from Guangzhou. Built on the west bank of the Liuxi River which runs at the foot of the pretty Qingyun Mountains, it is a pleasant resort town whose main attraction is the hot springs, a few miles to the north. The guesthouse is an elegant recent building roofed with green-glazed tiles, built at the edge of the water. Ideally, one would like to spend a week-end there to rest and go walking in the hills, but one-day excursions are usually made from Guangzhou.

ZHAOQING (4) 肇庆

The drive from Guangzhou west to Zhaoqing (Original Blessings) is picturesque though rather long and slow (100 km, three hours); the Bei River has to be crossed by ferry. The area around Zhaoqing resembles the beautiful mountainous landscape around Guilin in Guangxi province, but on a smaller scale.

The Seven-Star Crag is a wide expanse of water interrupted by causeways, bridges and sugar-loaf shaped hills overgrown with trees. Halls and pavilions dot the shores, including Five-Dragon Pavilions which perpetuate the memory of the Five Dragons of Learning, five brothers who lived in Shandong province in the second century B.C. and all became great scholars. Fog is frequent in the area and amateur photographers will have an opportunity to capture the mist-shrouded hills so often depicted in traditional Chinese landscape paintings.

At Dinghu, a little way downstream from the town, the hills rise on the west bank of the river with their feet in the water, and spectacular springs cascade down the rock.

6 Guangxi

Guangxi, or the Guangxi-Zhuang Autonomous Region as it is properly known, is west of Guangdong province; it has a short coastline to the south and a long border with Vietnam to the southwest. It is watered by the Xijiang and its tributaries, which constitute the third major waterway in the country. Some 300 million years ago, the region was below sea level and its thick layer of limestone has been eroded into karst formations which account for its beautiful landscapes and numerous natural caves. The climate is sub-tropical to tropical. Rice paddies and clumps of bamboo grow in the low-lying areas and the hills are sparsely populated.

The Guangxi-Zhuang Autonomous Region, established in 1958, has an area of 230,000 square km and a population of about 30 million. Of the numerous minority nationalities inhabiting the region, the principal ones are Yao, Dong, Miao, Mulao, Maonan, Hui (Moslem), Jing, Yi, Shui, Gelao and Zhuang. The Zhuang, who belong to the Thai linguistic group, are the largest minority in China, totalling about 12 million; 90 per cent of them live in Guangxi-Zhuang, where they occupy about 60 per cent of the land.

GUILIN (Kweilin) 桂林

Guilin (Cassia Forest) is perhaps the most touristic place in the whole of China; its lone sugar-loaf mountains rising among the paddy fields and rivers have been a source of inspiration for generations of Chinese painters.

Guilin is forty minutes away from Guangzhou by air and about forty hours by train from Beijing and eighteen from Wuhan. If you are intending to visit Guilin as the last stop on your itinerary before leaving the country via Guangzhou, you will do better to fly out to Guangzhou rather than go by train, which means making a detour of 260 km north to the junction at Hengyang, since Guilin and Guangzhou are not connected directly by rail.

Guilin has a mild winter season and it rains on average every other day in May and June. The average annual rainfall is 1900 mm. Temperatures stay between 18° and 28°C. from April to October, and the best seasons to visit are the autumn, winter and early spring when the visibility is good and the water level in the rivers high enough to allow boat trips downstream to Yangshuo.

The *Lijiang Hotel* is a 14-storey building completed in 1976, situated in the heart of the city on the shore of Ronghu (Banyan) Lake, and every room of which has a magnificent view of the hills which rise in and around the town. It offers the usual range of services and its lobby shop sells a selection of the local handicrafts. Both Western and Chinese food is served. The hotel is heated in winter.

The Friendship Hotel, south of Fir Lake, is now rather old and decrepit, owing to the high humidity and bad maintenance. The food is excruciating and the more you pay per day for your meals, the greater number of greasy dishes will appear on your table. It is also famous for its hard beds.

The *Banyan Lake Hotel*, usually reserved for official delegations, is very comfortable and serves reasonable local cuisine.

History. The town was founded in the third century B.C. when the construction of the Lingzhu canal gave it a great impetus. The canal, dug around 214 B.C., is 33 km long and links up the Yangzi and the Pearl River systems through two major tributaries, the Xiang and Li respectively, bringing Changsha into indirect contact with Guangzhou. It proved a major asset in the conquest and control of the southern provinces in imperial times.

Guilin became the capital of the province early in the Ming when Hong Wu, the founder of the dynasty, sent one of his sons there to be king of Jingjiang. The Taiping failed to take the town in 1852 because they lacked artillery. Sun Yatsen stayed in Guilin during the early 1920s while discussing an alliance with the Comintern. Though Nanning had been the provincial capital since 1914 (and is so again now), in 1936, under the Nationalist government, the capital was once again moved to Guilin. The Japanese during their 1944 offensive almost razed the town to the ground. It was one of the last cities to be taken by the Communists in 1949.

The hills. There are hundreds of hills in and around Guilin. Duxiufeng (Peak of Solitary Beauty) rises in the centre of town, where the Ming palace used to be. A moat and portions of wall, including a gate flanked by a pair of stone lions buried up to their bellies, are all that is left of the palace which is now a teacher training college. The climb up the peak is very steep.

Diecaishan (Folded Brocade Hill) is in the north, covered with trees, topped by a small pavilion and pierced with a hole. It can be climbed without too much difficulty. Several pieces of calligraphy from the Tang and the Song are engraved in the rock. Fuboshan (Underground Water Hill) is by the side of the Li River. It has a cave, Huanzhutong (Returning the Pearl Cave), with Buddhist carvings and calligraphy from the Tang and the Song dynasties. A column of granite descends to within a few centimetres of the ground.

Yinshan (Hidden Hill), in the west, is famous for the nunnery which was built at the foot, the Huagai'an, and Laorenshan (Old Man Hill), north of it, has carvings of Buddha. The West Hill, west of Hidden Hill, also has Buddhist carvings. There are over 2,000 cliff carvings and sculptures in Guilin but many of them were damaged or destroyed during the Cultural Revolution, in particular those of Yinshan, Laorenshan and West Hill.

The Seven Star Cave, a very large natural cave in the south-west of town, is one of the chief attractions. The trip round its interior takes two hours, and if you dislike dark and damp places, you should elect to visit the Crescent Hill near by instead. The Dragon Refuge Cave inside it, which takes its name from the dragon scales produced by water eroding the rock face, has a crack in the ceiling which lets the light filter through. In this cave, as in the Seven Star, illustrious visitors were moved to compose poems which are engraved on the rock. The approach to the Seven Star Cave and the Crescent Hill is over Floral Bridge, a recent reconstruction of a Song dynasty bridge, surmounted by a covered gallery of elegant and sober design.

To the south lie several other hills: Elephant Trunk Hill, drinking the water from the west bank of the Li River, and Pagoda Hill, topped with a pagoda of the Ming dynasty now overgrown with weeds; Tunnel Hill, pierced through by a long cave, and South Creek Hill, a pleasant hill for walking, with a teahouse at the water's edge.

Reed Pipe Cave, 8 km to the north-west of Guilin, is a natural cave near Peach Blossom River, a tributary of the Li. It takes its name from the reeds growing at the bottom of the hill which were used for making reed pipes. It had been known since the Tang dynasty but was only made accessible to a large number of visitors in the 1960s. The delicate colours of its stalactites and stalagmites, lit by electricity, have retained their freshness, and are not blackened by smoke as in the Seven Star Cave, through which generations of candle-bearing visitors passed. The visit to the Reed Pipe Cave is fairly short, just over half an hour to cover the 500 m long path, and although it is damp and deep, it is enjoyable. If you have a choice, go to this cave and avoid the Seven Star Cave.

Other sites. Banyan Lake and Fir Lake, in the centre of Guilin, were once part of the city moat. Their retaining walls fell into disrepair and they were dredged and landscaped after 1949, contributing to the charm of the city. A temple of the Tang dynasty, the Kaiyuansi, once stood south of the Peach Blossom River, west of Elephant Trunk Hill; all that is left now is a small stone stupa. You can visit the place easily from the hotels.

The Yao Mountains, rising some 15 km north-east of the town, are perhaps the most interesting area in Guilin, though your guide may be reluctant to take you there. There used to be many temples, both Taoist and Buddhist: the Zhusheng Nunnery at the foot of one hill, the Baiyunguan (White Cloud Temple), an important Taoist temple, the Shoufoan, Nunnery of the Buddha of Longevity, the White Stag Temple, and the Jade Emperor Pavilion. There is also the tomb of the wife of the king of Jingjiang, son of the Ming emperor Hong Wu.

The river trip to Yangshuo. The descent by boat of the Lijiang, Peach River, will be the best part of your visit to Guilin, or even of your entire China tour. In high water season, the trip starts from Guilin itself and takes seven hours. Gently towed by a tugboat which, if you are lucky, will not broadcast loud music for too much of the time, you can enjoy the extraordinãry panorama of hills, river

THE GUILIN-YANGSHUO RIVER TRIP

mist rising in gauze-like layers, and the unhurried river traffic of fishermen and paddle boats powered by men turning a big wheel on the deck. Along the way, groups of people carrying bundles on poles wait for the small ferry which will take them across the river, and buffalo cool themselves in the shallow water bordering the paddy fields, immersed up to their muzzles. You may even see cormorants diving and bringing back their catch to a solitary figure sitting on a long and flimsy boat carrying a big tub, or perhaps a train of logs with a few men balancing on the edge and steering the rafts with long poles. Many strangely shaped hills, most of which have names which your guide will be only too eager to tell you, line the banks of the river which at times is contained between steep cliffs, and at others spreads lazily to the edge of the fields. The excursion ends at the small town of Yangshuo (see below) 85 km downstream, and you will return by road to Guilin.

On the way back, a detour 6 km south to the village of Gaodian is usually included. It is a courtesy call on a 1300-year-old banyan growing by the river, opposite a small island where buffalo graze. At the end of the day, they swim back to the river bank and hoist themselves out of the mud. Paddy fields, reflecting the sky like window panes, surround the venerable tree which spreads its branches almost to the ground. Near by is a hill pierced with a round hole to which people come at night to see the full moon shine through. Not a parcel of level land is wasted along the road back to Guilin and family graveyards cling to the sunny side of the hills, their tombstones and circular walls barely distinguishable from the rocks and stones.

The boat excursion itself, which includes lunch on board, is not too expensive, but if you travel by taxi back to Guilin, the fare will be extortionate, and you should enquire about the possibility of joining a tourist group or another small party and returning by bus or minibus.

YANGSHUO (6) 阳朔

Yangshuo (Bright New Moon) was founded in the Sui dynasty (sixth century A.D.) and existed — as it still does — as a market town along the river. It is in the centre of a rich agricultural area where the main crop is rice, but where bamboo, sugar cane and tropical fruit abound. The Yangshuo pomelo (a rubbery cousin of the grapefruit) are well known throughout the South, but kumquats, persimmons, chestnuts and mangosteen, which has medicinal virtues, also grow.

In town, the large People's Park encloses a green area with

several hills and a stream. The best view is from the Pavilion Nestling in the Clouds (Woyunting), a Southern extravaganza brightly painted and decorated with murals on the outside. West Youth Hill rises in the park, projecting a rock in the shape of a human silhouette, above which is the Hillside Pavilion. The boat from Guilin anchors alongside a pretty spot on the river bank. You can climb the hill to the Yingjiangge (Pavilion by the River) and gaze at the river and the hills through the six openings between the columns on its upper floor. They are framed with carved wood, creating the illusion of six landscape paintings.

There are several famous hills in Yangshuo: the Green Lotus Peak by the river, shaped like a lotus bud; the Scholar's Servant Hill (Shutongshan), a small hill standing alone by the river and dwarfed by a much taller hill; and Mirror Hill next to the Pavilion by the River.

LIUZHOU (5) 柳州

Liuzhou (Liu Country) is a fairly large town situated in the heart of Guangxi — by the river Liu, hence its name. To the south rise the Ma'an Mountains, dominating the city which spreads on both sides of the river. The old town is at the tip of a peninsula formed by the sharp bend of the river.

Liuzhou was founded during the Qin dynasty (third century B.C.) and was then known as Kunzhou. In 634, it took its present name. In the Tang dynasty, it was a small trading town surrounded by uncultivated land, living mainly off the exploitation of its forests. Indeed, Liuzhou's claim to fame is its timber and carpenters, sought after for the making of coffins. Wood had become rare in the eastern provinces of China, and it took a certain amount of wealth to be able to afford a coffin from Liuzhou.

A Tang dynasty official, Liu Zhongyuan (773-819), posted to Liuzhou for four years in 815, undertook great improvements in the town: he had wells dug, the city walls rebuilt and tried to discourage banditry and bondage. He was a talented poet who wrote about his disillusionment in politics and the life of the people in the province. Liu died in Liuzhou and a temple, built in his memory in 822, is now in a park which is also named after him, the Liu Zhongyuan Park, together with a symbolic tomb in which his official hat and gown are buried.

Liuzhou is predominantly an industrial city and a major railway junction, but its beautiful natural setting makes it unexpectedly pleasant. There is a large park on the south bank of the river, the Yufengshan Park, and a natural cave, the Dule cave, in the suburbs.

NANNING 南宁

Nanning (Tranquillity of the South), the capital of Guangxi, is situated in the south of the province along the railway line which goes to Vietnam. It is twenty-four hours by train from Changsha and is linked by air to Hanoi, Beijing, Guangzhou and Changsha. It is located on one of the main tributaries to the Xijiang, the Yongjiang, in a plain surrounded by hills to the north and the south.

Founded in the third century B.C., it was an outpost on the road to North Vietnam during the conquest by the Tang who gave their southern protectorate the name of Annam (Southern Peace). From the eighth century, the west of Guangxi province was ruled by Thai people, and it was not until 1253, when the Mongols, bypassing the southern provinces of the Southern Song empire, took what is now Yunnan province, that the Thai retreated south. With the empire again in control of the south, Nanning's importance as a market town increased, but still it remained an outpost. It is only in the twentieth century that it grew into a large town, and in particular since 1949. Having been the provincial capital from 1914 until 1936, it became so again shortly after liberation. The urban area is now twelve times what it was in 1949. The population is about 500,000.

Nanning is above all an industrial city, processing produce from the province and exploiting the resources in bauxite and coal. In addition, it has chemical and machine and engine factories, tanneries, refineries and a tractor plant.

The city is built on the north shore of the Yong river and has several lakes, including South Lake in the south-eastern suburbs, where the Dragon Boat Festival (see p.181), which no one was allowed to celebrate from the Cultural Revolution until 1978, has been revived. On the fifth day of the fifth month of the lunar calendar (around 15 June), dragon boats, elaborately decorated, compete in regattas; the winning team is selected not only on its performance but also on the decoration of its boat.

Nanning has an Institute for Nationalities for training students from the minority nationalities which constitute nearly 40 per cent of China's population.

Near the town of WUMING, 50 km north of Nanning, is the Zhuang Autonomous Brigade of the Two Bridges, to which day-long excursions are now organized by CTS. The drive there is superb and the Zhuang people colourful and hospitable. A five-minute walk from the rest house will take you to a small Qing dynasty pagoda.

A large natural cave can also be visited near the village of Iling, 20 km south-west of Nanning.

IV
THE SOUTHWEST AND THE BORDER PROVINCES

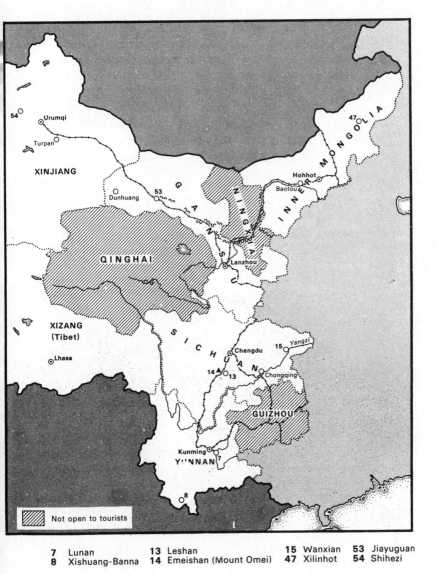

Not open to tourists

7 Lunan	13 Leshan	15 Wanxian	53 Jiayuguan
8 Xishuang-Banna	14 Emeishan (Mount Omei)	47 Xilinhot	54 Shihezi

1 Yunnan

Yunnan, west of Guangxi province, shares a border with Vietnam, Laos and Burma. Southern and south-western Yunnan are a plateau which lies between 500 and 2,000 m above sea level in which geological faults have left depressions often filled by lakes. Western Yunnan has very high mountains along a north-south axis, deeply cut through by powerful rivers: the Nujiang (Salween), the Lancang-jiang (Mekong) and Yuanjiang (Red River), and the Babianjiang (Black River). Western Yunnan is often shaken by earthquakes and there are volcanoes in the Baoshan area near the Burmese border. The climate varies greatly according to the altitude, from tropical in the valleys of the south-east and temperate on the plateau, to very cold towards the northern border with Tibet.

Yunnan has vast forests and a small population. The Han Chinese are concentrated in the valleys and on the plateau; the mountains are thinly settled by many different minorities who until this century often lived in complete isolation from one another. Unlike neigh-bouring Guangxi, Yunnan is not an autonomous region because no one of its minority groups has a sufficiently large population to be dominant; but within the province there are some twenty auto-nomous zones and districts, created in the 1950s and '60s. Minorities include the Bai around the town of Dali, the Dai (Thai) in the south and south-west, the Yi, scattered over a vast area south and east of Kunming, the Miao in the east, the Zang (Tibetan) in the north, the Naxi in the north-west, and many others; they constitute about one-third of the total population of Yunnan.

History. The Han Chinese penetrated Yunnan in the third century B.C. but they controlled only the plateaus, while the minority peoples in their often inaccessible valleys enjoyed complete autonomy. In A.D. 751, the Chinese armies were defeated in Yunnan by the emerging Nanzhao kingdom, founded by ancestors of the Thai, and for the next five centuries China lost control over the Southwest. When the Mongols conquered Yunnan in the thirteenth century, Moslem administrators were sent in and a portion of the population converted to Islam; there is still a sizeable Hui (Moslem) minority in the province. But the Naxi people in north-western Yunnan rejected Mongol rule and formed the independent Mu kingdom, which lasted into the 1730s, when the whole of the province was finally brought under Manchu control.

With the rebuilding of the palace in Beijing, Yunnan timber was in great demand, and its wealth in non-ferrous metals, in particular copper and tin, attracted the foreigners. The Zhifu (Chefoo) Convention of 1876 gave the

British trading rights in the province. The French, already occupying Indo-China, obtained similar rights in 1896, and in the hope of draining the province's resources southwards built the Kunming-Haiphong railway. In the Second World War the Japanese invasion forced the Nationalists to retreat into Sichuan, where they were cut off from the rest of the country and later, when the Japanese took Hong Kong and French Indo-China, from the rest of the world. The only tenuous link was the Burma Road, 1,000 km of dirt road over high mountains and deep precipices, from Lashio in Burma to Kunming, following the southern branch of the old Silk Route, which was opened to motor vehicles in 1939; when it was cut by the Japanese offensive in 1942 supplies had to be airlifted to Kunming from India.

KUNMING 昆

Kunming (Brilliance for Generations), capital of Yunnan, is almost in the centre of the province, on the Yunnan plateau 1,800 m above sea level, north of a large lake, the Dianchi. It is linked by rail to Sichuan and Guizhou provinces, and to Hanoi in Vietnam, but as Guizhou is still (1979) closed to tourists, it is only worth travelling by train to Kunming if one is also visiting Sichuan. There are regular air services between Kunming and Nanning, Chengdu, Xi'an and Zhengzhou. The city can be visited in three to five days.

Kunming is also known as 'Spring City' because the weather is mild the year round. It is one of the very few Chinese cities pleasant to visit in any season. January is the coldest month, with temperatures averaging 9°C., and May the warmest, with temperatures averaging 21°C. This temperate climate is due to the altitude. Being in the sub-tropical to tropical zone, the city receives abundant rainfall, in particular in the summer, and is often shrouded in mist.

Foreigners stay at the *Kunming Hotel*, in East Dengfeng Road, in the city centre, tel. 3919. The rooms are spacious and clean and the food adequate. A new hotel for tourists is being built (1979).

Local culinary specialities include Yunnan ham and steamed chicken. Vendors in the streets sell roasted lemon seeds and thin pancakes stuffed with soy paste.

A number of original handicrafts are produced in the province, largely by and for the minorities. Miao embroidery, swords and daggers made by the Achang people near the Burmese border, boots, hats and sashes for minorities costumes, and cotton batik can be found in the Minorities Store, the Arts and Crafts Store and the hotel lobby shop; everyday Chinese traditional clothing can be obtained in the Department Store. A Friendship Store is being built.

History. Under the Han Chinese Kunming, founded in 109 B.C., lived off trade: timber, salt, silver and gold were sent to the North and silks and manufactured products of the North exported via the Silk Route. The city was the secondary capital of the Nanzhao kingdom founded in the eighth century A.D., and did not fall to the Mongols until 1274. The Ming took Kunming in 1382, and rebuilt a walled town to the north-west of the former site. In the mid-nineteenth century Du Wenxiu, leader of revolts in the mining regions of the north-west, created an Islamic kingdom with Dali — the former capital of the Nanzhao kingdom — as his capital. Although the Sultan of Dali never took Kunming, he besieged it several times, inflicting great damage before his rebellion was suppressed in a bloodbath in 1873.

Places of interest.   Kunming itself has few interesting buildings or sites, though the town has kept a flavour of the old Yunnanfu (its former name), with its narrow cobbled back streets where chickens peck amongst children playing in front of two-storey houses and open markets. On its outskirts are a number of places worth visiting:

Cuihu (Green Lake) and Yuantong Hill, in the north-west quarter of the city, have both been turned into public parks. The Yuantong temple, on the southern slope of the hill, which is covered in lush green trees, dates from the third century A.D. There is also a zoo with some 400 species of animals, and the Provincial Museum, at present closed (1979). The lake is bordered with willows and fragrant cassia trees; a small palace with red walls stands on the north shore.

The Daguanlou (Tower of the Great Perspective) and Daguan Park are south-west of the city, on the north shore of the great lake Dianchi, also called Kunming Lake, twenty minutes by car from downtown Kunming. The tower, built in 1690 on the lake shore, is a three-storey whitewashed building with grey tiled roofs and galleries running round the second and third floors from which one can gaze at the lake and hills: hence its name. A long poem by a Qing dynasty poet, Sun Ranweng, praising the beauty of the lake is inscribed on the façade of the tower.

The West Hill, by the lake shore, is best visited in the morning when the eastern slope overlooking the lake is in the sunshine. From West Hill, you can take a boat tour on the lake, having brought a picnic lunch from the hotel which you will eat on board. A walk to the highest point of the Hill at the Dragon Gate takes two hours, the path at first running through thick woods and then emerging towards the top, cut through the barren rock face.

On the way you pass the Huatingsi (Temple of the Flower Pavilion), built in the fourteenth century. During the Song dynasty, when Yunnan was ruled by the Nanzhao kingdom, it was a country villa for the king. It has been restored recently. Celestial guardians about 6 m tall stand on either side of the entrance, protected by the roof of the gate building. The first hall contains the statues of the Four Heavenly Kings, vividly painted, and of Maitreya Buddha. In one of the halls, there is a wooden model of a pavilion of the Nanzhao country villa. Further along the path, the Taihuasi (Great Flower Temple), built in the early fourteenth century, is situated at a particularly good spot for viewing the sunrise. Many beautiful flowering trees grow within the temple compound, including magnolias, camellias and cassia trees. Its Hall of the Precious Hero contains three beautiful statues of Buddha with two disciples and rows of Lohans, all carved with individual expressions, probably dating from the Ming and in an excellent state of preservation.

The Longmen, or Dragon Gate, stands across a path hacked out of the cliff face, the result of twenty-nine years of difficult labour. The carvings were made by the Taoist monk Wu Laiqing and a number of stone cutters between 1781 and 1843. The path passes several caves, the Ciyundong (Cave of the Compassionate Clouds), Yunhuadong (Cave of the Splendour of the Clouds), then the Dragon Gate, a lacquered wooden portico built on an overhanging terrace, from which one can view the Dianchi lake below, and finally the Datiange (Tower which Reaches Heaven). The last grotto on the way up is dedicated to a deity who helps students taking the Imperial Examinations. His weapon is a brush and the walls of the cave are engraved with inscriptions by grateful graduates.

The Sanqingge (Tower of the Three Pure Ones) is a Taoist temple built in steps against the vertical drop of the cliff. It was once a country villa for Prince Liang of the Yuan dynasty, and was later named Yuhuangge (Tower of the Jade Emperor). It was repaired and added to several times during the Ming dynasty, but no more halls were added after the end of the nineteenth century. The temple is dedicated to the three main deities of the Taoist pantheon, but within the compound are halls dedicated to many deities.

Environs of Kunming. About 12 km to the north-west of Kunming, on a quiet, wooded slope of Mount Yufeng, is the Qiongzhusi, Monastery of the Qiong Bamboo (a variety of bamboo from Sichuan), said to have been founded under the Tang. It was burned down in 1419, rebuilt in 1422, and restored again between 1883 and 1890. The hall of the Five Hundred Lohans is the most interesting part of the temple. In 1884 the abbot of the temple hired a master sculptor, De Shen, from his native province, Sichuan, to depict the Five Hundred Lohans. The sculptor set to work with three local craftsmen, often searching for inspiration amongst the people of Kunming and the neighbouring villages. The result is a collection of highly individualistic and realistic figures, made of painted clay over a wooded frame, which were considered in bad taste by contemporary scholars and devotees. His work completed, De Shen vanished and was never heard of again.

The Jindian (Golden Palace), about 10 km north-east of Kunming, dates from the end of the Ming. It was considerably enlarged by the rebel general Wu Sangui (see p. 75) who, sent by the Manchu rulers in 1659 to subdue the province of Yunnan, made himself master for twenty years of the southwest of the country, and used this as a summer palace. The entrance is marked by four triumphal arches (*pailou*) which lead to the Hall of the Great Peace. The Golden Hall, which gives its name to the palace, is built on a terrace of white marble. The pillars are made of bronze which once was gilded, as were the wood beams supporting the roof; the roof itself was covered in thin copper tiles. Near by is the Black Dragon Pool, a garden graced with pavilions in which there are two adjoining ponds, one with clean, one with muddy water, but which do not mix. The Jindian and Black Dragon Pool can be visited in one morning.

LUNAN (7) 路南

Lunan (South of the Road) is a county town in an autonomous district inhabited by people of the Yi nationality, some 100 km south-east of Kunming. The local attraction is the Stone Forest, known all over China — a quite extraordinary sight. A tour of the strange stone formations takes two to three hours. Limestone towers and columns rise vertically from the ground in thick formations resembling, from a distance, a forest of pine trees. Some of them are inscribed with large characters carved in the stone by admiring visitors over the centuries.

The journey by road from Kunming takes nearly three hours, and visitors who have time to make the excursion usually stay the night in a guesthouse which is rather primitive.

2 Sichuan and the Yangzi River Gorges

Sichuan, with 10 per cent of the country's inhabitants, is the most populous province of China. The Tibetan population alone numbers more than 1 million. This westernmost of the eighteen provinces of imperial China is bordered by Tibet and Qinghai to the west, and isolated from its eastern neighbours by high mountains. Agricultural activity is concentrated in the fertile Red Basin, surrounded by mountainous ranges 2,500 to 3,500 m high. The basin lies at an altitude of about 600 m and is watered by the Ming River and its tributaries. Though the name Sichuan means 'Four Rivers', the province is actually watered by the Yangzi River and seven major left-bank tributaries, all flowing in a north-south direction. The Red Basin, named after the colour of the soil, enjoys a moist and temperate climate and does not have severe frost. The average January temperature is about 10°C. and July, 20°C. Rain falls most heavily in June, July and August, but also throughout the year. Most of the basin is shrouded in mist from October to March. April-May and September-October are the best months for visiting the province.

Agricultural production is more efficient in Sichuan than in some other parts of the country. Rice is grown in summer and wheat in winter in the lowlands, and millet, corn and sorghum in the dry terraced fields. Cotton and silk are also produced in large quantities, together with a variety of vegetables and fruit, making the province completely self-sufficient agriculturally. Citrus fruit and sugar cane grow in the southern sub-tropical region of the Tuo River basin.

Sichuan has abundant mineral resources: coal, iron ore, petroleum, natural gas, copper, asbestos and salt, and its industrial development was given a great impetus when the Nationalist government retreated to Chongqing after the Japanese invasion during World War Two. Chengdu and Chongqing, the two major cities of eastern Sichuan, were linked by rail in 1952 and the line prolonged north to Baoji (towards Xi'an) in 1956. The connection to the south-east, with Guizhou province, was only completed in 1966, thus ending the reliance on transportation by waterways.

The journey by train from Beijing to Chengdu, via Xi'an and Baoji, takes about two and a half days — and another twelve hours (unfortunately possible only by night train) to Chongqing. The last third of the journey from Baoji to Chengdu, is through beautiful and unspoiled mountains along the course of the Jialing River, through Shanxi, Gansu and north-east Sichuan. Small hamlets or isolated farms huddle in small valleys, and for miles only slender suspended rope bridges span the river. The Tang dynasty Buddhist carvings at Guangyuan, sculpted out of the cliff face, can be seen from the train but the area is not open to tourists.

CHENGDU 成都

Chengdu (Perfect Metropolis), formerly Huayang, capital of the province, is situated in a plain watered by the Min and Tuo Rivers and their many tributaries and surrounded by heavily populated and meticulously cultivated countryside. Chengdu municipality has a population of over 3 million, with over 1 million in the city itself.

The best times to visit Chengdu are in the spring and autumn; summers are hot, humid and unpleasant, and fog settles for four months at the end of October. In three to four days you will have time to see the most interesting sites, even distant ones. Chengdu is linked by rail to Xi'an and Kunming; it is the point of departure for flights to Tibet and is linked by air to Lanzhou (Gansu province), Wuhan, Changsha, Guiyang (in Guizhou province, at present closed to tourists) and Kunming.

Chengdu has two hotels which accommodate foreign tourists. The *Jinjiang* (Brocade River) *Guesthouse*, tel. 4481, named after one of the local rivers, is in the south of the old town, on the west side of Renmin Road South. It was built in 1956 for Soviet experts and is fairly well run and comfortable, with a well-appointed lobby shop, post office, barber and same-day laundry service. The *New Chengdu Hotel*, completed in 1979, has 500 rooms; it is situated opposite the Jinjiang, also in Renmin Road South. Both hotels serve reasonable food with a fair proportion of local dishes. Sichuan cuisine, one of the great cuisines of China, with hot, peppery dishes, can be sampled at the *Chengdu Restaurant*, in Shengli Road East, or at the *Furong Restaurant*, in Renmin Road South, near the hotel.

There are several colourful shopping streets in the eastern district of the old town. The old Chunsi Road, now renamed Fandi (Anti-imperialist) Road, north section, has several interesting shops and a small open-air flower market in a tiny square presided over by a statue of Sun Yatsen. There is an arts and crafts shop at No. 10, a pot shop, and a fan shop which sells hand-painted fans and original paintings by local artists at sky-high prices. There is also a painting shop, equally expensive. Local handicrafts include bamboo and silk articles, lacquerware, brocade, embroideries and Tibetan handicrafts (silver jewellery).

The old Salt Market, re-named the Workers', Peasants' and Soldiers' Market, is in Jiefang Road, central section. It has a store selling articles for the minorities: silk sashes, knives, hats, boots, gold braid, etc., most of which are made in Sichuan province, and not in the minorities regions. An antique shop is being opened in the Nanjiao (South Suburb) Park.

History. Sichuan province has the reputation of being the first to rebel and the last to submit. In the period of the Three Kingdoms, Chengdu, then known as Yizhou, was the capital of the kingdom of Shu Han, ruled by Liu Bei, a descendant of the fallen Han dynasty who in the middle of the third century A.D. tried unsuccessfully to reconquer the empire and restore the dynasty. With the help of a valiant general, Guan Yu, and of the minister strategist Zhuge Liang, Liu Bei fought continuously against the rival kingdoms of Wu in the south and Wei in the north, but the Wei emerged victorious and the Shu Han kingdom fell in 263.

In 745, Emperor Xuan Zong of the Tang, already in his sixties, took for his concubine the beautiful Yang Guifei (see p.103). A 'barbarian' general, An Lushan, who had become the concubine's protégé, staged a revolt in 755, and the Emperor had to flee to Sichuan. On the way, his soldiers threatened to abandon him unless Yang Guifei was executed, and she had to commit suicide. During the seven years of the rebellion, the Emperor and the court resided in Chengdu while the north of the country was being torn apart. Eventually, in 762, the Emperor abdicated in favour of one of his sons. Chengdu put up a fierce resistance against the Mongols and the city was almost destroyed during the fighting.

During the Ming dynasty, to guard against rebellion, the viceroy of Sichuan was always chosen from among the members of the Imperial clan. In 1644, a troop of 100,000 rebels led by Zhang Xiangzhong, nicknamed 'Yellow Tiger', invaded the province through the Yangzi gorges. They first took Chongqing, and then Chengdu, where they established an independent kingdom at the same time as the North was being conquered by the rebel Li Zicheng and the Ming dynasty terminated. Zhang's government had ministries and a Grand Secretariat, held examinations and minted money, but it sought to control the gentry by terror. Historical records say that Zhang killed 600 million people (no doubt an exaggeration) before he was himself killed by the Manchu in 1647. During the Qing dynasty, Chengdu had a permanent garrison of 4,000 Bannermen, living in fortified quarters within the city.

Places of interest. Chengdu is a charming old provincial city, once surrounded by a wall (now demolished) and a moat, still largely intact. Most of the houses are built of wood with an overhanging upper floor, reminiscent of Tudor houses or old cottages in Normandy. The Palace of the Viceroy, built in the Ming dynasty for a son of Emperor Hong Wu, used to stand at the centre of the city, in what is now the People's Park. To the shame of the municipality, it was demolished and replaced in 1973 by a Palace of Culture in pure Stalinist style.

The Tang dynasty poet Dufu (Tu Fu) (712-70) served for ten years as a minor official in Chang'an (Xi'an); when the An Lushan revolt broke out, he was captured by the rebels and later fled to Sichuan. In 759 he arrived in Chengdu, where he spent three years in a modest cottage, writing hundreds of poems, mostly inspired by the sufferings of the people during the civil war. Here is one of them:

A GUEST ARRIVES

South of my cottage and north, spring streams are flowing,
Gulls alone are my daily visitors.
The garden paths have not been swept for guests.
For you alone the thatched door is open now.
Shopping has been perforce at distant markets,
And all delicacies cannot be purchased.
Since I am poor, all I can provide
Is the wine in the old jar.
If you are willing to drink with my neighbour,
I shall ask him to come over the fence and join us.*

Dufu left Chengdu after 762 and wandered in the southern provinces and eventually died in exile. After his death, the people of Chengdu built a shrine on the site of his garden and it became the custom to visit it on the seventh day of the first lunar month (around the middle of February), when the plum blossoms for which the garden is famous are at their best. The original cottage no longer exists and the buildings within the cottage compound, south-west of the city, have been repaired and added to thirteen times since the eighth century.

The halls and side buildings in the forecourt contain calligraphy by famous persons from Ming times to the present. A small hall in the eastern section of the grounds, dedicated to the memory of the poet, contains a statue of Dufu flanked by those of two other poets: Huang Tingzhen on the right and Lu You (1125-1210) on the left. In a small building to the south-west of the Memorial Hall is an exhibition of many editions, some very old, of Dufu's poems. Leaving the grounds of the cottage by the Flowery Path, one comes to the former Dufu Temple, now desecrated and dedicated to the memory of a visit by Chairman Mao on 7 March 1958. A screen wall at the entrance to the Flowery Path is decorated with the characters *Caotang* (Thatched Cottage) in fragments of old blue and white ceramic.

The Wangjianglou (Pavilion for Viewing the River) is in what is now a public park next to Sichuan University, in the south-east

---

101 Chinese Poems, trans. Shih Shun-liu (Hong Kong, 1967).

suburbs overlooking the Jinjiang (Brocade River). Over a hundred varieties of bamboo are grown in this park which, apart from the four-storey Wangjianglou, also contains two smaller pavilions, all three built out of fragrant and durable cedar wood, with sharply upturned roof-ends and decorated with pieces of broken ceramics in the local fashion. The present buildings date from the Qing dynasty. From these towers court officials and their ladies viewed the changing colours of the river and the Dragon Boat Festival Races which are traditionally held on the fifth day of the fifth lunar month (early June), in memory of the poet Qu Yuan (see p.181). In the park, there is a well named after the Tang dynasty poetess Xue Tao, who is said to have drowned herself in it. Near by also is the tomb of Wang Jian, a rebel who at one time set himself up as emperor of the kingdom of Shu. The tomb was excavated in 1943; a small museum on the site was due to reopen in 1979.

The Wuhousi, in the south-west suburbs, is a temple dedicated to Zhuge Liang (A.D. 181-234), the great strategist of the Three King-doms period. A native of Shandong province, he was living in Hubei when the Emperor Liu Bei visited him, three times, to ask him to join in the reconquest of the Han empire, which he agreed to do in 207, when he was only twenty-six years old. Several later emperors have visited the temple and left inscriptions on tablets preserved there.

The first hall is dedicated to Emperor Liu Bei whose statue stands behind the front altar, flanked by his son and grandson. To the right of the main shrine is the red-faced image of Guan Yu, the brave general subsequently raised to the status of God of War, with his four sons; to the left is General Zhang Fei, another valiant general of the state of Shu Han, represented with a black face, accompanied by his grandson. In two galleries along the sides of the first courtyard are Qing dynasty terracotta figures, forty-seven in all, of generals on the right and ministers on the left. The courtyard of the second hall, dedicated to Zhuge Liang, has a Bell Tower on the right and a Drum Tower on the left of the entrance. A most unusual cast-iron incense burner in the middle of the path leading to the hall has handles in the shape of two little figures peeping over the top. Zhuge Liang's statue, accom-panied by his son on the right and his grandson on the left, stands in the middle of the hall. The two bronze drums on pedestals used to be struck before every battle. Among the stone tablets embedded in the north wall of the hall is one by the poet Dufu.

The temple, which was already in existence in the Tang dynasty, has been restored many times and the present buildings date from the Qing dynasty. Immediately to the west of it is the site of the Emperor Liu Bei's tomb, of which all that is left is a tumulus, 80 m in circumference and about 12 m high, surrounded by a circular wall. There are no statues, only some steles.

The Nanjiao Gongyuan (South Suburb Park), to the west of the temple and the tomb, is a green and peaceful haven by comparison, with a lake and a small temple now used as a teahouse for distinguished guests. You can have a cup of tea in its shaded court-yard, where potted plants and trained shrubs grow. Local artists and craftsmen exhibit their works in a gallery within the park.

Environs of Chengdu. The Baoguangsi (Monastery of the Precious Light), a Buddhist temple about 30 km north-east of Chengdu, in Xindu county, was already in existence during the Tang dynasty, and once had a community of 3,000 monks. In the late Qing dynasty, the number was reduced to 300 but it was still the main teaching monastery of the province. Only nineteen monks live there now (1979) and the temple is no longer open for worship.

A dragon screen, two incinerators for burning paper offerings and two red sandstone lions mark the entrance to the temple, and two ferocious-looking statues of Guardians stand inside the gate-house.

The first hall is dedicated to Maitreya Buddha, accompanied by the statues of the Four Heavenly Kings. Immediately behind it, at a somewhat slanted angle, is a small fifteen-storey pagoda, each level adorned with a row of twelve little Buddhas, which dates back to the Tang dynasty. The Seven Buddha Hall, which can be seen next, has a roof of grey tiles decorated with broken pieces of ceramic, supported by unpainted pillars each made of a single tree trunk, two of which, at the centre, also date from the Tang dynasty. Inside the hall, two rows of eight rubbings of Lohans hang on the walls.

The third hall contains a Sakyamuni Buddha with two Bodhisattvas, and a two-foot-tall white jade statue of Buddha, of the Ming dynasty. The ceremonial gong, carved out of a single piece of wood, and decorated with a pair of gilt goldfish on red lacquer, still rests on the left of the altar, and, on the right, one can see a cast-iron drum and a bell. The Bodhisattva Guanyin (Kuanyin) stands at the back of the altar; the walls are decorated with paintings of sixteen Lohans and four Bodhisattvas.

The fourth hall bears the inscription 'When you are awakened from a long sleep, you are not far from the banks of eternal bliss'. It is empty of any sculpture, but the walls are hung with paintings, some of them very large, and protected after a fashion by sheets of plastic pinned directly through them. The hall to the right of the fourth hall has some paintings and carvings, including a One Thousand Buddhas stele dated A.D. 540, found in the vicinity of Chengdu. In the hall to the left are various relics kept in the temple since its foundation.

To the east of the fourth temple hall, a gateway leads into a shaded courtyard with numerous potted plants. In a reception room, tea is served in two-centuries-old china mugs, with the Tang dynasty pagoda of the temple painted on them. The eastern part of the temple is a maze of courtyards and buildings, including the monks' living quarters, a hall of the Five Hundred Lohans, a hall built around a little pagoda carved out of a single block of stone and another containing a thousand-year-old statue of Guanyin.

The Guihu Gongyuan (Cassia, or Cinnamon, Lake Park), also in Xindu county, is usually visited together with the Baoguang monastery but is not worth a special excursion. It is the garden of an old country house which used to belong to Yang Shen, a Ming dynasty scholar of the sixteenth century who was put in prison for having dared to criticize Emperor Jia Jing, and later sent into exile in Yunnan. His wife stayed in the Cassia Lake garden and used to send him poems about the fragrant cassia trees, of which there were said to be five hundred planted around the lake. Yang Shen returned to the garden only after his wife's death, when he was seventy-one; he then returned to Yunnan, where he died a year later. The park has a small lake overgrown with lotus and is surrounded by a thick old wall from the top of which one can survey the gentle countryside. A small museum (closed in 1979) is housed in the former residential quarters.

The Guangxian Waterworks, 45 km north of Chengdu, are a technological wonder of the country. They were designed by a Qin dynasty engineer, Li Bing (c. 250-200 B.C.) who was sent to Sichuan at the end of the Warring States period, and designed and built several water control projects. The most famous of these, the Guangxian waterworks, were started in 256 B.C. to divert the waters of the river Min, which used to flood the valley, and channel them into irrigation canals. The project is currently being expanded, and by 1980, there will be 11 million *mu* (c. 1.8 million acres) of land under irrigation, supporting a population of 7 million.

At the site a Taoist temple, the Fulongguan (Temple of the Harnessed Dragon), commands a magnificent view of the river valley where the dragon — in Chinese mythology master of underground water — has been harnessed, and has a statue of Li Bing. A short drive away, through the irrigated area and over a hill, is the Two Kings Temple, set in the woods by the river Min, near an old suspension bridge. Li Bing and his son were granted the posthumous title of Wang (King), hence the name of the temple built in their honour just over a thousand years ago. A stone tablet is engraved with a famous eight-character quotation from Li Bing: 'When the river flows in zig-zags, cut a straight channel/When the river bed is wide and shallow, dig it deeper'. The temple, in which seven or eight Taoist monks still live, is a popular stopping place for sightseers. It is built up the side of the hill and one can enjoy a good view of the most modern parts of the water conservation project from its top.

LESHAN (13) 乐山

Leshan (Happy Mountain), at the confluence of the Min, Tatu and Chingyi Rivers, is 120 miles (190 km) south of Chengdu by road; the two places are also connected by ferry. Leshan, with less than 100,000 inhabitants, is in a naturally fortified position, built on a rocky promontory almost cut off from the land by the three rivers. Foreigners stay in a small but comfortable guesthouse.

Across the river is the Temple of the Great Buddha, which has a colossal seated figure carved in the eighth century out of the red sandstone on the face of the hill. The Buddha is 70 m high; the big toes of his feet are larger than a human being. Steps are carved out of the rock on the side to enable visitors to see the figure up close, but the best view is from the river or from the opposite bank.

Further downstream is another large temple, the Wuyousi, founded in the Tang dynasty and repaired during the Ming and Qing dynasties. It contains among other pieces the statues of eighteen Lohans, particularly lifelike. The temple is not open for worship but houses a small archaeological museum. An art gallery for local painters has been opened in the former hall of the Five Hundred Lohans.

EMEISHAN (Mount Omei) (14) 峨眉山

From Leshan one goes by car to Omei (Emei), some 40 km to the west, for the climb to Emeishan, highest of the four sacred mountains of Buddhism. There were already some temples on Mount Omei in the Eastern Han dynasty (second century A.D.), although most of the existing ones were founded in the sixth century when Buddhism spread to northern and western China. Emeishan became one of the four Buddhist sanctuaries in the sixteenth century, when a great many of the seventy or so temples still standing were rebuilt and enlarged.

Emeishan (High Eyebrow Mountain), which is very wild and unexplored in parts, is also a nature reserve for some 3,000 species of animals including monkeys and small pandas, and giant butter-flies. Wild azaleas and tall *nanmu* (a species of cedar) grow in abundance. In clear weather, the snow-capped mountains of Tibet are visible from the summit.

Visitors have to register at the bottom of the trek to give advance notice for catering and lodging, as well as for their safety. The path, cut out of the green rock, is quite dangerous and difficult to follow in places and all visitors are accompanied by a local guide. Accommodation in the temples is, of course, rudimentary. The summit is at an altitude of 3,137 m, but foreigners are not allowed to go all the way to the top.

The trek begins at the Baoguosi (Temple for Protecting the Country) (**1**), at an altitude of about 600 m. The temple was built in the sixteenth century On the ground floor of the Library of Sutras is a porcelain figure of Buddha 3.4 m high, made in the Yong Le era, in 1416. In front of the hall of the Seven Buddhas stands a bronze pagoda 7 m high decorated with rows of little Buddhas, 4,700 in all, and inscribed with the Huayan (Garland) sutra.

Taking the left-hand path after leaving the Baoguosi, one arrives after a walk of about 2 km, to an altitude of 800 m at the Fuhusi (Temple of the Crouching Tiger) (**2**), surrounded by very tall cedars. Founded during the Sui dynasty (sixth century), the temple was rebuilt in 1652. Its name comes from the shape of the mountain at this spot.

The path continues past the Temple of the Sound of Thunder, Leiyingsi (**3**), built at an altitude of 900 m in front of the Pagoda Mountain. The way parts into two main branches at a particularly beautiful spot called the Little Gate of the Sound of Clear Water, Qingyingge (**4**), behind which rises the Ox Heart mountain range, Niuxinling.

The right-hand path leads after about an hour's walk to the Wanniansi (Temple of Ten Thousand Years) (**5**), dedicated to the patron saint of Emeishan, the Bodhisattva Puxian. A guesthouse at this point is equipped to receive visitors for meals and overnight. The temple, one of the oldest and most famous on Emeishan, was founded in the fourth century. It was almost entirely destroyed by fire in 1946. Only the Brick Hall (Zhuandian)

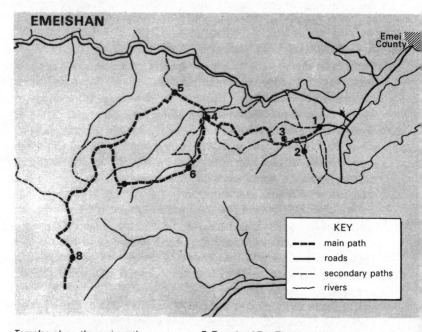

EMEISHAN

Emei County

KEY
- - - main path
—— roads
- - - - secondary paths
〜〜 rivers

Temples along the main path
1 Temple for Protecting the Country
2 Temple of the Crouching Tiger
3 Temple of the Sound of Thunder
4 Little Gate of the Sound of Clear Water
5 Temple of Ten Thousand Years
6 Hongchun Temple
7 Temple of the Magic Peak
8 Temple of the Golden Summit

containing the famous statue of Puxian seated on an elephant survived. This bronze and cast-iron image, made in 980 A.D. is 9.1 m high; the elephant is brightly painted while the Bodhisattva, seated on the Lotus Throne and wearing a heavy crown, is entirely gilded. The square walls and dome-shaped roof of the Brick Hall are decorated inside with rows of small seated figures of Buddha.

Hongchun Temple (6) is named after the tall trees of the cedar family growing all around it. The temple was founded in the fourth century A.D. but the present halls were built in 1790. It has dining rooms and bedrooms and is about two hours' walk on the left-hand path from the Little Gate of the Sound of Clear Water. After a walk uphill of about 3 km, one arrives at the Temple of the Magic Peak, Xianfengsi (7), built in the middle of the seventeenth century. To the right of the temple, nine caves have been hollowed out of the rock. They are much more ancient than the temple and are inhabited by large bats.

The two paths to the Golden Summit meet after about two hours' walk from the Temple of the Magic Peak. The Jindingsi (Temple of the Golden Summit) (8) crowns the mountain; built in the sixteenth century, it contains a large bronze statue of Buddha made in Hubei province in 1890 and hauled to the top.

From the summit of Emeishan, at present inaccessible to foreign tourists, one can see the sun rise over the Ocean of Clouds. At about 3 or 4 p.m., a phenomenon known as the Precious Light of Buddha occurs, when rings of rainbow colours, produced by the light deflected through particles of water suspended in the air, shine against the cliff face. The shadow of a person against the Precious Light is projected upside down. Devout Buddhists have been known to jump off the precipice in order to attain Nirvana.

CHONGQING (Chungking) 重庆

Chongqing (Noble Good Fortune) is situated in eastern Sichuan province, at the confluence of two mighty rivers, the Jialing and Yangzi. The whole city is built on rocky promontories, with little wooden houses clinging to the rockside and steep steps leading down to the river. The Chongqing municipality has a population of about 6,000,000 (including the suburbs).

Thick fog settles over the city, as over most of the province, from October to March and the summers are scorching hot: Chongqing is one of the 'three furnaces' of China (the other two being Nanjing and Wuhan). April and September are the best months for tourism. Chongqing, an overnight journey by train from Chengdu, is the starting point for the down-river Yangzi Gorges cruise. A day is sufficient time to spend in the city before boarding the cruise vessel, or after disembarking from it.

At present, three hotels receive foreign tourists. The *Chongqing*

Binguan (Chungking Guesthouse) in Minsheng Street, built in 1944, is very run-down and dirty. The *People's Hall Hotel*, in Renmin Street, has recently been renovated and affords decent accommodation in the centre of the town. It is in a wing of the People's Hall, built in 1954, which is used for large conferences. The *Yuzhou Hotel*, set in a park in the south-eastern suburbs, near the Chongqing Medical College, provides comfortable accommodation for large delegations, but is far from the centre of town. In addition to these three, a new hotel is being built with state funds and should be completed in 1980.

Places of interest. Chongqing, called Yuzhou (Yuchow) during the historical period of the Three Kingdoms, is a natural stronghold to which the Nationalist government of Chiang Kaishek retreated from the invading Japanese armies in 1938. Today it is a black industrial town with very few buildings of interest, still bearing the marks of the last war, when it was heavily bombed by the Japanese, and neglected by the government in the decade before 1976. Owing to its dramatic natural setting, however, it is not entirely without beauty. Take a walk through the narrow streets and watch from the Chaotianmen (Gate towards the Sky), at the tip of the peninsula, the skillful navigating of the ferries across the muddy and turbulent waters of the Jialing and Yangzi Rivers as crowds of people carrying baskets and bundles climb the long steps leading to the piers. The now abandoned airstrip on the little island of Shan Hu Ba in the middle of the Yangzi was for several years a lifeline for the besieged city.

The Red Crag Village, in the western suburbs, along the Jialing, was the site of the Eighth Route Army's Chongqing office and the Southern Bureau of the Central Committee of the Chinese Communist Party, headed by Zhou Enlai. When Chairman Mao came to Chongqing in 1945 to negotiate a truce with Chiang Kaishek, the Communist delegation stayed at No. 50 Cengjiayan Street, in the north-west of town, which can also be visited.

Two former SACE (Sino-American Special Technical Co-operation Organization) prisons, in the Shaping district north-west of Chongqing, are a grim reminder of how the Nationalists treated their Communist captives. These two prisons, the Beigongyuan (Mr Bei's Summer House), formerly the residence of a Sichuan warlord, and the Zhazedong (Cave of Coal Cinders), once a coal pit, used to be known as 'coffins for the living'.

Some distance from Chongqing are two parks which may be visited. The Beibei (Northern Hot Springs) park, about 75 km north of the city, was opened to the public in 1927. A Ming dynasty temple on the site, dedicated to General Guan Yu of the Three Kingdoms period (see p.220), was partly destroyed by rockfall and rebuilt during the Qing dynasty. Three swimming pools contain water which comes out of the ground at a temperature of 38°C. The Beibei are not worth the time and expense of a whole day's excursion, but at the Nanbei (Southern Hot Springs), about 20 km south of the city, one can go boating on the Flowery Creek and visit the Caves of the Fairies.

THE YANGZI (Yangtze) GORGES

Scheduled cruises down what the Chinese call Chang Jiang (Long River) depart from Chongqing on odd days of the month and arrive in Wuhan two and a half days later. Up-river cruises take four and a half days. In addition CTS organizes special tourist cruises on well-run modern boats, with cabins for two and simple but clean facilities. Following is an account of a down-river cruise.

Day One. After leaving the industrial suburbs of Chongqing — the view of the city from the river is quite spectacular — the Yangzi, heavy with soil, flows fast through a landscape of fairly steep hills with terraced fields, ugly towns and pretty villages. The first stop is at Fuling, after a four-hour journey. At each stop, the boat turns round and anchors facing the current.

The next stop, two hours later, is at Fengdu, on the north bank, a mediaeval-looking small town. After a further two hours, the boat stops at the industrial town of Zhongxian, west of which, around the next bend of the river, stands a sugar-loaf shaped rock with a temple, called the Shibaozhai, on top. Its entrance, cut through the rock, is surmounted by a ten-tier roof, and its many halls are built on the flat top of the rock. Thereafter the river narrows and flows between massive rocks. Only villages appear along the river for the next two hours of the journey until one arrives at the big town of WANXIAN (15) where the boat anchors for the night. Passengers can go ashore for a walk in the town.

Day Two. The first stop of the day, in the early morning, is at Yunyang, a pretty small town built high above the river, with a long flight of steps leading to the water. After Yunyang, the river bed narrows and the water flows rapidly between the walls of the mountains. It enters the Qutang Gorges, about 8 km long, just after the small town of Fengjie, still very mediaeval-looking with its old walls and its forbidding gate by the river side. The famous Baidicheng (Wall of the White God) rock bears many inscriptions, sometimes carved in almost inaccessible places. The Baidi-miao (Temple of the White God), on the north bank, where generations of Taoists used to pay sacrifices, is remarkably well preserved.

After the large town of WUSHAN, the river enters the second set of gorges, as it cuts through the Wushan (Wu Mountains) which separate the province of Sichuan from that of Hubei. The Yingfengguan (Welcome the Peak Temple) stands at the beginning of the gorges, which are about 40 km long, with the mountains reaching up to about 300 m casting dark shadows on the smooth surface of the water, broken at intervals by rapids. Further downstream, the river flows past the much-photographed Shennüfeng (Fairy Peak).

The town of Baodong, where the boat stops next, is built in a valley where the river widens briefly before flowing through the Xiling Gorges, about 25 km long, with their layered rocks containing the tumultuous river. Some fishermen's huts cling on the rock, and a few farmers cultivate tiny scattered plots on the steep slopes. The little town of Huanglingmiao (Temple of the Yellow Mound) with its brick-red temple lies in a valley. High rock formations, the Sanmatou (Three Horses' Heads), appear after a bend of the river, followed by the Dengying Gorges, with scattered rocks at the top looking like lanterns. The rock face turns to grey with yellow patches and, as one approaches the large industrial town of YICHANG, stone quarries in large numbers completely disfigure the scenery.

After Yichang, the river widens and slows down, turning chocolate brown. The boat stops three more times, at Zhijiang, SHASHI (**16**) and Jiangling, before arriving in Wuhan.

3 Xizang (Tibet)

The Tibetan highlands, which lie for the most part more than 4,000 m above sea level, have earned this land-locked region the name of 'Roof of the World'. Tibet is bordered to the north by the Xinjiang Autonomous Region, but is separated from it by the Kunlun Mountains which tower at 7,723 m. The only route into Xinjiang skirts the border with Kashmir. Communications with Qinghai province to the north-east are more direct, through the Tanggula Mountains, rising 'only' at 5,000 or 6,000 m above sea level. Sichuan and Yunnan provinces lie to the east of the Hengduan Mountains which follow a general north-south direction, channelling between their folds three powerful rivers: the Yangzi, Mekong and Salween. To the south the Himalayas at 8,848 m separate Tibet from India, Nepal and Burma.

Tibet can be divided into two natural regions: the Qing Zang plateau (Qinghai-Tibetan plateau), which stretches into Qinghai province and occupies two-thirds of the region, and the valley of the Yarlung Zangbo River to the south. Glaciers are the source of four powerful rivers, but the highlands where they originate are at an altitude such that almost no vegetation can survive, and no people can settle. Herding is the main activity in the valleys below 3,000 m, where most of the sparse population live.

In June, July and August — the only months during which tourists are allowed into Tibet — temperatures in Lhasa average 17°C., with a great difference between night and day. Summer rainfall can be heavy.

Very few people have as yet been able to visit Tibet. Permission to visit is granted sparingly, and only to special-interest groups: politicians, journalists and long-term 'friends of China'. Applicants must not only belong to one of these groups, but also be not too old, able to pass a stringent physical examination, and lastly have plenty of money and time. The average day's expenses in Tibet (room, board and transportation) are about eight times more than in most provinces of China, and this without taking into account the flight there. There are flights to Lhasa daily except Sundays from Chengdu in Sichuan, and daily from Lanzhou in Gansu; the inward flights depart early in the morning and the planes fly back to their base the same day. Flights operate only in optimum weather conditions and are often cancelled or delayed at short notice — usually while you are waiting at the airport — further decreasing your chances of getting to Tibet. Similarly, return flights can be delayed and unscheduled extra days will further increase the cost of the visit.

History. Little is known of Tibet before the seventh century A.D. when King Songtsan Gampo (Srongbtsan Sgam-po) unified Tibet for the first time, introduced an alphabet based on Sanskrit and administered his country on the Tang model. Tibet remained a small but strong military power, paying tribute to the Tang empire and raiding its neighbours — Nepal, India and also China — until the ninth century. Meanwhile, Buddhism took root in Tibet and, amalgamated with an early form of superstition called *Bon,* produced Lamaism. In the tenth century the assassination of the last lay king, Kang Darma, marked the beginning of the rise of the temporal power of the lamas, who accumulated land and serfs, fortified their monasteries, and attracted the sons of the nobility into their ranks.

In 1260, Basba, the head of the Red Hat sect (Sakya) paid a visit to the court of Kublai Khan in Beijing and was given the grand title of Imperial Tutor to the Tibetan people and paid tribute to the emperor. In the fourteenth century, a reform movement led by the lama Tsong Khapa created the Yellow Hat sect — named after the long conical hats worn by its lamas — which emphasized celibacy and discipline, and the two sects soon found themselves in conflict. Tsong Khapa turned to the Mongols, still powerful north of the Great Wall, and in 1572 the so-called third incarnation of Tsong Khapa's first disciple, head of the Yellow Hat sect, visited the court of Altan Khan in Mongolia, where he had conferred upon him the title of Dalai Lama (All Embracing Lama). The Dalai Lama, in turn, created a permanent head of the Lamaist church in Outer Mongolia, resident in Urga (Ulan Bator), who was the reincarnation of Tsong Khapa's third disciple. The Panchen Lama, who resides in Xigaze (Shigatse) west of Lhasa, is the reincarnation of Tsong Khapa's second disciple. Thus it was in the late sixteenth century that the principle of reincarnation was established and it is still in force today, after a fashion.

In 1641-2, the Mongols intervened in Tibet to crush the Red Hat sect and unified the country under the newly installed fifth Dalai Lama whom they had chosen. During his tenure, the Ming dynasty collapsed; the Manchu, seeing in the control of Tibet the key to subjugating the fierce Mongols, intervened militarily in Tibet until they were able to manipulate its government. In 1720, Qing armies penetrated into Tibet for the first time to chase an army of western Mongols, bringing with them the new seventh Dalai Lama, but it took another thirty years to restore order in the country so that the Dalai Lama could rule it with the help of two Qing viceroys backed by a garrison of 1500 men.

As the power of the Qing dynasty declined, military interventions ceased and in 1856, when the Gurkhas invaded Tibet, they were not chased out as they had been by the Qing armies in 1789, but instead were able to exact tribute from Tibet. The thirteenth Dalai Lama's attempt to break away from Chinese rule, with the help of Czarist Russia, prompted the last Qing armed intervention in Tibet in 1910. The dynasty was on its last legs, however, and the Dalai Lama declared independence of the territories in Tibet proper in 1913, leaving under Chinese control Xigang province, since abolished, and Qinghai.

When the Communists took power in 1949, they promptly re-asserted the former Manchu claims of sovereignty over Tibet. In 1950, fighting broke out between Chinese and Tibetan armies and the fourteenth Dalai Lama, then only a youth of fifteen, fled to India. After a year-long campaign, the Tibetans agreed to recognize Chinese suzerainty and the Chinese for their part undertook to let the Tibetans introduce reforms at their own pace and to respect the status of the Dalai and Panchen Lamas. Thereupon the Dalai Lama returned to Lhasa.

The People's Liberation Army began a gigantic task of road building — between 1952 and 1958 major highways were completed linking Tibet with Sichuan and Qinghai, western Xinjiang, Pakistan and Nepal. At the same time social and land reforms were introduced which alarmed the Dalai and Panchen Lamas so much that they both went to Beijing in 1954 to protest. While they were there, a revolt broke out among the Khamba, a Tibetan tribe living in western Sichuan province. This revolt spread to central Tibet with the help of monasteries where the lamas not only recruited men for the rebels, but also stored and supplied arms, and even took up arms themselves. The Dalai Lama returned to Lhasa only to leave again for India to gather support for Tibet. More arms flowed over the Himalayas. In 1959, a People's Conference held in Lhasa declared the independence of Tibet and gave the signal for an insurrection.

As the fighting began, a Preparatory Committee was set up by the Chinese to administer Tibet, which remained in charge until the Tibet Autonomous Region was established in 1965. The Chinese began by curtailing the monasteries' power: 2,500 were closed down or destroyed, a great portion of their land was redistributed to the serfs who were cultivating it, and novices, nuns and monks were induced to leave the monasteries. However, efforts at stamping out religious beliefs were not too successful and the monasteries are now open again for worship a few days a week.

LHASA 拉萨

Lhasa, situated on the banks of a tributary of the Yarlung Zambo (Brahmaputra), is at 3,800 m above sea level, and the first thing you are told after you land is 'take it easy'. At this altitude, oxygen is scarce and most people feel dizzy, short of breath, sick and irritable. CTS guides greet you with a smile and an oxygen pillow with a tube which you can insert into your nose to relieve the symptoms of altitude sickness. The trip from the airport to town takes an hour and a half and is spectacular, with mountain ranges outlined against the crisp blue sky. The guesthouse for foreigners is situated in the main east-west street which runs at the foot of the Bodala, palace of the Dalai Lama. It has only sixty rooms — which explains why tourists cannot come to Lhasa in large numbers — and is moderately comfortable. When the hotel is filled to capacity, however, the boiler runs out of hot water. The food, Chinese-style, is mediocre. Unfortunately, every view of the Bodala from the hotel windows has a factory chimney or a telephone pole in the foreground.

Visitors usually spend about five days in Lhasa. The old town, which is only ten to fifteen minutes' walk from the hotel, is delightful. The traditional houses are low, built of white-washed stones and their door and window frames are carved and painted. Almost every house is a shop and has a small courtyard at the back with a well. Goats wander about and there is an open-air market where the merchants sit on rugs or heaps of hay, displaying their wares: pots and pans, vegetables, junk. There are also commission shops which sell old and new Tibetan wool clothes, rugs, silver bowls, saddle rugs, fur hats, daggers, boots. There are also some 'luxury' shops run and owned by Nepalese — once there were 10,000 Nepalese living in Tibet, now there are 500 — where bargaining is part of the transaction and the goods tend to be of better quality, often imported from India or Nepal. Some people can be seen fingering prayer beads or spinning prayer-wheels and occasionally old women even stick their tongue out in respect, a reflex reaction to seeing rich people.

The Bodala (Potala). The palace-temple of the Dalai Lama — the name means 'Mountain of Buddha' — was first built by King Songtsan Gampo in the eighth century, who named it the Red Palace. The present structure, however, dates back to the time of the fifth Dalai Lama (1617-82). It took about fifty years to build and has a thirteen-storey tower above the city, visible from almost everywhere. Tourists are not made to climb the 125 steps which lead from the main street to its lower storeys, but driven up a back road on the northern slope. The approach to the zig-zagging staircase on the south slope is lined with houses once occupied by noblemen and lay ministers of the Dalai Lama.

This fortress-like palace, consisting of the red palace at the centre, and the white palace which was added in the twentieth century by the thirteenth Dalai Lama, is said to contain 1,000 rooms, 200,000 statues and 10,000 chapels. Because the Bodala is built on a hill and has been added to and remodelled many times in its 1,200 years of existence, no two storeys are continuous, and access to a large audience hall can be found through a small door hidden behind a pillar. Except in the upper storeys where the Dalai Lama used to live, the rooms are in almost total darkness, and CTS guides press the visitors from room to room with the dire warning that if they linger behind, they might get lost and locked up. The private apartments of the Dalai Lama at the top in the red palace, draped in silk and brocade and with Tantric paintings on the walls representing the Tibetan pantheon, contribute to the oppressive effect.

Of the several tombs, or Halls of Funerary Pagodas, built inside the Bodala, the largest and richest are those of the fifth and thirteenth Dalai Lamas. The tomb of the fifth is 20 m high, rising through three storeys of the building. The hall at the base of the tomb is filled with an accumulation of offerings; among them is a belt adorned with no less than 200,000 small pearls. The tomb is surmounted by a dagoba covered with gold leaf, and the walls of the hall painted with murals. In front of the altar in the tomb of the thirteenth Dalai Lama, 22 m high and made of solid silver covered with gold leaf and studded with precious and semi-precious stones, are two solid gold butter lamps. Offerings left by wealthy pilgrims include old ceramics, ritual vessels and banners.

And there are also the torture chambers and the dungeons at the bottom of the hill. The view from the terrace roof will take your breath away — if the climb hasn't already done so.

Other places of interest. The Zuglakang (also known as the Jokka Kang, Jokhan, Dazhaosi — the last being the Chinese version), the oldest building in Lhasa and the holiest of its temples, was founded in 652 to house the Tang dynasty statue of Sakyamuni Buddha brought by the Chinese Princess Wen Cheng, wife of King Songtsan Gampo. Situated in the main circular street, the Parkor, in the old town, within walking distance of the hotel, it is now open three days a week for worship. The architecture is a mixture of Chinese, Indian and Nepalese, and the roofs, surmounted by gilded copper dagobas, glisten under the pure blue sky.

It is a rather small temple and its main hall, three storeys high, is the oldest part. The walls and windows outside are shaded with dark yak-wool screens. Pounds of yak butter used to be burned as offerings every day, and some of the walls are still covered with a thick layer of grease. Frescoes have been discovered under the layer of dirt.

In the main hall (Dazhengdian) is the statue of Sakyamuni Buddha, enshrined in a small room; only the face, gilded, is visible. The statue, 2 m high, is seated on a golden throne between pillars of solid silver. Behind it is a flaming aura, also made of gold studded with precious stones. There are several other shrines, including one dedicated to the memory of King Songtsan Gampo who is represented with two of his wives, Princess Wen Cheng and his Nepalese wife.

The Norbu Lingga (Norbulingka) — the name means 'Jewel Park' — is the former summer palace of the Dalai Lama, where he lived from April to September to escape from his prison-palace at the Bodala. Now renamed the People's Park, it is a few kilometres west of Lhasa, in the valley. A small stream runs through the park, which is planted with many trees and contains scattered groups of buildings and pavilions, some destroyed by fire in 1956. The buildings have little architectural interest, when they are not simply ugly. People go there for picnics, and to see the erotic pictures decorating the Dalai Lama's private apartments.

The Drepung (Zhaibung Goin) monastery, about 10 km north-west of Lhasa, is where the Yellow Hat sect was founded by the reformist Tsong Khapa; it became a stronghold for the Tibetan patriots during the insurrection of 1959. This cluster of white buildings rising on a hill (the name means Rice Heap), once housed 10,000 lamas and employed a population of 40,000 as serfs, herdsmen, and servants. Three hundred monks live there now and the monastery still owns enough land to support itself.

The Drepung was built in 1416 and its style is purely Tibetan. The Great Hall contains some magnificent murals, unfortunately heavily restored; there are many ornate and bejewelled statues of Buddhas and Bodhisattvas, and a rich collection of ancient books. The monastery is open for worship three days a week, but usually closed when foreign visitors are expected.

The Sera Monastery (Sera Goin) is on Iron Hill, 6 km north of Lhasa, in a strategic position from which the Tibetan rebels shelled the capital during the insurrection. There are four temple halls in the compound, the buildings of whitewashed stone with carved and painted lintels. Few frescoes have been restored, and one can still discern the delicacy of the original design. People of all ages come here to pray, making their round of the altars from left to right, arriving with their jars of yak butter which they deposit in bowls. Huge statues of Buddhas are carved out of the rock face behind the monastery, which also houses the inevitable museum of history and atrocities.

The Yalin (Emancipation) yak commune is five hours away to the north-east, on the Qing Zang plateau. An hour and a half out of Lhasa, the surfaced road ends and the rest of the journey can be very uncomfortable. At the commune, you are received by Tibetans in their bright national costume, washed and smiling, who put on a song-and-dance show. Delicious yogurt, Tibetan yak milk tea — an acquired taste — and rubbery white cheese is offered to the guests.

4 Xinjiang (Sinkiang)

Xinjiang (the New Dominion) is the north-westernmost region in the country, sharing a long border with the Soviet Union. It is the largest political unit in China, though the population is only 11 million. In 1955 it was made an autonomous region on the basis of its large population of Uighurs, who in 1953 accounted for 75 per cent of the total; they now represent only 60 per cent of the total, thanks to an influx of Chinese. The population is concentrated in the Tarim Basin oases and in the Junggar Basin (Dzungaria), separated by the Tianshan mountain range.

The Uighurs, who today number around 5.4 million, are a Turkic people who still speak a language intelligible to the Turks. The next largest minority, numbering 700,000 are the Kazakhs, also a Turkic people, spread on both sides of the border, in China and the Soviet Union. Another important ethnic group is the Hui, who speak Chinese but practise the Islamic religion. A large group of Hui live in the Ningxia-Hui Autonomous Region.

Xinjiang's mineral resources include non-ferrous metals, petroleum, gold and uranium. China's nuclear industry is situated in the Lop Nur (Lopnor) desert in the west of the Tarim Basin. The region has a seven-month growing season, but agriculture, depending on the availability of water, is possible only in the strings of oases circling the Tarim and Junggar Basin deserts. The main cereal is wheat, and the second most important, corn. Cotton, sugar beet and a variety of fruit (grapes, melons, pears, apricots, etc.) are also grown. Traditionally, the Junggaria grasslands and the western highlands bordering the Tarim Basin were the home of nomadic stockherders of Kazakh, Mongol and Kirghiz nationality. They now represent only 5 per cent of the population and are pressured into settling in villages. However, the low level of rainfall still makes moving the herds necessary.

It is in Xinjiang, in the Turpan (Turfan) depression, that the highest temperatures in the whole of China are recorded: 33°C. on the average in July. There are two climatic zones in the region: in the Tarim Basin, January temperatures average −7°C., and in July, 27°C.; in Junggaria the average is −15°C. in January, and 20 to 24°C. in July. Occasional spring and early summer storms sprinkle Junggaria (about 250 mm per year in Urumqi), but the Tarim Basin receives almost no rain (110 mm per year).

Xinjiang is to be avoided in the middle of summer and winter.

The incidence of stomach disorders among foreign visitors is particularly high and it is wise to bring adequate supplies of relevant medicine.

URUMQI 乌鲁木齐

Urumqi (a Uighur name meaning 'Beautiful Grassland'), in southern Junggaria, is the capital of the province. The Tianshan (Celestial Mountains), separating the area from the Tarim Basin, rise to the south and the desert of Junggaria stretches to the north. The city is also the economic and cultural centre of the region, if one can talk about a centre in this area made up of inhabited oases and large tracts of arid or mountainous land, only loosely linked by the northern and southern branches of the Silk Route, and connected by rail with Gansu province. Thirteen different nationalities live in the city, which has about 500,000 inhabitants.

It is possible to travel by train to Urumqi but it takes two and half days. Flying is obviously faster, five hours from Beijing, but very expensive. Accommodation is provided in a fairly comfortable guesthouse which was once a hostel for Russian experts. The food, when Chinese-style, is bad and it is wise to stick to lamb kebabs in the local style. However, you are seldom given a choice. Fruit at the end of the summer and beginning of autumn is beautiful and abundant, but be careful not to eat too much of it if you have a sensitive stomach.

Xinjiang is famous for its carpets, the best ones having been made in Kashi (Kashgar). But those produced today are spoilt by the mechanization of the weaving process and the use of gaudy chemical dyes reflecting Chinese taste, and old ones are almost impossible to find; your interpreter will be very reluctant to take you to a second-hand shop. Hides and skins (fox, wolf, sheep) are cheap but a good selection is not always available. If you have bought a good skin (usually assembled in the rough shape of a coat), take it home to have it tailored because Chinese cuts are poor. Other items to buy include leather boots and embroidered skull caps worn by the men and women of Uighur nationality. Each locality has its own particular design.

History. It was only in 1873 that Xinjiang was given the status of a province and a Chinese governor posted to Urumqi. Before that, the region was under the suzerainty of several khans each of whom ruled a portion of territory around his own oasis. Yang Zengxin, appointed governor in 1911, managed to keep the Gobi caravan routes open and safe from brigands in the troubled years when the rest of the empire was torn apart by warlords; but he was murdered in 1928 by his own Foreign Minister and this, added to the death of the Khan of Hami, set the stage for a Moslem rebellion in 1930 which spilled over into neighbouring Gansu, then moved westwards to Hami. Urumqi was eventually seized by White Russian émigrés who had served in the governor's army defending the city against the Moslem rebels. A bloodbath resulted before Chinese and Manchu reinforcements arrived and the Moslem rebels were driven south to Hotan (Khotan), where they dispersed.

Places of interest. Urumqi was renamed Dihua, 'City of Enlightenment, by a Manchu emperor of China, but it might more fitly have been called the City of Dark Intrigue. . . . The town has no beauty, no style, no dignity and no architectural interest. The climate is violent, exaggerated, and no season pleasant. . . . Urumqi's shop-keeping class lives to make money, and its official class lives for promotion.' Thus was Urumqi of the 1920s described by two missionaries, Mildred Cable and Francesca French, in *The Gobi Desert* (1942). Thirty years of Communist rule have brought about a number of improvements, but no architectural beauty. The city now has a People's Park on the west bank of the Urumqi River, with a lake, bridges and pavilions, completely in Chinese style. The city also boasts a People's Theatre, in neo-classical Russian style, which is quite impressive. Visitors are also taken to a carpet factory, and to a factory which makes traditional musical instruments. The town's activities centre around its industries, almost all developed after 1949.

From Urumqi, a drive to the north-east will take you to the Tianchi (Lake of Heaven) half-way up to the majestic Bogda Feng (Peak of God), which rises 5,445 m above sea level. Boat tours on the lake are organized.

It is possible to visit a horse-breeding commune, some three hours drive from Urumqi in the Baiyangge (Valley of the White Poplars). The Kazakhs, whose occupation has traditionally been breeding horses, live in colourful and comfortable circular felt *yurts* (tents) about 8 m in diameter, which they move to new pastures when required according to the season. At the commune they display their horsemanship with demonstrations of *buzgashi*, a game in which the riders compete for possession of the beheaded body of a sheep, and engage in shooting competitions on horse-back. Both men and women display equal virtuosity and the show is worth the long but interesting journey. Guests are invited into the *yurts* to partake of fermented mare's milk, *balsac*, a sour-milk bread deep-fried in oil, *hert*, a hard cheese, and boiled mutton. The chief delicacy is the eyes, and when the meal is over, the custom is to throw the sheep's head through the hole in the roof of the *yurt*, usually serving as a chimney.

TURPAN (Turfan)　吐鲁番

Turpan lies some 200 km south-east of Urumqi, at the junction of the northern Silk Route (north of the Tianshan mountains), which goes to Xining (Guldja or Kuldja) and then on to the Soviet Union, and the southern route to Kashi (Kashgar) leading over the Pamir to India. Turfan is an oasis lying in what is the deepest dry depression (−154 m) in the world. To the south are salt marshes, beyond, the Dry Mountains, and to the north, the majestic Bogda Peak covered in eternal snow.

Turpan, which is not watered by any significant river, relies for its survival on an irrigation system known as the *Karez*, originally from Persia, which consists of rows of wells dug from the foot of the mountains to the plain, connected by tunnels and dug at a depth which diminishes as they get near to the plain, until the water finally emerges in the open. This unique system of irrigation produces luxuriant crops of fruit, grain and cotton, which Turpan exports to the rest of the country. *Karez* water is suitable only for irrigation, and drinking water is supplied by the small river outside the town. Temperatures reach 50°C. (130°F.) in the summer and the people retreat to underground shelters dug in their back gardens during the day, emerging in the evening. Minimum winter temperatures reach −17°C. (0°F.)

The journey from Urumqi takes half a day by road. Accommodation for foreign guests is provided in a 'caravanserai'. The rooms are built of thick brick, with vaulted ceilings, in two rows along a courtyard with creeping vines growing over covered walks. There are no luxuries, but the rooms are cool and clean. The area abounds in poisonous snakes, scorpions and spiders, cockroaches and mosquitoes, but they have been successfully kept outside the boundaries of the guesthouse.

The Turpan bazaar, covered over with straw mats in the summer, offers a great choice of dried fruit (raisins, apricots, nectarines, mulberries, jujube, melon and walnuts), as well as fresh. Knot-dyed cotton goods and brightly coloured silks are also available, and embroidered skull-caps.

The majority of the people in Turpan are of Uighur nationality and are devout Moslems. There are many mosques in town, some still in use; the most beautiful one, to the south-east of the Chinese quarter, dates from 1760 and was built by the Khan of Lukqun (Lukchun, 70 km south-west of Turpan, secondary residence of the Khan of Hami, also known as the King of the Gobi).

The ruins of GAOCHANG (Kaochang), to the south-west of

Turpan, rise from the plain which is now a desert of gravel. The city was founded in the Han dynasty when the Chinese conquered the Xiongnu (Huns) and imperial troops were stationed there, sharing the land with farmers. In the late fourth century, Gaochang became an independent kingdom until the Tang dynasty, when as capital of the Xizhou, or Western Province, of Central Asia, it began paying tribute to the emperor of China. Again in the middle of the tenth century Gaochang became an independent Uighur kingdom. It was abandoned several hundred years ago when its wells dried up.

What remains of Gaochang indicates a master plan, familiar to those who have already visited Beijing or Xi'an, of an Outer City, an Inner City and a palace to the north. The outer wall is about 1.5 km long on each side and the total circumference about 6 km. The walls are built of stamped earth rising to 11.5 m at the highest point, and with a base which is 12 m thick. Battlements jut out at intervals and the city gates are protected by a crooked barbican. Around the ruins of the palace are stupas and tall buildings decorated with niches. There are also ruins of temples to the south-east and south-west of the outer city. Fragments of frescoes have been found in the ruins, some of which depict European people (the best examples are now in the Berlin Museum), perhaps brought by the armies of Alexander the Great who disbanded and settled along the Silk Route. In Gaochang too the earliest images of Buddha were found — his features have a great resemblance to Apollo's — and also the remains of monasteries of Persian architecture, brought by Nestorian missionaries in the fifth century A.D.

Half a day is sufficient to visit Gaochang; from there one can either go to the ruins of Jiaohe or to the Turpan grape commune.

JIAOHE, which means 'confluence', is known amongst the Uighurs as Yar Kotho, Junction of the Yars or Streams. Its walls rise above the dry beds of two rivers, on a terrace at the limit of the irrigated land to the west of Turpan. The plan of the city is more confused than that of Gaochang and it appears to have been smaller. The walls are also made of stamped earth, in a fairly good state of preservation owing to the extreme dryness of the climate. Some ancient tombs with murals have been found, cut out of the rock, which are possibly those of Nestorian Christians. A visit to Jiaohe, including travelling time, takes around two hours.

The Turpan grape commune is situated in the centre of the county, south of the Flaming Mountains. It grows cereals, cotton and fruit. Grapes, the most abundant fruit because of the dry and sunny climate and the difference in temperature between day and night, have a high sugar content, and are seedless and delicious. They are trained on high frames, a canopy of foliage under which one can walk. An afternoon's visit is almost a visit to paradise: imagine groves of poplars with a path of brilliant antique carpets on the ground, and bowls of fruit placed in the middle for the refreshment of the thirsty visitors. The commune relies on water from the Karez well system and has 220 frost-free days per year.

SHIHEZI (54) 石河子

Shihezi (Stony River), proudly called the Pearl of the Gobi, is a bleak and dusty modern city lying about 180 km west of Urumqi; like Urumqi and Turpan, it is situated in the string of oases which lie between the Tianshan mountain range and the desert-like Junggar (Dzungaria) Basin. The first settlement in Shihezi was a KMT unit which had surrendered to the PLA in the area and was given no choice but to stay. Development began in 1950, when several reservoirs were built across the small rivers which run from the Tianshan range; in twenty years, 4 million *mu* (about 66,000 acres) of land were brought under cultivation.

Shihezi, a grain and cotton base and one of the most important industrial towns in Xinjiang, has food processing industries, wool and cotton mills and an agricultural machinery plant. The population is about 750,000. There is little to interest the tourist in Shihezi.

Buddhist caves in Xinjiang.   To date, some 900 caves have been found in Xinjiang. They follow exactly the southern Silk Route and are hollowed out of the sandstone cliffs which border the Tianshan mountain ranges. From east to west, they are: the Shanshan (Piqan) Grottoes, about 100 km east of Turpan; the Turpan Grottoes; the Yanqi Grottoes, near the Bosten (or Bagrax) Lake; in Kuqa county, the Kumtura Thousand Buddha Grottoes, which, with the recent discovery of seven more caves, now contain 106 shrines; and the Baicheng group of caves. The latter, the most important in Xinjiang, extend for 2 km from east to west and are 200 to 300 m high. Newly found caves in the lower section of the Kirzil Thousand Buddha Grottoes bring the total to 236, built between the third and the tenth century. They are to be opened to the public, but it is not clear (1979) whether foreigners will be permitted to visit them. There are two more groups of caves, still further west, in Xinhe and Wensu counties.

5 Gansu and Inner Mongolia

Gansu is a province carved out of natural regions for political considerations. (For regional administrative purposes it and the adjoining Ningxia Hui Autonomous Region — not open to tourists — are considered part of the North.) Gansu province comprises a small part of the Alashan desert, part of the Ningxia irrigated plain, the Gansu Corridor proper, the Lanzhou basin and part of the Shaanxi loesslands. The climate is continental, with January mean temperatures ranging from −10 to −6°C., and 21 to 26°C. in July. Precipitation is insufficient, ranging from 400 mm in the Lanzhou basin to 60 mm in the Alashan desert. Agricultural production varies according to the region, including wheat, millet, gaoliang, cotton and tobacco. The province is rich in mineral resources and has growing steel and petroleum industries.

History. During the Han dynasty, the Great Wall was extended to the pass of Yumen, at the western extremity of the province, and 700,000 Han Chinese were sent to settle in the Gansu Corridor. A Protector General was appointed for the region but by the middle of the third century A.D. the areas under his control had shrunk to the Lanzhou basin. At the beginning of the fourth century, Xiongnu tribes invaded the north of the country, looting and killing, and a Chinese general defending the Gansu Corridor founded the Earlier Liang dynasty (313-73) with its capital in Lanzhou. The Silk Route remained vulnerable to attacks until the beginning of the Tang dynasty and Lanzhou served as capital for a succession of short-lived tribal states. It is during this troubled period that Buddhist art flourished. Gansu was first counted as a Chinese province in the Yuan dynasty and three garrisons of Bannermen used to be stationed there to defend the Silk Road against attacks by Central Asian nomads.

LANZHOU (Lanchow) 兰州

Several sites of neolithic Painted Pottery Culture have been found in the vicinity of Lanzhou (Orchid Country) and it appears that, unlike in other parts of the country, this primitive culture lasted into historical times.

Lanzhou, capital of Gansu province, is a natural centre for communications between China proper and the west and north. It is the chief crossing point over the upper Yellow River and its role as a communication and distribution centre has been enhanced by the building of the railway in 1952. From traditional activities such as processing and distribution of natural products (wool and skins),

Lanzhou has diversified its industrial production to include petro-chemical plants, fertilizer plants, and machine-building. Today, the city has a population of 1.6 million, including about 1 million living in the city proper; the built-up area stretches for 50 km along the Yellow River gorges. The pollution is catastrophic.

Lanzhou is linked by rail to Urumqi in Xinjiang, Baotou in Inner Mongolia and Xi'an in Shaanxi. The journey by train from Beijing takes under twenty hours. There are flights from and to Beijing, Xi'an, Chengdu, Urumqi, Hohhot and Yinquan. Lanzhou is linked to Tibet by road via Xining, the capital of Qinghai province, which is only 20 km to the west and closed to tourists. Visitors usually stay at the Lanzhou Guesthouse. The airport is about 70 km from the city.

The best Chinese carpets — made for the imperial palaces, temples and rich households — came from neighbouring Ningxia-Hui Autonomous Region, but Gansu is also the source of some beautiful carpets. The designs are geometrical like those of the Persian carpets, but the colours are particularly glamorous. Pale shadows of these beautiful carpets are still made, but the old ones are difficult to find.

An important group of cave temples can be visited from Lanzhou. The Binglingsi, near the town of Yongjing, some 40 km west of Lanzhou, were started around A.D. 513, during the Northern Wei period, and contain carvings and frescoes from the Wei dynasty through to the Ming. The Upper Bingling monastery has a giant statue of a seated Buddha, carved in the Tang dynasty, and the Lower Bingling monastery, stretching to the bank of the Yellow River, contains frescoes of particular brilliance, of the Song and Ming dynasties.

JIAYUGUAN (53) 嘉峪关

Jiayuguan (Pass of the Pleasant Valley) is over 500 km north-west of Lanzhou, on the Lanzhou-Urumqi railway line, and on the way to the Dunhuang Grottoes. It is one of two westernmost strategic passes through the Great Wall, which stretches for 6,000 km between Shanhaiguan, the Pass between the Mountains and the Sea, and Yumen (Jade Gate) in the Gobi desert. The original wall in this area dates from the beginning of the Han dynasty, but the fortress at Jiayuguan was rebuilt in 1372 during the reign of Ming emperor Hong Wu, and from then on it was the westernmost pass; Yumen was abandoned. It was known locally as Guimenguan, the Pass of the Demons Gate, and a mound of earth used to shield its west gate from evil influences carried by the wind of the Gobi desert.

Jiayuguan consists of an outer city in which the inns, black-smiths' and other shops used to be, and an inner city — a citadel — the last Chinese outpost on the Silk Road — in which the commander of the pass and his family lived. The outer city has grown into a town with a population of about 100,000 and some industry.

The inner city is surrounded by a brick and stone wall over 11 m high and 730 m long, with two main gates, each surmounted by three-storey watch towers. The east gate leads to Qiuquan, a county town where the civilian magistrate used to live; in former times, couriers used to run every day across the plain to fetch delicacies for the commander and his ladies. The west gate, once used only by travellers, opens on to the desert. The local people speak of those who have passed beyond the gate of the citadel as being 'outside the mouth', and the long vaulted corridor under the wall is carved with many inscriptions left by exiles and disgraced officials. Outside there is a stele inscribed with the words, 'The Greatest Barrier Under Heaven.' Before setting off, travellers used to throw a stone through a gap where the bricks of the wall had crumbled. If it bounced back, it was a good omen. Legend says that the plans for building the fortifications at the pass had been so carefully designed, and the quantity of material needed so exactly calculated, that when the work was completed, only one brick was left over. A brick, said to be this very one, is still kept in a watchtower.

The Jiayuguan exhibition hall, in the grounds of the old Yamen (the commander's house) has an archaeological exhibition of objects unearthed in the area, mainly from Wei and Jin dynasty tombs. Among the most interesting finds are several hundred bricks decorated with hand-painted scenes of everyday life in the Wei and Jin period (fourth to sixth century A.D.).

DUNHUANG 敦煌

Dunhuang (Blazing Beacon) was one of four commanderies (*jun*) created in 111 B.C. by Emperor Wu Di of the Han, along the Gansu Corridor. It was an important caravan stop on the Silk Road, over which circulated not only goods but also technology and ideas. Buddhism, which brought the new ideas of the immortality of the soul and of reincarnation, took root easily amongst the people of the oases, and monasteries and cave temples sprouted along the Silk Route thanks to the donations of converts amongst the local gentry. It is to them that we owe the earliest and most beautiful examples of Buddhist art.

The people of Dunhuang, blessed with sufficient water supplies and a dry climate, have always enjoyed a prosperous life. Some of the largest and best maintained buildings in town are the granaries, and the climate is such that wheat can keep for several years. Not only was the town self-sufficient in food, but also in brides and bridegrooms: local chauvinism made it an offence for anyone from Dunhuang to marry someone from another oasis. And in the troubled decades of the 1920s to '40s, Dunhuang merchants were able to carry on commercial transactions in the currency of their choice.

The Mogao Caves. Among the many important cave temples in western Gansu are the Maijishan caves, south-west of Tianshui in the south of the province; the Binglingsi caves near Lanzhou (already mentioned); the Matisi (Horseshoe Temple) near Zhangye; the Qingyang caves also near Zhangye, at the confluence of the Ru and Pu rivers; Wenwushan (Culture Mountain) near Jiuquan; and the Changma caves near Yumen. In the north-west, belonging to the Dunhuang group, there are the Mogao caves, the most important and best-known of the group; the Yulinsi, with its cliff of the Ten Thousand Buddhas, near the village of Tashi; and the Qianfoya (Thousand Buddha Cave), near South Lake, which was rediscovered in the late 1920s and is also known as the West Thousand Buddha Cave.

Work on the cave temples of north-west China went on almost uninterrupted from A.D. 366, during the Sixteen Kingdoms Period, until the great Buddhist persecutions of the late Tang (841-5). Renewed religious fervour under the Yuan expressed itself in a fresh wave of cave carving which was maintained until the next great persecutions during the reign of Ming emperor Jia Jing (1522-67), which spelt the end of the magnificence of Buddhist art.

Lying in a dip between the Sanwei and Mingsha mountains, carved in a sandstone cliff over a distance of about 1600 m, the Mogao caves near Dunhuang are the most often visited. Simple accommodation is provided in a guesthouse on the site of the grottoes.

The Mogao caves were discovered by a monk, Wang Yuanlu, early in this century. Finding them abandoned, he settled there, diverted the waters of a little stream into a channel flowing at the bottom of the cliff, planted some poplars, went on begging tours to collect money for repairs, and built a guesthouse. He discovered a library of ancient manuscripts in a cave which had been sealed off in the eleventh century; among the first to be brought to light were some sutras brought from India by the monk Xuan Zang in the seventh century.

In 1908, Sir Aurel Stein arrived at Dunhuang and began to study the manuscripts and rolls of Tibetan paintings. The same year, the French

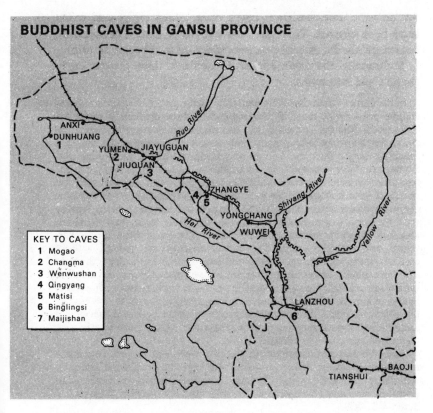

BUDDHIST CAVES IN GANSU PROVINCE

KEY TO CAVES
1 Mogao
2 Changma
3 Wenwushan
4 Qingyang
5 Matisi
6 Binglingsi
7 Maijishan

sinologist Paul Pelliot came to Dunhuang, and between them they bought some 13,000 manuscripts and several hundred paintings and rolls of silk brocade for a very small amount of money; it represented a lot, however, for Abbot Wang, who could spend it on restoring and beautifying the caves, which the Imperial government, finding it too costly to have the manuscripts and paintings removed to Beijing for study, had ordered resealed. The Dunhuang Institute for the study of the caves and manuscripts was finally set up in 1943, but, in the interval, a large number of precious documents found their way into foreign museums.

The Mogao caves, begun in 366, according to an inscription dating from the Tang dynasty, contain the oldest Buddhist shrines in the country. Dunhuang was a centre for the study of Buddhism from the fifth to the eleventh century, attracting not only scholars and pilgrims, but supporting and training generations of sculptors and painters, most of whom have remained anonymous. There are several hundred caves carved out in several rows, sometimes five storeys high, and balconies and galleries have been built to render them accessible to visitors without the risk of breaking their necks.

At the same time, the lower caves, often closed off by sand drifts, have been cleared. There are now 492 caves, carved between the fourth and the fourteenth centuries in a good state of preservation.

Stylistically, the caves can be divided into three groups: early, mature and late styles.

In the earlier caves (366-580), generally on the third row in the south and middle portions of the cliff, the main decorative element is sculpture. Sakyamuni Buddha is usually the central figure, massive and with the draperies of his robe following the body closely. He is represented seated or standing, larger than the Lohans and Bodhisattvas accompanying him. Some caves have a central pillar decorated on its four faces with figures and low-relief decorative motifs; others are built on an open plan with the main group of statues along the far wall. In the Mogao caves frescoes decorate the walls, which are not found in the Yungang and Longmen caves. Painted with tempera (water-based emulsion), they have kept their freshness thanks to the extreme dryness of the climate. The colours used are browns, white, red and blue-green. The earlier frescoes are painted without outlines, the faces wide and highlighted with white on the bridge of the nose and the eyeballs, while the cheekbones and eyes are outlined with a colour which was originally brown but has turned black with oxidation. The effect is that of a mask and the Chinese call it the *xiao face* because it resembles the character *xiao*. The landscapes, smaller than the figures and serving as a transition between the scenes, are a pretext for brilliant improvisations on themes of everyday life and animal life.

Cave 285 is a particularly good example of early grotto art. One mural represents devotees, drawn in outline with very fine brushwork, lining up with their wives and bearing offerings. They were probably rich merchants and their servants are represented smaller than the masters. This cave is dated A.D. 539.

During the Sui (581-618) and the Tang (618-907), Buddhism penetrated the peasant population and became ideologically simplified. Colossal statues were made during that period, including a Buddha 33 m high in cave 96, and another 26 m high in cave 130, both of the Tang period. The technique was to carve a figure from a cave wall, only grossly outlined, and to coat it with clay which was moulded into detailed features and then painted, resulting in refined and detailed figures of exquisite proportions, as represented in cave 45.

In the murals the technique of outline drawing comes back into use to render scenes of great complexity. For the first time, elaborate court scenes appear which are very like the few paintings of the Tang dynasty which have survived on scrolls. The activities depicted in the murals include weddings, funerals, scenes of torture and presentation of tributes from non-Chinese people to the emperor. In this more urbane setting, dancers, acrobats and singers are painted with particular flamboyance. In cave 217, one mural represents travellers in the mountains, some arriving at the city gate, some setting up a camp, some riding donkeys. The mountains and trees have grown in proportion, compared to the earlier frescoes, but the figures still appear larger in relation to the landscapes.

After the fall of the Tang dynasty, Dunhuang went into a decline; nevertheless, the governors continued to patronize the arts and more caves were added while a greater number were redecorated. The changes from the mature Tang style appear in simpler drawing techniques and the beginning of portrait painting. In the late murals (907-1368), pictures of devotees include inscriptions detailing their names and positions. Among them are not only Han Chinese but also kings from Central Asia.

During the Western Xia and Yuan dynasties (eleventh to fourteenth centuries), a small number of caves were added which reflected the split of Buddhism into a number of sects. The Yuan caves feature circular altars, an idea borrowed from the Mongols, and frescoes representing creatures from the Tibetan pantheon. After the Yuan, no more caves were added, but some redecoration took place until the Qing dynasty.

Most visitors spend two or three days in Dunhuang but for those who are interested in Buddhist art, there is no limit to the amount of time or the number of visits they would wish to devote to the caves. It is, alas, not permitted to take pictures.

The Lake of the Crescent Moon. A popular saying at Dunhuang goes: 'The skill of man made the cave of the Thousand Buddhas, but the Hand of God fashioned the Lake of the Crescent Moon'. To the east of Dunhuang, stretching into Xinjiang, high sand dunes rise, so high that they look like mountains. About 6 km to the east, hidden between two dunes of shifting sand, lies a beautiful lake, small, crescent-shaped and deep blue, with a small temple built on its south-facing shore. The sand dunes round the lake make a rolling sound of thunder under the action of the wind or when someone walks on them. Marco Polo mentions these 'rumbling sands' in the narrative of his travels.

Inner Mongolia is made up of four natural regions: the Mongolian Plateau, rising about 1,000 m above sea level, which occupies the whole eastern half of the region, the Yin mountain range on the south-western edge of the plateau, the Yellow River valley and the Ordos desert to the south, and the Alashan desert to the west. The population is around 10 million, only 20 per cent being Mongols.

The Autonomous Region of Inner Mongolia is a political unit which goes back to the creation of Manchukuo by the Japanese in 1932. It was then called the Autonomous Mongol province of Xingan. In 1937, an autonomous government was established in Inner Mongolia until the invasion by Soviet and Outer Mongolian troops in 1945. The Communists regained control over it and established the Inner Mongolia Autonomous Region in 1947, two years before they set up a government in Beijing.

The borders of Mongolia, once stretching from the Junggar Basin (Dzungaria) in the west to the Great Khingan Mountains in the east, have undergone many changes, the most recent being the return to Inner Mongolia in 1979 of part of the Alashan desert which since 1969 had been shared with Gansu and Ninxia. Outer Mongolia, theoretically a sovereign state, is under the control of the Soviet Union. Thus, the Mongols, the most powerful nation on earth from the twelfth to the fourteenth centuries, are now scattered over several political units: Outer Mongolia, Inner Mongolia, Xinjiang, Gansu, Ningxia, Heilongjiang, Jilin and Liaoning.

The Mongols are a nomadic people who live off cattle herding. The political dismemberment of their natural grazing grounds has made life difficult for them. The nomadic population represents 26 per cent of the Mongol ethnic group, or about 340,000 herdsmen. The Chinese have encouraged them to give up their 'backward' nomadic life and to settle in permanent houses; however, extensive cattle herding as it is practised in Mongolia demands that the herdsmen move six times a year to different pastures.

Two other types of cattle-herding are practised: summer grazing combined with winter stall-feeding, practised in agricultural areas with mixed Chinese-Mongol population, and stall-feeding in the agricultural areas settled by Chinese. About half the herds are made up of sheep and goats and the rest include cattle, horses and camels. Agriculture is confined to the alluvial plain of the Wujia River, west of Baotou, and to the Hohhot plain where the population is almost entirely Chinese.

Baotou is the largest and most industrialized town in Inner Mongolia, with a population of about 800,000. It grew with the exploitation of coal mines in the area.

HOHHOT (Huhehot) 呼和浩特

Hohhot (Huhehot), a Mongolian name meaning 'Blue Town', is the capital of the autonomous region, with a population of about 500,000. It is about 425 km northwest of Beijing and can be reached by train in ten hours or by plane in just over one hour. The Friendship Hotel in town is simple but adequate. Mongolian food consists almost exclusively of mutton, served boiled in chunks, but Chinese food is available in the hotel.

The local department store has a Friendship Store counter for foreigners where the local handicrafts sold include boots, skins, knives, braid and costumes. Mongolians wear an outer gown bordered with several lines of contrasting colour, girded with a long bright sash, over trousers which they tuck inside their boots.

Hohhot has some food-processing and mechanical industries. It is linked by rail to the two other major centres of the region: Jining, which is on the Trans-Siberian railroad via Outer Mongolia, and Baotou, beyond which lie the western provinces.

Summer, which is also the rainy season (May to September) is pleasant with temperatures around 20°C. Winter is prohibitively cold and dry (mean January temperatures −8 to −12°C.) and does not allow tourism.

Hohhot, which has been the capital since 1952, was founded in 1581 by the Altan Khan, the last of the great Mongol conquerors. After the Manchu conquest, it was renamed Guihua (Return to Civilization) and a Chinese walled town developed to the north-east which was called Suiyuan (Pacified Distant Place). The two towns have now merged, but a portion of the walls of the Chinese town still remain. The former name of Hohhot was restored in 1952.

Like all the Mongolian towns, Hohhot grew around its temples and there are still a few, but they are not usually included in the tour. Instead, visitors are given a tour of the underground shelters, erected against the permanent threat from the 'Polar Bear' on the country's border; these are equipped with hospitals and factories to enable life to continue in case of Soviet attack.

While in Hohhot, you will probably have a chance to see a local rodeo, held in a fairground in a suburb. The Mongols, great horsemen, enjoy equestrian competitions: races, trick riding, rounding up of ponies.

XILINHOT (Abagnar Qi) (47) 锡林浩特

Xilinhot is 500 km due north of Beijing and accessible only by plane; the flight takes a little over one hour. It is the major city in the Xilin Gol League (there are four leagues in Inner Mongolia), an administrative region which regroups four Banners or tribes: the Sonid, Abag, Ujimqin and Abagnar Banners. The Xilin Gol League still has relatively little Chinese colonization and was the stronghold of Mongolian nationalism in the 1930s.

At the end of the Ming dynasty, the Yellow Hat sect of Tibetan Buddhism spread to Mongolia and the lamaseries which were built across the land became the nucleus of today's towns. From the sixteenth century the power of these lamaseries grew until in the nineteenth century, the priests owned half the cattle and the land in the country and lamas represented one-fifth of the population, employing another fifth in the lamaseries and dependent farms. Today, the lamasery-towns are the headquarters of the Banners, and until 1953, Xilinhot was known by the name of its lamasery Beizimiao. The population is under 100,000, and it has few industries. The city's role is still principally marketing and processing the natural products of the region: hides and wool.

The Beizimiao is a large lamasery which once had several hundred resident lamas. It dates from the Qing dynasty and its buildings are in the Chinese style. The main hall is two storeys high and is surrounded by a gallery under which are sheltered the long copper horns which the monks blow at certain times of the day (they wear dark reddish-brown gowns cut in the local fashion). The hall contains some richly ornate statues with bejewelled crowns. The temple now operates a carpet factory within its walls, employing reformed monks as well as lay workers. Outside the temple is a curious construction found throughout Mongolia, an *obo* (in Chinese *ao bao*). It is a row of tumuli made of piled-up stones, flattened at the top, and one larger one, making a kind of platform on which are erected staffs and poles. Inside the hollow structure is a space for offerings such as coloured stones, shells or fossils, and the staff on top may have a banner or strands of coloured hair or wool. *Obos* are found everywhere and used as landmarks by travellers. These shrines are for the shamanist cult, much more ancient than Buddhism.

APPENDICES
SELECT BIBLIOGRAPHY
INDEX

The Climate of China

TEMPERATURE (*in degrees of Fahrenheit and centigrade*)

	AVERAGE WINTER/ SUMMER TEMPERATURES				MIN./MAX. TEMPERATURES SPRING AND AUTUMN*	
	January		*July*		*April/October low/high*	
NORTHEAST						
Harbin	−2 F.	−19 C.	72 F.	22 C.	30/62 F.	−2/16 C.
Shenyang	2 F.	−16 C.	76 F.	24 C.	32/64 F.	0/17 C.
NORTH						
Beijing	23 F.	−5 C.	79 F.	26 C.	32/68 F.	0/20 C.
Xi'an	15 F.	−9 C.	80 F.	27 C.	30/66 F.	−1/19 C.
SOUTH						
Shanghai	38 F.	3 C.	84 F.	29 C.	40/80 F.	4/27 C.
Nanjing	40 F.	4 C.	86 F.	30 C.	40/88 F.	4/31 C.
Wuhan	40 F.	4 C.	85 F.	29 C.	38/88 F.	3/31 C.
Guangzhou	56 F.	14 C.	84 F.	28 C.	52/90 F.	15/32 C.
SOUTHWEST						
Chongqing	42 F.	5 C.	85 F.	29 C.	42/88 F.	5/31 C.
XINJIANG-INNER MONGOLIA (approximate)						
Turpan	14 F.	− 9 C.	91 F.	32 C.	20/62 F.	−7/16 C.
Hohhot	−20 F.	−29 C.	73 F.	22 C.	15/59 F.	−9/14 C.
XIZANG (Tibet) (approximate)						
Lhasa	−22 F.	−30 C.	60 F.	15 C.	5/40 F.	−14/4 C.

* Spring and autumn are very short seasons. Temperature changes are sudden and steep, the extremes greater in the north and west.

PRECIPITATION*

	ANNUAL AVERAGE RAINFALL	WETTEST MONTHS (10 OR MORE DAYS OF RAIN)
NORTHEAST	(approximate)	
Shenyang	20 in./400 mm	July, August
NORTH		
Beijing	25 in./500 mm	July, August
Xi'an	21 in./420 mm	July, August
SOUTH		
Wuhan	39 in./780 mm	April, May, June, July
Shanghai	45 in./900 mm	February, March, April, May, June, July, August, September, October
Guangzhou	63 in./1250 mm	March, April, May, June, July, August, September
SOUTHWEST		
Chengdu	36 in./720 mm	April, May, June, July, August
XINJIANG-INNER MONGOLIA (approximate)		
Urumqi	7 in./150 mm	

*The winter is very dry in low-lying areas in the Northeast, North and Xinjiang. Rain falls almost throughout the year in the South and Southwest, where in July and August there can be up to 20 days with rain. Significant snowfall occurs only over the mountainous areas in the Northeast, Xinjiang-Inner Mongolia, Tibet and the Southwest.

The Chinese Language

The official phonetic transcription of Chinese characters (Pinyin) does not always correspond to the usual pronunciation of the letters in English, French or other European languages. It is useful to try and memorize some basic phonetics if you want to be understood, even when saying the simplest things. Each syllable, represented by a Chinese character, is made of an initial consonant — occasionally omitted — and a vowel or diphthong, sometimes nasalized with the ending *n* or *ng*. Thus, each syllable transcribed phonetically ends with a vowel, *n* or *ng*, but never with a consonant. The letter *r* at the end of a syllable indicates a retroflection.

Initials

T, P and H	are strongly aspirated.
G	is a guttural consonant pronounced as in 'go'.
C	is strongly aspirated as *ts* in 'its'.
Z	pronounced softly as *ds* in 'weeds'.
ZH	pronounced as *j* in 'jug' or *dg* in 'bridge'.
CH	is similar to the English *ch* as in 'charming'.
SH	is similar to the English *sh* as in 'sheet'.
R	is like *su* in 'leisure'. The English or French *r* sound does not exist in Chinese and is rendered by *l* in the transliteration of foreign names.
J	is like *g* in 'gin'.
Q	is a tricky consonant, more strongly aspirated than *ch* but has no equivalent.
X	is a strongly aspirated hissing consonant which has no equivalent but can be rendered approximately by *hs*.

Finals

IAN	(spelled YAN where there is no initial consonant) is pronounced like *ien* in 'Vienna'.
IANG	(spelled YANG where there is no initial consonant) sounds like the word 'young'.
IAO	(also spelled YOU where there is no initial consonant) sounds like *iaow* in 'miaow'.
IU	(spelled YOU where there is no initial consonant) sounds like *yo* in 'yoyo'.
I	is like *e* in 'me', and when there is no initial consonant, it is spelled YI and pronounced as *y* in 'yes'.
IE	(also spelled YE where there is no initial consonant) sounds like *ye* in 'yes'.
O	is short as in 'stop'.

OU   is the long version of the sound O as *oa* in 'boat'.
U   is like a French *u* or German *ü*.

Examples
A list of well-known place names with their pronunciation rendered in English phonetic spelling:

Hangzhou	Hong-jo
Suzhou	Soo-jo
Guilin	Gweilin
Nanjing	Nan-ging (as in 'gin')
Zhengzhou	Jeng-jo
Chongqing	Chong-ching
Qingdao	Ching-daow
Tiananmen	Tienn-an-men
Xi'an	Hsi'an
Guangzhou	Gwong-jo
Dazhai	Da-jai (as *gi* in 'giant')
Beijing	Bay-ging (as in 'gin')
Zhongguo	Jung-gwoh (China)

Tones
Each syllable is pronounced with a particular pitch, or variation of the voice, called tone. There are four tones: (1) – even, high-pitched voice; (2) ╱ rising pitch; (3) ∪ dipping, then rising pitch; (4) ╲ falling pitch. The neutral tone is marked by a dot (·).

USEFUL WORDS AND PHRASES

with a guide to pronunciation

Numbers

0	*líng*	〇		23	*èrshi-sān*	二十三
1	*yī*	一		24	*èrshi-sì*	二十四
2	*èr*	二		25	*èrshi-wǔ*	二十五
3	*sān*	三		26	*èrshi-liù*	二十六
4	*sì*	四		27	*èrshi-qī*	二十七
5	*wǔ*	五		28	*èrshi-bā*	二十八
6	*liù*	六		29	*èrshi-jiu*	二十九
7	*qī*	七		30	*sānshi*	三十
8	*bā*	八		31	*sānshi-yī*	三十一
9	*jiǔ*	九		32	*sānshi-èr*	三十二
10	*shí*	十		33	*sānshi-sān*	三十三
11	*shíyi*	十一		34	*sānshi-sì*	三十四
12	*shi'ér*	十二		35	*sānshi-wu*	三十五
13	*shísān*	十三		36	*sānshi-liù*	三十六
14	*shísì*	十四		37	*sānshi-qī*	三十七
15	*shíwǔ*	十五		38	*sānshi-bā*	三十八
16	*shíliù*	十六		39	*sānshi-jiu*	三十九
17	*shíqī*	十七		100	*yībǎi*	一百
18	*shíbā*	十八		200	*liǎng*bǎi*	两百
19	*shíjiǔ*	十九		300	*sānbǎi*	三百
20	*èrshí*	二十		500	*wǔbǎi*	五百
21	*èrshi-yī*	二十一		1,000	*yīqiān*	一千
22	*èrshi-èr*	二十二		10,000	*yīwǎn*	一万

Money, quantity

5 cents	WǓ FĒN	五分
25 cents	LIANG MÁO WǓ (FĒN)	两毛五（分）
13 dollars, 55 cents (¥13.55)	SHÍSĀN KUÀI, WǓ MÁO WǓ	十三块五毛五
one pound (lb.)	YĪ JĪN (500 g.)	一斤
half a pound (lb.)	BÀN JĪN (250 g.)	半斤
one meter	YĪ MǏ	一米
2 meters 50 centimeters (2.5 m)	LIANG MǏ WǓSHI FĒN	两米五十分
How much? (quantity)	DUŌSHǍO	多少
How much? (price)	DUŌSHǍO QIÁN	多少钱

---

*liǎng is used instead of *èr* in the adjectival form.

Time, days of the week, months of the year

one o'clock	YĪ DIĂN(ZHŌNG)	一点（钟）
two o'clock	LIĂNG DIĂN(ZHŌNG)	两点（钟）
half-past eleven	SHÍYĪ DIĂN BÀN	十一点半
quarter past five	WŬ DIĂN YĪ KÈ	五点一刻
quarter past eight	BĀ DIĂN YĪ KÈ	八点一刻
quarter to two (three-quarters after one)	YĪ DIĂN SĀN KÈ	一点三刻
week	XĪNQĪ	星期
Monday	XĪNQĪYĪ	星期一
Tuesday	XĪNQI'ÈR	星期二
Wednesday	XĪNQĪSĀN	星期三
Thursday	XĪNQĪSÌ	星期四
Friday	XĪNQĪWŬ	星期五
Saturday	XĪNQĪLIÙ	星期六
Sunday	XĪNXÍTIĀN or XĪNXĪRÌ	星期天 星期日
day	TIĀN	天
today	JĪNTIĀN	今天
tomorrow	MÍNGTIĀN	明天
yesterday	ZUÓTIĀN	昨天
month	YUÈ	月
January	YĪYUÈ	一月
February	ÈRYUÈ	二月
March, etc	SĀNYUÈ	三月
December	SHÍ'ÈRYUÈ	十二月
morning	ZĂOSHĀNG or SHÀNGWŬ	早上 上午
noon	ZHŌNGWŬ	中午
afternoon	XIÀWŬ	下午
evening	WĂNSHĀNG	晚上
night	YÈLĬ	夜里

General conversation

Hello, how are you?	NÍ HĂO, NÍ HĂO MÀ?	你好，你好吗？
Goodbye	ZÀI JIÀN	再见
Please	QĬNG	请
Thank you	XIEXIE	谢谢
You're welcome	BÚ KÈQI	不客气
Comrade	TÓNGZHI	同志
Friend	PÉNGYOU	朋友
I am sorry	DUÌ BÙ QĬ	对不起
I do not understand	WŎ BÙ DŎNG	我不懂
Slowly	MÀNMÀNDE	慢慢地
Please, write it down	QĬNG NÍ XIĚYIXIA	请你写一下
Is there an interpreter?	YŎU MÉI YŎU FĀNYÌ?	有没有翻译

yes	yes, that's right	DUÌLE	对了
	yes, I am, you are, it is, etc.	SHÌ	是
	yes, I have, you have, there is	YǑU	有
no	no, it's wrong	BÚ DUÌ	不对
	no, I am not, you are not, it is not, etc.	BÚ SHÌ	不是
	no, I have not, you have not, there is not, etc.	MÉI YǑU	没有

Travelling*

(Turn) towards the north	WÀNG BĚI ZǑU	往北走
. . . south	WÀNG NÁN ZǑU	往南走
. . . east	WÀNG DŌNG ZǑU	往东走
. . . west	WÀNG XĪ ZǑU	往西走
Please wait (for me)	QǏNG NǏ DĚNGYIDĚNG	请你等一等
(I want to go) back to the hotel	HUÍ DÀO FÀNDIÀN QÙ	回到饭店去
Please stop here (briefly)	QǏNG ZÀI ZHÈRLǏ TÍNGYITÍNG	请在这儿停一停
(I want to) go to	DÀO . . . QÙ	到…去
. . . Peking Hotel	BĚIJĪNG FÀNDIÀN	北京饭店
. . . Friendship Store	YǑUYÌ SHĀNGDIÀN	友谊商店
. . . International Club	GUÓJÌ JÙLÈBÙ	国际俱乐部
. . . Airport	FĒIJĪCHǍNG	飞机场
. . . Railway Station	HUǑCHĒ ZHÀN	火车站
. . . British Embassy	YĪNGGUÓ DÀSHÍGUǍN	英国大使馆
. . . U.S. Embassy	MĚIGUÓ DÀSHÍGUǍN	美国大使馆
When do we arrive in Beijing?	SHÉNMOSHÍHÒU DÀO BĚIJĪNG?	什么时候到北京

At the hotel

What is my room number?	WǑDE FÁNGJIĀN JǏHÀO?	我的房间几号？
Can you help me carry my luggage?	QǏNG BĀNG WǑ NÁ XÍNGLI?	请帮我拿行李
Please come in	QǏNG JÌNLÁI	请进来
This is dirty (not clean)	ZHÈIGE BÚ GĀNJÌNG	这个不干净
Please return my laundry tomorrow	QǏNG NǏ BǍ WǑ XǏHǍODE YĪFU MÍNGTIĀN NÁHUÍLÁI	请你把我洗好的衣服明天拿回来
Can you call me tomorrow at 6.30 a.m.?	QǏNG NǏ MÍNGTIĀN ZǍOSHÀNG LIÙ DIǍN BÀN JIÀO WǑ	请你明天早上六点半叫我
Please would you bring me	QǏNG NǏ GĚI WǑ . . .	请你给我…
. . . some cold water	LIÁNGKĀI SHUǏ	冷开水
. . . some ice cubes	BĪNGKUÀI	冰块
. . . a soft drink	QÌSHUǏ	汽水

*Directions are always given with reference to the points of the compass, even inside a building.

. . . a bottle of soda water	YĪ PĪNG SŪDÁSHŬI	一瓶苏打水
. . . some ice-cold beer	LĔNG PÍJIŬ	冷啤酒
. . . some boiling water	KAI SHUI	开水
. . . a bar of soap	YĪ KUÀI FÉI-ZÀO	一块肥皂
This is broken	ZHÈIGÈ HUÀILE	这个坏了
Please call someone to mend it	QĬNG JIÀO RÉN LÁI XIŪLI	请叫人来修理
Be careful	XIĂOXĪN	小心
The (hot) water is cold	SHŬI LIÁNGLE	水冷了
The room is cold, please turn the heating on	WŪZI LIÁNGLE. QĬNG NĬ KĀI NUĂNQÌ	屋子冷了，请你开暖汽
To have a rest	XIŪXÌ	休息
Where is the dining room?	CĀNTĪNG ZÀI NĂR?	餐厅在哪儿？
Where can I change money?	HUÀNQIÁNCHÙ ZÀI NĂR?	换钱处在那儿？
I want a haircut	WŎ YÀO LĬFĂ	我要理发
I want a shampoo	WŎ YAO XĪ TOU	我要洗头
Not too short, please	QĬNG BÚYÀO TÀI DUĂN	请不要太短
I want to make a long-distance phone call	WŎ YÀO DĂ CHÁNG TÚ DIÀNHUÀ	我要打长途电话
Is there a taxi? or (more commonly used)	YŎU MÉI YŎU CHŪZŪ CHĒ?	有没有出租车
Is there a car?	YŎU MÉI YŎU QÌCHĒ?	有没有汽车
I am leaving tomorrow morning	WŎ MÍNGTIĀN ZĂOSHÀNG ZŎU	我明天早上走
Can I have the bill please?	QĬNG NĬ GĔI WŎ SUÀNZHÀNG?	请你给我算账
first floor (ground floor)	YĪ LÓU	一楼
second floor (first floor)	ÈR LÓU	二楼
after breakfast	CHĪ ZĂOFÀN YĬ HÒU	吃早饭以后
after lunch	CHĪ WŬFÀN YĬHÒU	吃午饭以后
after dinner	CHĪ WĂNFÀN YĬHÒU	吃晚饭以后
during dinner	CHĪ WĂNFÀN DESHÍHÒU	吃晚饭的时候
before dinner	CHĪ WĂNFÀN YĬQIÁN	吃晚饭以前

In a restaurant or restaurant car

We are four people	WŎMEN SÌGE RÉN	我们四个人
We would like four dishes and a soup	WŎMEN YÀO CHĪ SÌGE CÀI YĪGE TĀNG	我们要吃四个菜一个汤
Do you have any fruit?	YŎU MÉI YŎU SHUĬGUŎ?	有没有水果
Please bring three bowls of rice	QĬNG NĬ LÁI SĀN WĂN MĬFÀN	请你来三碗米饭
I (we) do not like too peppery (food)	WŎ(MEN) BÙ XĬHUAN TÀI LÀDE (CAI)	我（们）不喜欢太辣的（菜）
Fruit juice	GUŎZI ZHĪ	果子汁

I would like western-style breakfast	CHĪ ZĂOFÀN, CHĪ XĪCĀN	吃早饭，吃西餐
. . . Chinese-style lunch	WŬFÀN, CHĪ ZHŌNGGUO CÀI	午饭，吃中国菜
. . . Chinese-style dinner	WĂNFÀN, CHĪ ZHŌNGGUO CÀI	晚饭，吃中国菜
I will drink beer	WŎ YÀO HĒ PÍJIŬ	我要喝啤酒
. . . soft drink	QĪSHUĬ	汽水
. . . black (red) tea	HÓNGCHÁ	红茶
. . . green tea	LǛCHÁ	绿茶
. . . mineral (spring) water (in the North you can ask for Laoshan water)	(KUÀNG) QUÁN SHUĬ LAŎSHĀNSHUĬ	（矿）泉水 （崂山水）
. . . yellow wine (the best comes from Shaoxing)	HUÁNGJIŬ SHÀOXĪNGJIŬ	黄酒 （绍兴酒）
Please bring an ashtray	QĬNG NĬ LÁI YĀNDIÉ	请你来烟碟
Please bring another bottle of beer	QĬNG NĬ ZÀI LÁI YĪ PÍNG PÍJIŬ	请你再来一瓶 啤酒
Please bring two more glasses	QĬNG NI ZÀI LÁI LIĂNGGE BŌLIBĒI	请你再来两个 玻璃杯
Bottoms up	GĀN BĒI	干杯
hot milk	RÌDE NÍUNĂI	热的牛奶
cold milk	LIĂNGDE NÍUNĂI	冷的牛奶
sugar	TÁNG	糖
lump sugar	FĀNGTÁNG	方糖
Very good (to eat)	HĚN HĂO CHĪ	很好吃
I have eaten my fill	CHĪ BĂOLE	吃饱了
a cup of coffee	YĪ BĒI JIĀFĒI	一杯咖啡
I do not like (to eat) . . . (in southern restaurants)	WŎ BÙ XĬHUAN CHĪ . . .	我不喜欢吃…
. . .sea-slugs	HĂISHĒN	海参
. . .snake meat	SHÉROU	蛇肉
. . .dog meat (in northern restaurants)	GŎUROU	狗肉
. . .bear's paws	XIŌNGZHĂNG	熊掌
. . .thousand-year-old eggs	PÍDÀN	皮蛋
Where is the lavatory?	CÍSUŎ ZÀI NĂR?	厕所在那儿？
. . . ladies'	NŬ	女
. . . men's	NÁN	男

Shopping

To go shopping	QÙ MĂI DŌNGXI	去买东西
(I want to) buy this one	(WŎ YÀO) MĂI ZHÈIGE	（我要）买这个
Is there some more?	HÁI YŎU MA?	还有吗？
another one?	YŎU BIÉDE MA?	有别的吗？

(I want to) buy three	MǍI SĀNGE	买三个
I would like a bigger one	WǑ YÀO YĪGÈ DÀ YĪ DIǍN DE	我要一个大一点的
big	DÀ	大
small	XIǍO	小
too big	TÀI DÀ	太大
too small	TÀI XIǍO	太小
blue	LÁNDE	蓝的
red	HÓNGDE	红的
yellow	HUÁNGDE	黄的
green	LÜDE	绿的
dark blue-green	QĪNGDE	青的
black	HEĪDE	黑的
white	BÁIDE	白的
pink	FENHÓNGDE	米红的
grey	HUĪDE	灰的
May I try it on?	KĚYǏ SHIYISHI MA?	可以试一试吗？

Nations and nationalities

What country are you from?	NǏ SHÌ NÁRGE GUÓJIA?	你是哪个国家？
I am British	WǑ SHÌ YĪNGGUÓRÉN	我是英国人
I am American	WǑ SHÌ MĚIGUÓRÉN	我是美国人
I am French	WǑ SHÌ FǍGUÓRÉN	我是法国人
Australia	AÒDÀLÌYÀ	澳大利亚
Austria	AÒDÌLÌ	澳地利
Argentina	AGENTÍNG	阿根廷
Belgium	BǏLÌSHÌ	比利时
Brazil	BĀXĪ	巴西
Canada	JIĀNÁDÀ	加拿大
Denmark	DĀNMÀI	丹麦
France	FǍGUÓ	法国
Germany (Federal Republic of)	XĪ DÉGUÓ	西德国
Italy	YÌDÀLÌ	意大利
India	YĪNDÙ	印度
Japan	RÌBĚN	日本
Netherlands	HÈLÁN	荷兰
New Zealand	XĪNXĪLÁN	新西兰
Norway	NUÓWĒI	挪威
Soviet Union	SŪLIÁN	苏联
Spain	XĪBĀNYÁ	西班牙
Sweden	RUÌDIǍN	瑞典
Switzerland	RUÌSHÌ	瑞士

Thailand	TAÌGÚO	泰国
United Kingdom	YĪNGGÚO	英国
United States of America	MĚIGÚO	美国

GLOSSARY OF USEFUL WORDS

General terms

bei north
binguan guesthouse
cheng walled city, wall
cun village
da great
dajie (lit. large street) avenue, boulevard
dao* road, street (in Southern island; cities)
dong east
fandian hotel
feng peak
gang harbour
gaoyuan plateau
guan pass
guang wide
guangchang (city) square
guo kingdom
hai sea, lake
he river
hou back, rear
hu lake
hutong alley, narrow back street
jiang river
jie street
kou mouth (of a river), entrance (to a street)
lang covered way
lin forest
ling* mountain range; tomb

lou building with two or more storeys
malu (lit. horse's road) highway, main road
matou (lit. horse's head) pier
men gate
nan south
nei inside
qian front
qiao bridge
quan spring
riquan hot spring
sha sand
shamo desert
shan mountain
shang above
shi market
shi municipality, city, town
shui water, river (small)
shuiku reservoir
simao temple
tian* heaven, sky; field
wai outside
xi west
xia* gorge; under
xian county
ya cliff
yuan* plain; garden
zhong centre, central
zhou country, region
zhuang village, hamlet

Art, architectural and religious terms

an nunnery
apsaras (sg.), *apsarah* (pl.) flying angel in Buddhist iconography
Avalokitesvara *see* Guanyin
bei stele
Bodhisattva in his last incarnation

before attaining Nirvana
Buddha has attained Nirvana
celadon green-glazed ceramic
chop *see* seal
cloisonné enamel colours separated by copper threads on copper base

---

* Homophonic word, whose different meanings correspond to different Chinese characters.

dagoba   tall Buddhist monument in the shape of an inverted vase built as a reliquary; shape borrowed from India. *See also* pagoda *and* stupa.

Devarja   (Sanskrit) the four celestial kings in Buddhist temples

dian   hall

Dvarapala   (Sanskrit) guardians of the gate in Buddhist temples

fo   Chinese word for Buddha

Famille rose   ceramics with pink enamel decoration over the glaze

Famille verte   ceramics with green enamel decoration over the glaze

gong   palace

guan   Taoist temple

ge   pavilion or tower with two or more storeys

Guanyin (Kuanyin)   in Sanskrit, Avalokitesvara, Goddess of Mercy, a Bodhisattva

Lohan   Chinese name for Buddha's disciples

lou   building with two or more storeys

miao   temple, shrine or lamasery

obo   religious monument made of piled-up stones, only found in Mongolia

pagoda   Chinese architectural form of dagoba or stupa. Multi-storeyed tower built as a reliquary in Buddhist temples

pailou   triumphal arch or portal built at the entrance of palaces, temples, tomb sites, or across streets.

pusa   Chinese word for Bodhisattva

rubbing   design obtained by applying a piece of thin paper to a carved stone or brick and then rubbing it with ink

Sang de bœuf   monochrome deep red glaze on ceramics

scroll painting   Chinese painting mounted on paper and silk and which can be rolled up

seal (chop)   engraved with owner's name, used instead of signature

si   temple (Buddhist)

stupa   *see* dagoba

sutra   Buddhist scripture

ta   pagoda, dagoba

tang   hall

Taoism (Daoism)   Chinese religion

ting   pavilion

usnisa   bun on top of Buddha's head

zhuang   column or pillar engraved with sacred texts and images

Beijing: Plans of the diplomatic compounds

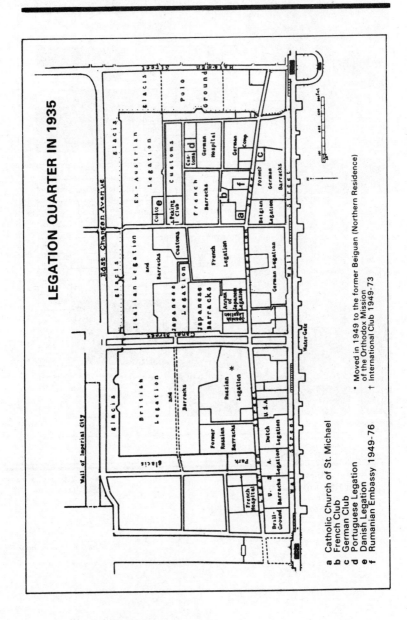

LEGATION QUARTER IN 1935

a Catholic Church of St. Michael
b French Club
c German Club
d Portuguese Legation
e Danish Legation
f Rumanian Embassy 1949-76

* Moved in 1949 to the former Beiguan (Northern Residence)
  of the Orthodox Mission
† International Club 1949-73

NEW DIPLOMATIC COMPOUNDS:
SANLITUN

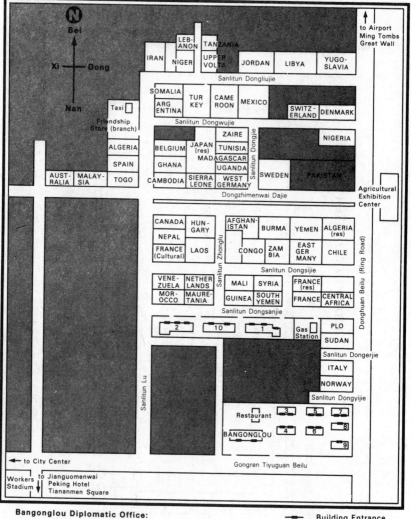

Bangonglou Diplomatic Office:
Equatorial Guinea: 2-41
France (Trade): 1-Ground Floor
Kenya: 1-82
Liberia: 2-62
Peru: 2-82
Venezuela: 2-72

➡ **Building Entrance**
▨ **Local Area**

©1980 The China Phone Book Co. Ltd.

NEW DIPLOMATIC COMPOUNDS: JIANGUOMENWAI AND QIJIAYUAN

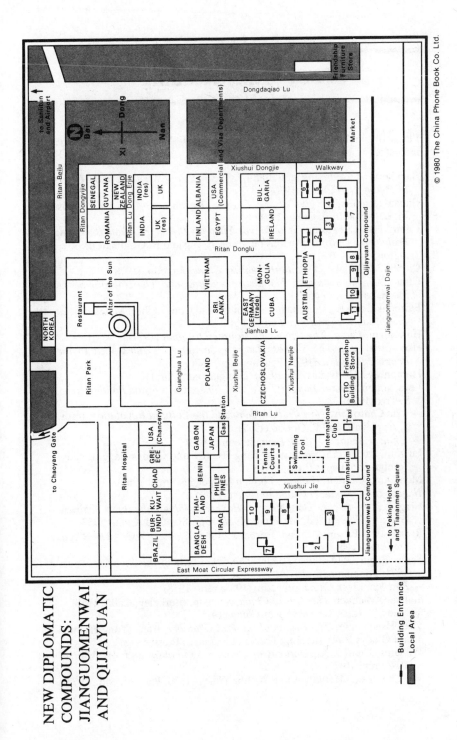

© 1980 The China Phone Book Co. Ltd.

For Further Reading

Place of publication is London and/or New York unless otherwise indicated.

Backhouse, Sir Edmund, and Bland, J.O., *Annals and Memoirs of the Court of Peking* (1914; repr. 1970)

Bianco, Lucien, *Origins of the Chinese Revolution, 1915-1949*, trans. M. Bell (Stanford, Calif., 1971)

Chen Johsi, *The Execution of Mayor Yin and other stories from the Great Proletarian Cultural Revolution*, trans. N. Ing and H. Goldblatt (Bloomington, Ind., 1978)

Clubb, O. Edmund, *Twentieth-Century China*, 3rd edn. (1978)

Confucius, *The Analects, The Great Learning, and The Doctrine of the Mean*, trans. J. Legge (1972)

Fairbank, John K., Reischauer, Edwin O., and Craig, Albert M., *East Asia: The Modern Transformation* (1965)

Han Suyin, *Lhasa, The Open City: Journey to Tibet* (1977)

Hsu Kaiyu, ed., *The Chinese Literary Scene: A Writer's Visit to the People's Republic* (1975; Penguin edn., 1976)

Humphreys, Christmas, *Buddhism* (Penguin edn., 1951)

Leys, Simon, *Broken Images: Essays in Chinese Culture and Politics*, trans. S. Cox (1979)

— *The Chairman's New Clothes: Mao and the Cultural Revolution*, trans. C. Appleyard and P. Goode (1977)

— *Chinese Shadows* (1977: Penguin edn., 1978)

Lu Xun, *Selected Stories*, trans. Yang Hsien-yi and Gladys Yang (Beijing: Foreign Languages Press, 1972)

Mao Dun, *Midnight* (Beijing: Foreign Languages Press, 1962)

Nagel's Encyclopaedia Guide to China (1979)

Ning L., Tai-tai, *A Daughter of Han: Autobiography of a Chinese Working Woman*, ed. Ida Pruitt (1945; repr. Stanford, Calif., 1967)

Reischauer, Edwin O., and Fairbank, John K., *East Asia: The Great Tradition* (1961)

Snow, Edgar, *Red China Today: The Other Side of the River*, rev. edn. (1971; Penguin edn., 1972)

— *Red Star Over China*, rev. edn. (1968; repr. 1978)

Sullivan, Michael, *The Arts of China*, rev. edn. (Berkeley, Calif., 1978)

Tregear, T. R., *A Geography of China* (1965)

Tsao Hsueh-chin, *The Dream of the Red Chamber*, trans. Yang Hsien-yi and Gladys Yang (Beijing: Foreign Languages Press, 1978)

Williams, Charles A., *Outlines of Chinese Symbolism and Art Motives* (1974; repr. 1977)

Wu Ch'eng-en, *Monkey*, trans. Arthur Waley (1958; Penguin edn., 1973)

Index